Circling the Great Karoo

A Back-roads Journey through History on an Old Scrambler

Nicholas Yell

Springbok Press

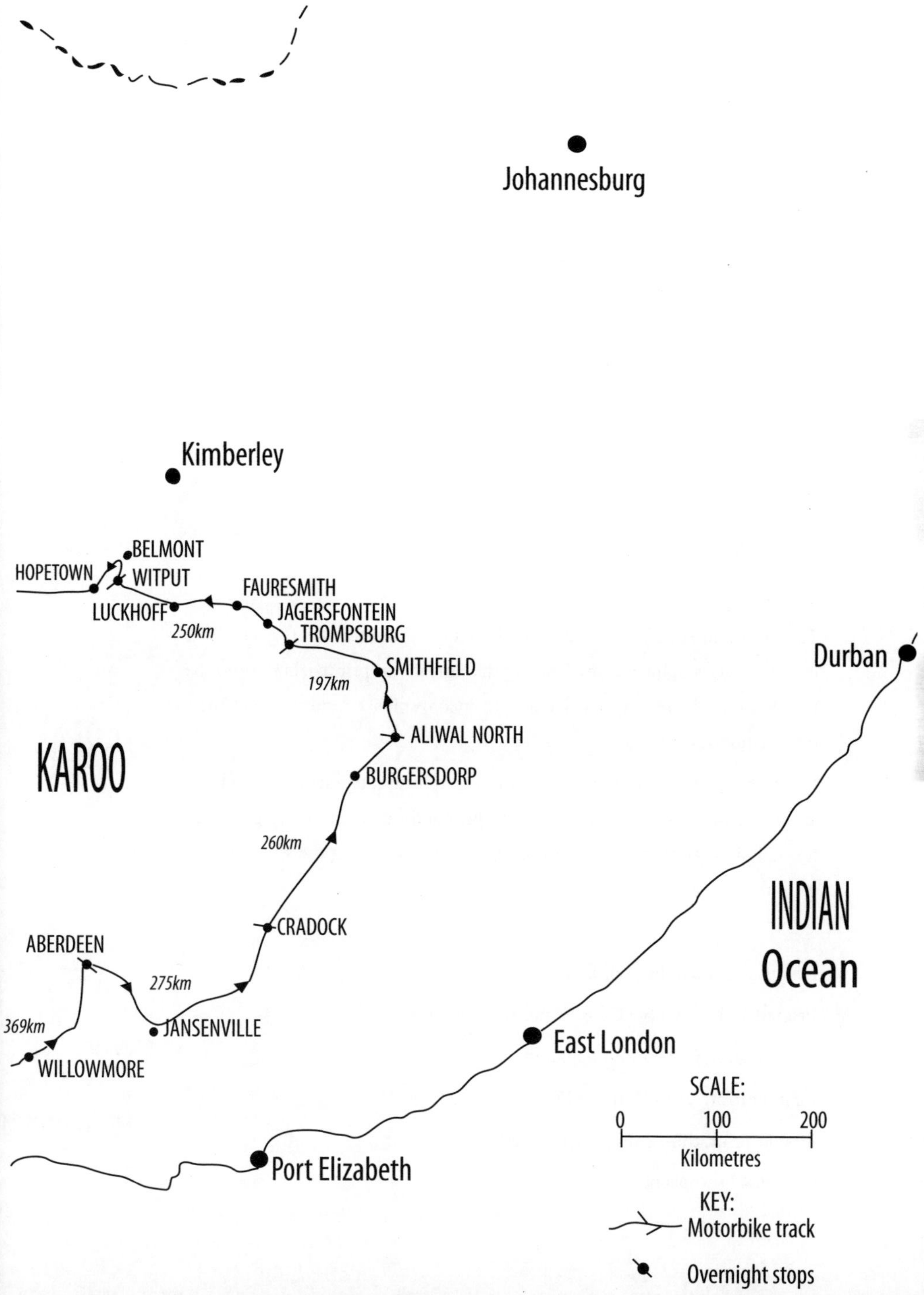

Johannesburg
Kimberley
BELMONT
HOPETOWN
WITPUT
FAURESMITH
LUCKHOFF
JAGERSFONTEIN
250km
TROMPSBURG
Durban
SMITHFIELD
197km
ALIWAL NORTH
KAROO
BURGERSDORP
260km
INDIAN
Ocean
CRADOCK
ABERDEEN
275km
369km
JANSENVILLE
East London
WILLOWMORE
SCALE:
0
100
200
Kilometres
Port Elizabeth
KEY:
Motorbike track
Overnight stops

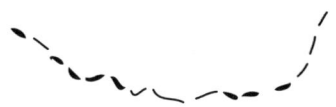

Published by Springbok Press, P O Box 252, Botriver, South Africa, 7185

© Copyright on all text, maps and photographs 2008: Nicholas Yell.
All rights reserved. No part of this publication may be reproduced, stored in a retrieval system or transmitted, in any form or by any means, electronic, mechanical, photo-copying, recording or otherwise, without the prior written permission of the copyright owner.

ISBN: 978-0-620-45351-6

The author and publisher have endeavoured to ensure the accuracy of all the information contained in this book at the time it was printed, but cannot be held responsible for any loss, damages or inconvenience resulting from the use of information it contains.

Whilst all quoted sources and other bibliographical references are listed in detail at the back of this book, the author and his publisher accept no responsibility for omissions and/or errors that may have occurred during the reproduction and printing process.

Layout & Design by: Yell Design

Printed and bound by: CTP Printers, Cape Town

First imprint, first edition September 2008

First imprint, second edition December 2008

First imprint, third edition January 2010

ISO 12647 compliant

for Harvey

Thank you for shining so much light on the path – and for the fun along the way.

Contents

Foreword		*xi*
Author's Note		*xiii*

1. **No Turning Back** — *1*
   (Aberdeen to Cradock: 275 kilometres)

2. **From Schreiner's Tomb to a Mineral Bath Spa** — *19*
   (Cradock to Aliwal North: 260 kilometres)

3. **Across the Gariep into the Highveld Karoo** — *46*
   (Aliwal North to Trompsburg: 197 kilometres)

4. **Battlefields and Diamonds** — *69*
   (Trompsburg to Witput, between Belmont and Hopetown: 250 kilometres)

5. **Railways, River Ways and a Well Full of Laxatives** — *99*
   (Witput via Belmont to Prieska: 221 kilometres)

6. **From the Place of the Lost Goat to a Dam of Peace** — *121*
   (Prieska to Boegoeberg Dam: 150 kilometres)

7. **From Cool and Rested to Hot and Bothered** — *142*
   (Boegoeberg to Kenhardt via Groblershoop: 160 kilometres)

8	**ACROSS THE LAND OF BEGIN AGAIN** (Kenhardt via Brandvlei to Loeriesfontein: 295 kilometres)	*163*
9	**MORE OF THE UNEXPECTED** (Loeriesfontein to Calvinia: 89 kilometres)	*184*
10	**OVER THE HILLS AND UP TO THE STARS** (Calvinia to Sutherland, with an excursion to Fraserburg: 404 kilometres)	*198*
11	**PASSES, POORTS AND PAUSING** (Sutherland to Kruisrivier: 270 kilometres)	*214*
12	**TAKING THE LONG ROAD HOME** (Rest day in Kruisrivier then the return trip home via Willowmore: 369 kilometres)	*237*

APPENDIX - 1 *260*
BACKGROUND TO THE KAROO'S
80-MILLION-YEAR-OLD UNBROKEN
FOSSIL RECORD *260*
    The Middle to Upper Permian Period *263*
    The Triassic Period *266*
    The Emergence of Dinosaurs *269*
    The Lower Jurassic Period *271*
    The First Mammals *272*
    The End of the Karoo Period *272*
    The Classification of Reptiles through the Ages *274*

Appendix - 2 — *276*
Other Karoo adventure-biking articles by the author
David and Goliath — *277*
Cruising the Camdeboo — *283*
To the Valley of Baboons — *289*

Bibliography — *301*
Endnotes — *306*
Index — *310*
About the Author — *316*

Foreword

He was seeking a challenge, an adventure. I assume this was prompted by the thought that he was approaching the half-way stage of an average life-time. Those over 40 know the feeling. Younger people seem hardly aware that such a feeling is possible.

Sailing to Rio in a 30-footer had been a great project for him years earlier. Exploring the islands off the Brazilian coast had been fun. Navigating a 4X4 across the roadless wilds of Botswana and the eastern edge of the Kalahari had been exciting - particularly with lions following his friend Lionel into their lonely camps, and one being so cheeky as to walk in and eat his camera bag.

But now he wanted something different: something to explore, including himself, he said. Something challenging, to be done entirely alone.

The Great Karoo, outside the front door of his new home, suddenly offered such a challenge - one of the few left for would-be explorers in an over-populated world with its smothering web of electronics and mobile phones and its pinpoint geographic positioning systems (GPSs).

The Great Karoo is a vast space that motorists hurry through as fast as they can in a day - or preferably at night. "It's hot, flat, dusty and dull," most people who traverse it will tell you. It's all of those sometimes... none of those for people who really know it. Yet few of the scattered farmers and others who live there are even aware of its many secrets, its history or its true nature. The challenge was to find a little of each.

In the Karoo, GPS would be mostly irrelevant, for he would have to follow meandering trails, two-track paths and back roads wherever they led him on his circumnavigation of this ancient basin. Mobile phones do not reach into vast tracts of semi-desert behind the hills and mountains that fringe the Karoo. The area is one of the least populated on this over-crowded planet. The few rugged people he had met beyond the Karoo's isolated villages knew little of the outside world - let alone how to chat on the Web.

A 3,000 kilometre journey among the scrub and rocks of this ancient land on a 15-year-old scrambler motorbike should offer the challenge he sought.

Harvey Tyson
2006

Author's Note

I have always loved books. But until I started writing myself I really had no idea about the amount of time, energy and perseverance that went into them — especially if you are intrigued by your subject matter and try to put it across in an easily accessible way.

In this book I have attempted to convey all that I have learnt from many varied sources, and in so doing, sincerely hope that I have represented and interpreted these works correctly. For those that I may have misunderstood, I would like to apologise up front.

There will no doubt be some readers who choose to differ with certain of my interpretations, opinions and nomenclature. With reference to the latter, the debate regarding terms such as "Bushman" and "Hottentot" being seen by some as pejorative still continues. I have used these terms, mostly in conjunction with their more socially acceptable equivalents of San and Khoi, respectively, in order to avoid confusion with the numerous historical texts I have quoted from. No offence is meant and I trust that none will be taken. Notwithstanding these and other issues that may arise, I believe I have done everything possible to check the veracity of the book's contents.

In the main, this is a book that is designed to appeal to the historically-inclined adventure motorbike enthusiast. Yet, I hope, it will also appeal to those lay travellers who simply love to explore the Karoo, as well as other out-of-the-way places in South Africa. But it should also be said that it is not a book aimed at the seasoned academic. What it is, is a travel starter pack for anybody interested in the Karoo; its modern and ancient history; its geology, fauna, flora and people; and everything else in between. For those who would like to find out more about specific topics raised, I suggest you refer to the comprehensive bibliography provided at the end of the book.

As for additional detail on palaeontological aspects, I have formulated a summary document as an appendix that attempts to explain the macro picture in this regard. Yet let me stress that I am not a palaeontologist, and suggest that those who require more than the summary detail I have provided again refer to the bibliography, as well as the excellent professors based at most of South Africa's larger universities.

I thank my wife for her love and assistance, Harvey for his tireless coaching and the rest of my family and friends for their enthusiasm and encouragement. I couldn't have done it without any one of you.

I hope this book brings you hours of vicarious pleasure and stimulates a thirst to know more about this mentally invigorating region — and yourself. At the very least, I trust it will whet your appetite for further exploration, wherever that may be.

Nicholas Yell, Botriver 2009

NB: With regard to all the prices mentioned in this book, please bear in mind that the actual journey took place over three years ago and these will have escalated significantly.

1

No Turning Back

(Aberdeen to Cradock: 275 kilometres)

*What availe it a man if he gain the
whole world and loses his soul?*

Matt. 26:I; Mark 8:36. Inscribed on a boulder
at Oukop, near Cradock.

*I*t was a cloudy day in early November when I waved goodbye to my small Karoo clan and settled into the saddle for the long and bumpy ride ahead. I had a pretty good idea of my route, but I'd decided not to book accommodation at any of my proposed destinations, in a determined effort to let go of my penchant for planning things down to the minutest detail. A long career in advertising can do that to one. So how the journey unfolded, whom I met and the stories that materialised were to be left to the universe. Perhaps I was starting to get the hang of this "New Age" stuff after all.

One thing I had probably been overly fastidious about, though, was the overhauling of my faithful old Yamaha XT250, which I called Rebeccasaurus. I'd named her after a fictitious female dinosaur species in anticipation of the numerous fossils I hoped to stumble across on the trip. Since arriving back home with my smoking machine after my 400 kilometre trial run, I'd discovered that the crankcase still had some mud in it. This was a hangover from a devastating flood we'd suffered in Napier six months previously. When I say "I discovered", I mean, of course, my trusty mechanic Johnny found it. I was still working on that "Zen and the art of motorcycle maintenance" thing. When I eventually collected the bike from Johnny, it had been completely stripped and rebuilt. She was purring like a thoroughbred — and she'd been just about as expensive to maintain as well. But who can put a price on true love?

I accelerated onto the dirt road turn-off and waved goodbye to some small snotty-nosed kids who almost collided with me in their exuberant farewell. And then the countryside opened up its ancient arms and welcomed me to my long-awaited appointment with nature — and, of course, myself. Just out of town, a relay of small steenbok started to escort the bike by running in the gap between the thorn bushes lining the road and the farm boundary fences a couple of metres on the other side of them. As one steenbok ended its frantic race with the bike by ducking under a gap in the fence, another would pop up out of the scrub and the game would begin again. Unfortunately the noise of the bike often seemed to flush them out like this. Yet there was little I could do, as even if I were to stop the bike and try and let them escape through the fence into the veld, they would wait for me to actually start "chasing" them again before they pushed through the fence further down the road.

But the kori bustards seemed less perturbed by my presence and simply lumbered up into the sky like lazy Antonov cargo jets when I got too close. Standing up to nearly a metre and a half tall and weighing in at over 16 kilograms, this is the heaviest flying bird in the world. When disturbed, it will walk away rapidly with giant purposeful strides, taking to the air with reluctant yet immensely powerful thrusts of its huge wings — but only if it really has to.

Numerous small puff-ball clouds scudded through the blue sky at low altitude. They played disco-ball tricks with the sunlight, highlighting a lone acacia tree on the veld and then allowing a brief cast of light to reflect off a dam in the distance. Setting out on this solo journey of close to 3,000 kilometres of predominantly dirt track riding around the perimeter of the Great Karoo, I thought of the early European explorers and naturalists who set out with such determination and optimism, but little idea of the real dangers and challenges that lay ahead of them. People like Gordon, Patterson, Thunberg, Barrow, Lichtenstein, Burchell and, of course, the lesser known early Dutch barterers and explorers of the Cape such as Corporal Cruse and Ensigns Bergh, Beutler and Schryver. How must these pioneers have felt as they set off into the hostile semi-deserts of southern Africa?

In writing of his thoughts on his upcoming "unfettered travels" into the interior from Natal in the 1860s, the stoical yet often rhapsodic "colonial" explorer Andrew Anderson made the following entries in his manuscript:

> for we know perfectly well before we enter upon these explorations, that we will not be living in the lap of luxury, or escape from all the perils that beset a traveller when first entering upon unknown ground — if any of these troubles should enter his mind, he had better stay at home.[1]

By contrast, the Bushmen (San) — whom the poet Pringle called "Lords of the Desert" — had no fear of the Great Karoo, which made up a large section of their home territories. It was their expansive backyard and it gave them life and succour. And, being hunter-gatherers, they depended on constant movement across the veld for survival; virtually nothing would hold them up. For instance, a woman who went into labour while the clan was on the move was said to have simply retired from the group, given birth and was then able to catch up with her people in just a couple of hours. Freedom of movement was everything to these diminutive aboriginal people. It is well documented, for instance, that when Bushmen were jailed (mostly for crimes they did not understand) they would often die within six months.

I'd been travelling all of half an hour when disaster struck. In awe of the landscape, as well as the freedom and adventure that lay ahead, I had decided to stop and draw out the pleasure in the silent surrounds. Walking contentedly around the bike and looking over the well-prepared rig, I was shocked to find that my prized clip-on "top-box" had come loose. To be precise, the beautifully made plastic lug holding the case to the carrier had sheared off. I cursed the Chinese manufacturers first. *I mean, what were they thinking using a plastic lug to hold down a heavy case on the back of a bouncing motorbike?* Then I cursed myself for cramming the case full of necessities such as a two-litre box of Chateau de Co-Op and far too many kilograms of "trail mix". Close to beating myself about the head with a cargo net, I decided to head back home and work another plan with a tog bag — or something. All the exuberant fauna that had just wished me on my way now reversed their timeframes and shepherded me back to Aberdeen.

I'm not sure whether my small Karoo clan were that happy to see me back so soon. After much knocking, my wife appeared in a towel, a face mask and a wreath of jasmine steam. Even the cats seemed put out by having to get off their dented cushions twice in one day. I quickly put the thought of sharing my wife's Japanese passion bath out of my head and rummaged around for a suitable receptacle to house my luggage. A commodious bright green travel bag seemed a good choice. Having hurriedly transferred my things, I waved goodbye once more to my incredulous — and slightly peeved — Karoo family.

The fences fell away from the dusty roadsides and retreated to where they were better utilised to demarcate cattle boundaries in the mountains. A Karoo korhaan — a smaller yet similar-looking bird to the kori bustard — catapulted itself noisily from its scrub-bush shelter, while a family of suricates, standing on their hind legs, craned their inquisitive necks to see what all the fuss was about. The horizons were expanding now and the vegetation grew more sparsely on tightly compacted soils. Lost in thought, I caught a subliminal flash of a signboard saying "Constantia School". Being so far away from the only "Constantia" I knew, the Cape Town suburb, this made incongruous reading. I was mulling this over when I rounded a corner and sailed into a river.

Yet sailing would be far too an elegant description for the type of crossing I made over the Sundays River. Only having seen the substantial stream of water hissing over the drift at the last minute, I lifted my legs into the splits position, screamed loudly and accelerated enthusiastically. There are times on a dirt-bike that you have no other option but to go like hell — and scream. Often, as in this case, you make it through or around what appears to be an insurmountable obstacle. And, of course, there are times when you don't. When I was still very much a novice dirt-biker racing around the forests of Mpumalanga with my stepfather and friends, I was travelling at great speed on a narrow logging road, trying my best to impersonate my motocross heroes' penchant for going around corners sideways. Coming around the blind corner from the opposite direction doing the same thing was my stepbrother Barry. At times like this there is no thought of taking evasive action or indulging in the luxury of a prolonged scream. A subdued "Oh fuck, here goes" was all I could muster before we collided in a tangle of handlebars and helmets. Amazingly, we were virtually unhurt, which was unfortunately more than could be said for our borrowed motorbikes.

Luckily, the river I had just come through was only about half a metre deep. The concrete drift's surface was thankfully also in good condition, because had it been potholed, I probably wouldn't have made it to the other side. Constantia School appeared through the fug of whooped-up adrenalin; scores of farm workers' kids were playing break-time games in the dusty yard. I was relieved they'd missed my inelegant crossing and waved cheerily at their squashed faces that were pressed against the diamond-mesh fence as I rode by.

A little way on, the topography of the countryside changed dramatically once more. Vast, open plains now gave way to rounded stony hills covered with many forms of native flowering euphorbia interspersed with alien cacti. Attractive as these cacti are in flower, the vast majority of them are invasive species and have already taken over large tracts of the Eastern Cape, rendering these areas virtually useless to farmers or indigenous game.

After my inauspicious start, I was beginning to thoroughly enjoy myself. I'd already encountered all manner of road surfaces, had one near swim and the recent tighter twists and turns over stony ground ensured that my mind was only focused on the road ahead. This "focussing" also freed up my mind from any extraneous thoughts other than those that directly affected the moment at hand; a pleasantly distracted Zen-like meditative state that meant I had little else on my mind.

I was starting to feel like James Dean on safari, slowly becoming one with my machine.

☙

I got off and crunched around the motorbike in the silence. Then, after hurriedly discarding my padded jacket in the heat, I stood dead still and just tried to absorb it all — the otherworldliness of the desolate landscape, the sense of timelessness and an understanding of the hardy people who populated it. A woman with curlers in her hair stepped out of a smartly painted labourer's cottage in the distance. Her movement caused momentary ripples in the baking semi-desert scene. And then we acknowledged each other through half nods and stifled waves — the awkward vocabulary of strangers.

All around me, numerous tiny succulents populated the dry veld. They defied the harsh and dry conditions by hanging on to every drop of moisture they possessed. From my travelling notes I read up on the three main kinds of succulents I saw: those that store water and manufacture carbohydrates via their leaves, their stem, or alternatively, their root structures. The stem succulents are often the most incongruous-looking of the three. Their leaves can wither and fall off, leaving the stem alone in its quest to create and store nutritious fluids for the plant. Having started off living permanently in water before making their move to land, all terrestrial plants had to evolve ways of absorbing and holding onto water before they could succeed "ashore". Unlike many plants in well-watered environments, succulents readily display the results of this remarkable ingenuity through water storage mechanisms such as fleshy leaf or bulbous root systems.

The Great Karoo basin often gives one hints of its ancient submerged past. On a superficial level, all sorts of seabed-type succulents and grasses waving in the breeze are reminiscent of ocean plants swaying to the play of underwater currents. On a more scientific, yet still simplistic level, Lawrence Green summed it up well when he described the formation of the Great Karoo region as follows:

> Millions of years ago the shallow basin of the Great Karoo was a vast glacier which became a lake when the ice melted. Then the pent-up waters burst through the escarpment and these Karoo rivers tore out the tremendous gorges of the Swartberg and other ranges: the gorges which we call poorts, where the precipices rise sheer above the traveller for three thousand, four thousand feet. Sometimes, as in Meiring's Poort, the mountain peaks are six thousand feet above the stream.[2]

Sitting on the side of the road crunching my trail-mix, I was mesmerised by the sunbursts of yellow flowers on the spiky columns of euphorbia around me. They were framed against a cobalt blue sky in super-real perfection, the absolute silence paying further tribute to this special moment in time.

Feeling a little guilty about disturbing this peaceful cloak of stillness, I cranked my bike into life and continued towards Jansenville.

It's difficult to know just where the Great Karoo begins and ends. Generally speaking, it's the elevated and parched semi-desert region forming the southern-central heart of South Africa. In the south-east, south and south-west, the area is mostly separated from its lower-lying and more fertile cousin, the Little or Klein Karoo, by many mountain ranges of varying size. Yet most South Africans simply regard it as the dry wasteland between the Hex River Pass in the south and the Gariep (formerly Orange) River in the north, on their hurried way to or from the northern provinces.

When planning my "circumnavigation" I'd consulted various recognised sources. My aim was to merge all these inputs into one route plan that would allow me to complete the journey predominantly on seldom-used dirt tracks. The upshot of this planning is the 2,940 kilometre perimeter trip indicated by the map at the front of this book.

The boundaries of the Great Karoo are difficult to define because the term Karoo describes a unique composite of different elements such as the type of soil, vegetation, topography, rocks and, most importantly, climate. It follows from this that the Great Karoo does not fall into a conveniently homogenous region with distinct borders that can be easily "circled" on a map. Because of this, there are probably still a number of Karoo-like regions that fall outside the area enclosed by my route plan. It is said that if all the individual Karoo-like regions were added together, the total area would take up around one third of South Africa's surface — well over 400,000 square kilometres and significantly bigger than Germany. The characteristics of the Great Karoo region vary greatly, but as far as a collective definition of the composite is concerned, the excerpt from a South African encyclopaedia that follows probably offers one of the better descriptions around:

> The Karoo, occupying the central and western interior of the country, is a region of low rainfall, clear and bone-dry air, blistering days and often freezing nights. Its plant cover is indeed sparse, but special in the way it has evolved and adapted to the harsh conditions. Its succulents — aloes, mesembryanthemums, crassulas, euphorbias and stapelias — are unique, surviving because they are able to store water in their thick leaves or root systems. Then there are the desert ephemerals, wild flowers whose seeds remain dormant for years, swiftly germinating and blossoming when the rare rains

come, sometimes — especially in the Namaqualand regions — producing glorious, expansive carpets of brilliant colour.

Geologically, the region is part of what is known as the Karoo System, which characterizes a much larger area, extending far to the north of the subcontinent. The shale and sandstone strata are horizontal, and huge tracts of the countryside are monotonously flat, but millennia of volcanic action have thrust up dolerite intrusions — dykes (ridges) and sills (kopjes) — which have been weathered by periodic floods into stark and often strange formations. Most prominent of the Karoo's uplands are the high mountains of its south-western and southern Cape boundary: the Cederberg, Cold Bokkeveld, Roggeveld, Nuweveld and Sneeuberg ranges.

Dry though the region is — rainfall varies from under 50 millimetres a year in the west to 375 millimetres in the eastern areas — there is good underground water which is trapped by wind pumped boreholes (windmills). This, together with the sweet grasses of the eastern parts, sustains huge flocks of sheep.[3]

(Having reflected on the route more on my return, it is arguable that I kept a little too far south and may have ventured slightly too much to the east. But then the extent of this deviation depends on whom you speak to and where their topographical loyalties lie.)

◌঩

I approached Jansenville from a completely unexpected direction. Since my last stop amid the stony hills of euphorbia about three-quarters of an hour ago, the landscape had transformed into large sparse plains of hard, tawny-coloured sand. The dirt track was deeply rutted and the bike and I were feeling somewhat battered by the time we arrived in the town. I found a petrol station on the edge of this small centre for sheep and angora goats and pulled in to fill up the bike. I was also in need of some large washers to secure my dangling number plate, which was fast threatening to run me foul of the law.

An uncomfortable-looking restaurant with cold stone floors and a tight-lipped manageress was squashed in between the workshop and showroom. The surly-looking lady suddenly sputtered into life:

"You on a bike, hey?"

Tempted to say that I was just wearing all my protective clothing and a helmet because I'd heard the sky was going to cave in at any moment, I flashed her a Jim Carey smile instead and replied: "Ja, on my way around the Great Karoo."

"Juslike, on that small scrambler; youse gotta be crazy."

On my way out the shop after that vote of no-confidence, I encountered a car full of traditionally dressed black Africans, their old-world attire contrasting sharply with their brand new Volvo sedan. The men wore loose-fitting "Madiba" mandarin-collared shirts with beaded headbands and the women were dressed in beaded tunics and skirts, their faces completely covered with a thick white paste. And in this remote and largely conservative town, this rare reflection of "New South African" opulence brought wide-eyed smiles to the petrol attendants who watched them.

How far we've already come in this country, I thought. But in the next breath I had to admit to myself that, sadly, especially in the rural areas I planned to travel through, very little had actually changed. Many black and coloured folk still refer to whites as "*baas*" or "master", no matter how many times you ask them to desist. Unfortunately, the embracing ethos of the "Rainbow Nation" has not yet made the journey into the outlying regions of the Karoo. Apart from the government needing to educate these indigent black and "coloured" folk as to their true worth and potential, it is surely the job of every educated South African to unyoke them from their outmoded patterns of the past. And it needs to start with the better educated white people, especially in rural areas, getting off their creaking pedestals and simply treating their black and "coloured" brothers and sisters on a more respectful and equal footing.

Complicating the situation further is the fact that all South Africans are, to a greater or lesser extent, recovering racists. And I'm not just talking about white South Africans either. If we can acknowledge this, we are surely on the path towards real and permanent healing. If we don't, and remain in denial, or worse still, are intolerant of the many cultural differences that divide us, we are undoubtedly doomed as a nation. The "New South Africa" will then be a certain disaster and there will be a regrettable, yet somewhat empirical basis for the Afro-pessimists to claim that racial harmony is merely the pipe dream of disingenuous political manifestos.

03

Founded in 1854 and named after the governor of the Cape Colony in 1803, Lieutenant-General Jan Willem Jansens, the small dishevelled town of Jansenville belies the apparently noble and valiant character of its namesake. It shows little sign of prosperity, and the community seems to be in a state of undecided transition — as if it is not sure whether it should hang onto its past conservative roots or move into a more cosmopolitan, African future. This is unfortunately true of so many small country towns in South Africa, where the majority of the white population refuse to embrace the programme of developing a non-racial and multicultural society. For the most part they simply ignore the fact that political changes have taken place. Yet, retarding the transformation process with almost equal vigour, is the fact that, after so many years of physical and economic segregation, the black and so-called "coloured" communities seem to prefer to stick to themselves as well.

General Jansens, on the other hand, appeared to conduct his difficult tenure as the new Dutch governor with a marked sensitivity towards all the inhabitants of the colony. Soon after taking over the administration of the Cape from the British in 1803, he set off on an expedition into the Cape's eastern hinterlands to inspect the living conditions of the colonists, Hottentots (Khoi) and Xhosas. He seemed impressed with the way he was received by the majority of the farmers — and particularly with how they fed him. But he was less impressed with a group of farmers near the Gourits River. They had experienced a run-in with the local Hottentots and some other native tribes and now they wanted revenge. As the historian Theal reports, Jansens saw their need for justice "as a lust for Kaffir cattle and a malicious desire for revenge." Jansens was also not impressed with the general idleness of the white farmer folk he encountered there. One of his aims in travelling up the coast was to look at reservation-style homelands for the Hottentots. In today's modern democracy, the thought of this action may hark back to the "Bantustans" (black homelands) implemented under apartheid, yet in the context of the era, it was seen as a move of compassion and protectionism. Once again, Theal elaborates:

> he was determined to treat these people, whom he looked upon as aborigines, with justice and kindness. Many of them made complaints to him of harsh treatment and violence by some of the frontier colonists, and this he resolved to put an end to. By placing them in small parties on reserves where they could maintain themselves, only those who wished to do so need have intercourse with the graziers, and for these he would make regulations that would fully protect them.

Apart from humanity and justice also, it was necessary to do this, for the colony was not strong enough to contend with the Hottentots and the Xhosas combined, and it was therefore necessary to conciliate the former and to detach them from alliance with the latter.[4]

General Jansens also set up terms with the various Xhosa chiefs in the Suurveld. He did this to encourage them to vacate the area and to move them across the agreed-upon border between themselves and the colonists: the Great Fish River. Various trade-offs were made and peace seemed assured for a time, yet as history has shown, the region was troubled by much enmity and bloodshed, which ultimately resulted in the British government at the Cape encouraging unwitting English settlers to establish a human barrier between the colony and the Xhosas in 1820.

General Jansens was to be faced with many other challenges in his short tenure as governor of the Cape. Probably the biggest was to try and defend the Cape against the imminent British invasion in 1806, when most of his regular soldiers had been taken to protect the Dutch's more lucrative trading interests in Java. While he was successful in putting together a reasonably competent army of Hottentots, burghers, German mercenaries, and some Dutch and French regulars of about 2,000 strong, the invading British force of seasoned campaigners under Lieutenant-Colonel Baird of well over 6,000 men was always likely to be victorious in the battle that followed, now known as "Blaauwberg".

When General Jansens took the remnants of his defeated forces to make a stand at the foot of the distant Hottentots Holland Mountains, the English command appraised him by letter that they had sent warships ahead to capture the settlement at Mossel Bay and that, as a result, his escape route into that region of the colony was effectively cut off. General Jansens knew then that further resistance would be futile, and just ten days after the hostilities began a truce was signed between the parties and the "war" was over.

Unfortunately, his positive influences and seemingly just intentions for the future of the Cape were also over. His more liberal policies towards the Hottentots in particular were soon to be replaced with more draconian laws under the conquering British. Whereas the Hottentots had largely enjoyed freedom of movement around the colony under Jansens, by November 1809 the then governor of the Cape, the Earl of Caledon, had issued a proclamation that, among other restrictions and new duties placed on them, required all Hottentots to carry a travelling "pass" as well. This "pass" was to be obtained "either from his commanding officer if he was in the military service, or his employer, or the magistrate of the district, under penalty of being considered and treated as a vagabond."[5]

It seems that "pass law" legislation was a South African reality long before the advent of apartheid.

ೞ

Leaving Jansenville behind, I worked my way up onto an elevated plateau via the gradual gradient of the Soutpansnek Pass. At a junction a little way on I felt like I'd entered a secret world of old farm roads and dirt tracks; I was in my element, because this was the pioneering sense of aloneness and the type of hidden adventure trail I had been hoping to uncover on my journey. I kept checking my rally-like navigation calculations, because out here, the only signboards you find are mostly ancient and completely rusted through, or point you in the direction of yet another farm called "Weltevrede" (well satisfied). And when you finally find one you can decipher, more often than not it alludes to a destination that isn't on the map — and probably never will be. Knowing the challenge I would be facing, I'd estimated, with the help of my old yachting dividers, the approximate distances between dirt track junctions and marked these off on the copies of the excellent Engen roadmaps I carried with me.

The fact is that if you don't practise rally-like directional concentration, you're likely to pass the same ant heap many times. And ants get edgy when this happens. On a 4X4 trip in the Kalahari some years back I had the dubious honour of being the only expedition leader in living memory to say goodbye to our game park hosts twice: I had journeyed in a wide circle and confidently re-entered the park for a second time — beaming proudly all the while as if it was virgin territory.

Just when I thought I finally had my radar under control, I coasted confidently towards a farmhouse that blocked my way forward. If you're travelling across the Karoo one day, always remember that a cement-filled 44 gallon drum with a pole sticking out of it means "a farm sign used to reside here, but I've been too busy shearing sheep or I just simply couldn't be bothered to replace it." It certainly doesn't herald the way to Cradock. Yet, after pursuing a number of dead end trails, I eventually found my way through the hazy blue light and headed towards what I hoped was Rossouw's poort in the distance.

A huge bird cast a shadow over the road in front of me; looking up at the enormous gliding form above, I was torn between identifying it as one of the snake eagles and the martial eagle. Without the binoculars and my faithful Newman's bird book on hand, I settled on the martial, mainly because of the sheer size of the bird — the biggest eagle in South Africa. Many people are at a loss as to why some of us folk need to classify birds in the wild. The reasons are often synonymous with many other forms of collecting. Yet for me it simply allows you to revel in the afterglow of your finds when you get back home and extend those rare moments that often pass so quickly out there. But I've not always been as astute at identifying birds. Some years back, I was sitting around a braai in Johannesburg. After a few beers, our host jumped up excitedly and pointed with great conviction to a rooftop some two blocks away. Against the sun, a silhouette of a large bird presented itself. Binoculars were trained on the mysterious creature and there was much debate as to what sort of heron, ibis or stork it was. Then the wind changed direction and the metal cut-out of a weathercock showed itself quite clearly. Even now I can see my host smirking — albeit out of harm's reach.

It was time to get off the bike and restore the circulation to my nether regions. Even though I was wearing cycling shorts underneath my home-made padded jeans, the hardness and shape of an old scrambler's saddle is certainly not the most groin-friendly platform. Aggravate that fact with many hours of hard riding and you understand why so many old bullets prefer the feet-up positioning offered by chopper-style Harleys. I was sure that I'd toughen up or just get used to this condition along the way, but I was certainly not prepared to become a eunuch in the process.

The flat-topped mountain of Bruintjieshoogte rose imposingly in the distance. My plan was to cut around it by first heading right towards Somerset-East, and a short distance later to turn north towards Cradock over an unnamed pass that runs parallel to the Swaershoek. By now I'd been on the road some six hours and had an estimated two to go. Miraculously, a sign at the turn-off onto the dirt road confirmed that I was actually heading in the right direction. It was turning out to be a wonderfully scenic route. A series of ascents led me through rough, yet lush mountainside vegetation, and the high game fences on either side of the track confirmed this to be a dedicated conservation area. I seemed to be on a natural roller-coaster ride, twisting ever upward before being able to, hopefully, descend sometime in the future towards Cradock. After about an hour I found myself on top of the world with my head, literarily, in the clouds. The various magnificent passes had eventually disgorged me onto a high plateau dotted with water-stained putty-rock mountains. It looked like it had received more than its fair share of rain in the past few days and — judging by the enormous build-up of anvil-shaped clouds ahead — was due to receive more any time soon. Growing up in Johannesburg, I'd once heard of a father and son mountain bike duo caught in an electric storm. Riding close together, they were both struck dead by a single bolt of lightning, their protective helmets split in two by the impact. Urban legend or not, I was not overly keen to put the wrath of Thor to the test, so I twisted the throttle a little wider than usual and got out of there — fast. With the weather chasing from behind and lakes of mud in front of me, I bolted along the high plateau like Charlie Tissen of old on the "Roof of Africa" rally. It was exhilarating stuff, and by the time I stopped to read an unusually lengthy farm sign, I was dripping with mud and having the time of my life.

(The sign, translated from the Afrikaans, read: "Here lives Andre Schoeman, his bad-tempered wife, his three beautiful daughters and his three strong sons.")

Getting back onto the bike with a broad smile, I was further cheered when I noticed that I'd left most of the weather behind me. A line of mountain reedbuck trailed skittishly up the steep side of a hill to my right. Things were clearly improving all the time. The top of the final pass before the rapid descent towards Cradock presented one of the most spectacular views I'd seen anywhere in the world. The land to the north led the eye through row after row of blue-brown mountains, the late afternoon light adding great dimension and depth through the effects of its dappled contrasts and golden aura.

In the middle distance lay Cradock and comforting thoughts of cold beer and hot baths.

2

From Schreiner's Tomb to a Mineral Bath Spa

(Cradock to Aliwal North: 260 kilometres)

Thy voice is on the rolling air,
I hear thee where the waters run,
Thou standest in the rising sun,
And in the setting thou art fair.

Samuel Cronwright-Schreiner quoted this verse from Tennyson's *In Memoriam* at the burial of his wife, Olive Schreiner, at Buffelskop, Cradock in 1921.

*A*fter my first day in the saddle, I was feeling pretty exhausted. Yet the commercial buzz of Afro-Victorian Cradock shocked my system into a semi-awake state and I coasted around the town looking for a modest B&B. There were many signs pointing to numerous establishments, yet once they had announced themselves in this way, they appeared to retreat back into obscurity, and I couldn't locate a single one. I put it down to my not being used to the intoxicating exhaust fumes, and headed back to the posh-looking Victoria Manor Hotel I'd seen soon after arriving in town.

Entering the plushly refurbished Victorian foyer, I had the distinct feeling it was going to be well beyond my modest budget. It was. But, while trying not to smear too much road mud onto the French-polished counter, I decided to try on some charm. Whatever I did seemed to have had the desired effect because the tough-looking Dutch lady manning the reception area conceded a third off the price of one of the hotel's cottages, just a little way down the road. Who said the Dutch were mean-spirited and frugal?

My cottage was aptly named "Forty-something", even though after bouncing around for a day in the wilderness on a vintage iron horse, I was feeling decidedly older than that. I'd been on the road for about eight hours and, including the "breakage" return trip to Aberdeen, I'd covered some 325 kilometres. This is certainly no great achievement on a road-bike, yet on a journey that was turning out to be a mixture of a wilderness rally and an enduro, not an inconsequential distance by any means. My little rented home was a picture of comfort. Every Victorian detail, from the interior design to the furniture and fittings, appeared to be totally authentic. Even the place settings on the table were period fine bone china. The bath was an oversized ball and claw, and I wallowed in it for some time, reflecting on the good start I had made on my long, lone journey around the Great Karoo.

Refreshed, I left my overnight cottage in search of some provisions for supper. In my luggage I always carried some standby provisions: tins of pilchards, crackers and, of course, my staple "trail-mix" for snacking and lunches on the road. But I'd resolved before I set out to always try and eat a substantial supper and breakfast at my overnight rest stops. And, of course, there was cold beer to find too.

The Olive Schreiner Tearoom appeared on my left to remind me of her long association with Cradock — and the Great Karoo as a whole. She was not only an exemplary author, who wrote, among other Victorian bestsellers, *The Story of an African Farm* (1883), but she was also an activist at heart. In fact, her first act of feminism was arguably to enter the male-dominated world of literature at a time when it was effectively taboo to do so. In order not to be snubbed by the world of male chauvinism, she chose to first publish under the rather macho pseudonym of Ralph Iron. She was a champion of feminism, better treatment for the Afrikaners during the Anglo-Boer War (1899–1902, now also more inclusively referred to as the South African War) and the equal voting franchise for men and woman — regardless of race. Schreiner was known for her vigorous intellect, and this, combined with her strength of conviction, made her appealing to other powerful personalities of her era as well. One such character was Cecil Rhodes. She was initially a great admirer of his — until he fell from grace after the abortive Jameson raid into President Kruger's South African Republic in 1895. In Lockhart and Woodhouse's biography of him, *Rhodes*, they note:

> Olive Schreiner, too ... was perpetually torn between contempt and admiration for him. When she first met Rhodes, about 1890, she said she felt "a kind of mysterious affinity with him" and added that: "He is even higher and nobler

than I expected; but our friends are so different (that) we could never become close friends. He spoke to me more lovingly and sympathetically of An African Farm than anyone has ever done."

In another quote from the same biography, Schreiner shows her characteristic self-confidence in a letter requesting Rhodes to come and visit her when she said: "You are the only man in South Africa I would ask to come and visit me, because I think you are large enough to take me impersonally."[6]

As a champion of human rights, she must have often been very restless in her nearby tomb in response to the many unsavoury antics of the local enforcers of the apartheid government. In one of his final attempts to crush the popular resistance, President P.W. Botha declared a state of emergency in 1985, and the apartheid police's ruthless handling of the many uprisings that followed around the country left over 500 people dead by the end of that year.

Yet, probably nothing would have made her angrier than the fate of the "Cradock Four". During 1985, four Eastern Cape activists were making their way to a United Democratic Front party meeting in Port Elizabeth. They were Matthew Goniwe, Fort Calata, Sparrow Mkhonto and Sicelo Mhlauli. After leaving the Cradock "township" of Vergenoeg on the morning of 27 June 1985, they were never seen again. Following a number of unsatisfactory inquests, the facts finally emerged at the Truth and Reconciliation Commission hearings in 1997. In applying for amnesty, five Port Elizabeth security policemen detailed how they'd ambushed the victims' car, killed them and burnt their bodies beyond recognition. Thereafter, the victims' families at least had the meagre compensation of the truth, and the certain knowledge that the perpetrators would never really be free of their deeds, "amnesty" or not.

These were not pleasant thoughts to occupy one's mind while choosing dinner, so I pushed them to the back of the queue and went in search of a ready-assembled stir-fry. A bottle of beer, a small wine carton and a packet of groceries later, I headed back along Market Street to "Forty-something". I could have trawled the local pubs for some interesting conversation, but I was guarding the novelty of my own company jealously — and loving every minute of it. Because for me this journey was as much about educating myself and getting to know myself better as it was about successfully completing the circumnavigation and meeting people along the way — and then, of course, trying to observe their lives in context as well. And it's certainly easier to understand yourself better when you spend quiet time alone — undisturbed and in the moment. It was essential for the success of this journey that I struck a balance between these goals.

Dinner for one was a crispy, crunchy, soy sauce sort of thing and definitely elevated in its final appeal by the fine bone china it was served on. After a bit of half-hearted route planning for the next day, I said good-night to Rebeccasaurus, who was parked safely off the road just outside my window, and collapsed heavily onto the luxurious double featherbed.

ᛰ

It was very tempting just to lie in that comfortable bed the next day and ignore the aspirations of my modern-day pioneering soul. It was only the thought of an egg breakfast that finally brought me back to my senses. On the way to the hotel, I lamented the lack of time I had to explore the many cultural and historical sites that Cradock had to offer, and made a mental note that I needed to return soon.

Of particular interest to me were certain Bushman (San) art sites at the farms Katkop, Spielmanskop, Normanskop and

Kaptein, the names of which reflect their ties with their Bushman past. The interior plateau, which I hoped to circumnavigate on my travels, is arguably the most prolific hunting ground for San artworks in South Africa, and these are to be found mostly as engravings on rocks, in riverbeds, or on clusters of boulders scattered across the veld, the better known paintings usually being found on the back walls of the mountain caves that sheltered them.

Reflecting on San artworks in caves reminded me about a motorbike trail I'd been on through a particularly remote mountain range in the heart of the Camdeboo. Tired and hungry, my friend Lionel and I decided to take a break in a cave we'd spotted from the dirt track. Peculiar things, especially regarding wild animals, occur when I'm with Lionel. Before inviting him on a Kalahari trip with me many years ago, I had no idea that his Christian name originated from the Latin for "small lion". I'd been to that particular end of Botswana twice before and both times I'd only had rare, distant sightings of lions. In fact, mostly I'd just heard them roaring from far away. With Lionel, we were not even in the reserve when we spotted one of the biggest black-maned lions either of us had ever seen. In fact, Lionel ended up attracting so many lions to every camp we made on that trip that I nicknamed him "Tau", which means lion in Setswana.

Back in the cave in the Camdeboo, getting our breath back after climbing a tricky scree slope, we noticed that it housed an intriguing collection of Bushman paintings. Among them was a series of geometric shapes and notches that we imagined to be some sort of lunar calendar. These were accompanied by what looked like a celebration scene of figures dancing around an eland antelope. Then, as we sat down to have a drink and a snack, we looked across the narrow poort — and a herd of seven eland strolled up the hill on the other side. Was this merely a coincidence …?

The Victoria Manor Hotel's excellent tourist information

dossier offered some insights into the possible origins of the Bushman paintings we'd observed:

> It is the trance dance, its associated beliefs and the experiences of the shamans which made up the subject matter of Bushman Rock Art. The shamans, after experiencing the spiritual world and after having recovered from the trance, would mix paint and depict their visions for all to see.
>
> Shamans entering the trance underwent three stages — Geometric shapes called entoptic phenomena included chevrons, zig-zags, dots, flecks, grids, vortexes, and U-shapes, were experienced during the first stage of trance. During the second stage, shamans now tried to make sense of the entoptic phenomena by turning the shape into something familiar to them. It was also during this stage that culture and local environment influenced hallucinations. During the third stage, the shaman's mental imagery underwent radical transformation. Here the trance becomes part of the experience.

The last recorded clan of Bushmen in the Cradock district was said to have been a group that made a courageous last stand in a nearby cave in 1850. As was their custom, Bushmen never openly surrendered, and in this desperate battle against the Boers, cornered as they were in a cave by sharpshooters, not one of them survived.

I made my way to a table with a plate of steaming poached eggs. The ornately decorated dining room was filled with travelling sales representatives from nearby Port Elizabeth and East London. A table of railway workers in overalls seemed a little in awe of their surroundings and ate their breakfasts in studied silence. I was just enjoying the novelty of being alone in a public place, able to thaw myself awake with detached observations of human behaviour, when an overly cheery voice said:

"Do you mind if I share this table with you?"

"No of course not," I lied horribly.

Nick was a travelling pie salesman from East London. He was also a self-confessed "hack" for a local East London newspaper, to which he submitted weekly surfing reports. It turned out that he was a devout Christian as well. And the light that shone from his bright blue eyes, coupled with his overall cheery demeanour, showed that his faith was obviously working well for him. Resigned to the fact that my lone dalliance with my observation powers was at an end, I entered reluctantly into some chit-chat.

"Did you perhaps know an East London surfer friend of mine, Steve Baker?" I ventured casually.

"The same Steve Baker who worked in Hong Kong and married a spunky Chinese air hostess?" the pie man enquired.

It turned out that Nick and Steve had virtually grown up together and had surfed countless spots on the same wavelength. The forces of synchronicity were clearly hard at work.

After a prolonged and chatty breakfast, I bade Nick farewell and he hurried off in search of the big pie order from the local Spar. I'd hoped to get away earlier and call in at the farm Lombardsrus where Kassie Blignaut had made some very important fossil discoveries in 1993, but there just wasn't time. Part of the uniqueness of the Karoo landscape I was to travel through was the fact that it showcases a virtually unbroken fossil record from 260 to 180 million years ago. Blignaut first discovered the fossilised remains of the herbivore lystrosaurus (a mammal-like reptile), which lived about 220 million years ago, and then later the hewittia skull, also of the synapsida group. This group eventually evolved into mammals and were the dominant land-living vertebrates of the Upper Permian times.

But to really understand the true significance of Blignaut's find, it is necessary to go back a few hundred million years. The predominant fossil-containing rock group I was to encounter during my circumnavigation was the Karoo Supergroup. This Supergroup is particularly well known due to its fossil record of mammal-like reptiles and dinosaur ancestors, as well as their evolutionary progeny: the first mammals (such as the megazostrodon: a mouse-sized, yet mongoose-like creature) and dinosaurs. The rocks of this group cover over 60 per cent of South Africa and were deposited from around 300 to 180 million years ago. The Supergroup is made up of five subgroups, which, listed from youngest to oldest, are the Drakensberg, Stormberg, Beaufort, Ecca and Dwyka. The subgroup, in turn, that dominated the footprint of most of my travels, was the Beaufort Group. In their authoritative account, *The Story of Earth and Life*, Terence McCarthy and Bruce Rubidge comment on the Beaufort Subgroup as follows:

> By about 250 million years ago the Karoo sea was largely silted up and rivers arising in the Cape Mountains meandered across extensive flood plains into an inland lake. Deposits formed at this time are known as the Beaufort Group. It is within the rocks of the lowermost Beaufort Group that the earliest terrestrial reptiles in South Africa are found, and on the floodplains of these river systems that the early evolution of the Permian fauna and flora played itself out.

Then around 251.4 million years ago, the greatest of the Earth's five main extinction events occurred. It has been termed the "Mother of all Mass Extinctions" and over 90 per cent of all marine life and 70 per cent of terrestrial life was destroyed forever. Unlike the meteorite strike that is said to have wiped out the dinosaurs about 65 million years ago, the exact cause of this event is still unknown. McCarthy and Rubidge record some of the theories that caused this catastrophe:

> A number of hypotheses have been put forward. These include: changes in the Earth's atmosphere brought on by

extensive volcanic activity; a major meteorite impact; and a decline in sea level caused by an ice age that exposed organic-rich sediments on the continental shelves to the atmosphere, causing sudden oxygen depletion and an anoxic ocean as the sea level rose again. But to date, little unequivocal evidence as to the cause has been forthcoming.[7]

Kassie Blignaut's find was seen as especially significant because lystrosaurus was the only dicynodont genus that survived the mass extinction.

The lystrosaurus grew to between one and two metres long, was up to one metre high and survived on plants that it broke up with its shovel-like, horny beak. To look at reconstructions of this mammal-like reptile is to witness a very strange beast indeed. It looks like an overgrown plump lizard with a stump-like tail, resting on short and bowed stocky legs. The head is tortoise-like and has two tusk-like protrusions, used for defence, emanating from its upper jaw. It is believed that lystrosaurus moved in herds along riverbanks and went on to become the dominant land-based herbivore of the Upper Permian and early Triassic periods.

But lystrosaurus also has another claim to fame. Its discovery in the Triassic rock strata of Antarctica in the 1970s added more evidence to the already well-substantiated continental drift theory. Adding even more credence to this theory were subsequent fossil discoveries of the animal in places as far apart as Russia, Australia and East Africa.

The therapsids, the umbrella group of all mammal-like reptiles (including lystrosarus), are recognised as the evolutionary source of all modern mammals. Seemingly, one of the most remarkable things of the South African fossil trail, with regard to mammals evolving from reptiles, is that one is able to start with fossils depicting the development of early therapsids near Laingsburg and follow their evolutionary development to the site of the first pure mammal fossil discovery in the Drakensberg Mountains of the eastern Free State.

The 80 million year long "Karoo period", as it is known, came to an abrupt end about 180 million years ago. Around this time, the Karoo basin experienced tremendous volcanic activity, and the age of Karoo sedimentation was largely over. The subgroup of rocks that resulted from this volcanic period, the Drakensberg, is basalt: a lid of hardened volcanic lava resting on top of all the other layers making up the Karoo Supergroup. The violent volcanic activity turned the Karoo into a wasteland, and this, combined with an increasingly arid climate, as well as the absence of consistent sedimentation, meant that the fossil trail in the region stopped almost altogether at this time.

I placated myself with the fact that in terms of evolutionary time, my delay in seeing Kassie Blignaut's fossil sites in person, would be less than the blink of an eye.

ᛤ

Walking back to my overnight *tuishuis* (home from home) to collect Rebeccasaurus, I reflected on the melting pot of cultures and people Cradock had housed over nearly 200 years since its formation as a frontier town in 1814. Besides being home to its founding fathers and their families, Cradock was also a place of refuge for unsuccessful English settler farmers, a home for those Boers who chose not to trek further north, and a town of increasing prosperity for travelling merchants, artisans and tradesmen. It was also frequently home to great popular dissent about the violation of human rights in general, and apartheid in particular.

Cradock also saw some action during the Anglo-Boer War. The town was at first a defensive position for the Boer commandos under leaders like Generals Kritzinger and Scheepers. Then the British swept in from Grahamstown, and many forts and lookout posts were erected to watch over Boer civilian and military movements. And because Cradock was part of the old Cape Colony, it also harboured its fair share of Boer "rebels": Afrikaner loyalists opposed to British rule and particularly the harsh treatment metered out by Lord Kitchener and his desperate and brutal "scorched-earth" policy.

These unpopular tactics, coupled with rising Boer deaths in the concentration camps, drove ten thousand Boer citizens of the Cape into rebellion. The British viewed "rebels" as traitors to the Crown and a number of those caught were executed for treason. One such case was the Cradock boy, 16-year-old Johannes Coetzee, who was tragically sentenced to death and hanged at the town jail.

I was eventually on the road by 9.30. On my way out of town I stopped on the bridge over the Great Fish River and was reminded of Guy Butler's vivid description of a typical Karoo storm, and the dramatic effect the torrential downpours could have on the slow-flowing, viscous water course I saw beneath me.

Mindful of what the weather may have in store for me later in the afternoon, I decided to hit the road in a hurry. When I was lying in the bath earlier that morning thinking about yesterday's long ride, the length of the journey still ahead had suddenly unfolded in ominous clouds of doubting steam. *Roughly 2,700 kilometres to go of back-breaking back roads — alone; I mean, who did I think I was? The iron man of the Karoo or what?* Luckily these mildly hysterical thoughts lost impetus the moment I got on the bike, and I set off in confident frame of mind once more. In fact, it never ceased to amaze me how, no matter how hard or how long the previous day's ride had been, I never seemed to resent getting back on the bike the next day. It was as if the allure of the road untravelled and the promise of more Zen dirt totally eclipsed any doubts that may have surfaced when I was resting at night. The journey always made me feel so invigorated, alive — and complete.

The dirt track out of Cradock was in pretty good condition and, for the first 45 minutes or so, followed the lazy meanders of the historically important Great Fish River. The dew-dampened smells of lush farmland wafted over the fertile alluvial plains that hosted huge tracts of lucerne and row upon row of fruit trees. Helping the region sustain its fertility are the three main irrigation dams in the vicinity, namely: nearby Lake Arthur; Kommandodrift, a bit further upstream; and Grassridge, halfway between Cradock and Schoombee, which, combined, provide ample water for a variety of cash crops.

The Great Fish River constituted the early colonists desired eastern boundary for the Cape Colony in the 1800s. But a misunderstanding between the negotiating parties at the time, Governor Van Plettenberg and the Gwali (Xhosa clan) chiefs during 1778, confused matters when the latter understood that they still had legitimate claim to the area between the Great Fish and the Bushman's River in the south-west. This was intentionally or otherwise labelled with the misnomer *"zuurveldt"* by the Dutch, indicating that the region would be useless for grazing, as the pasturage was deemed to be "sour". To complicate matters, the Khoi tribe, the Gonoqua, believed that they too had right to ownership of the *"zuurveldt"* because they were occupying it at the time the negotiations started. As a result, the whole region between the Bushman's River mouth (close to the present-day seaside town of Kenton-on-Sea) and Cradock gave rise to much enmity between white settler farmers (both Trekboere — itinerant Afrikaans farmers — and English immigrants) and the displaced Xhosa and Khoi people, who had laid claim to the area many centuries before. Over the hundred years between 1779 and 1878 there were nine main "frontier" wars between the two sides. Most of the confrontations were understandably about claims to the land and grazing rights, but many were due to cattle "theft" by Xhosa "raiding" parties and "retrievals" by the white colonists.

The raids and recoveries were so frequent and uncontrolled by any impartial governing body that, often, the authorities were never quite sure whose cattle they were in the first place. This became an issue that would have required the ongoing services of a very large and impartial army of detectives to resolve with any finality. The local Drostdy officials, based in the newly founded Graaff-Reinet region, certainly tried to draw some lines in the sand, but the small successes they achieved were often overturned by factions of disgruntled Xhosa clans or various mixtures of burghers (Afrikaans citizens) and English settlers.

Adding to the mess were the occasional opportunists on both sides who used the period of political uncertainty to settle old scores with their enemies. Some simply saw a gap to enrich their wealth through fraudulently "retrieving" stolen possessions. One such character was the well-known outlaw Coenraad de Buys. At nearly seven foot tall, this powerful and headstrong frontiersman was used to getting his own way. Frank Welsh in his *A History of South Africa* records:

> Coenraad de Buys raided for both cattle and women, shooting anyone who objected; nine were killed on one occasion, without the authorities being able to do more than complain. De Buys defended his actions, writing to the Landdrost: "men are pilfered and robbed, and I do not know that I am subject to the Kaffirs, and that they are to lord it over me."[8]

ଓ

Grassridge Dam shimmered large and silver in the distance and I decided to stop there to stretch my legs, and take in the tranquil scene. I'd left the lush plains of the Great Fish River about 15 minutes ago, and the countryside was steadily evolving into indigenous mixed grasslands, set against a backdrop of both flat-topped and conical koppies. A large bird of prey flew lazily over the distant shallows. I dived into my backpack for the binoculars and picked it up in the lenses as it hovered with purpose. Its barred tail and brown-trimmed, serrated wings were clearly visible as I wrestled with its identity. And then it plunged to the water and I lost contact. My bird book seemed to confirm a sighting I'd never had before, my first osprey. But I was little hesitant to celebrate the discovery, as these predominantly coastal "fishermen" are not normally found so far inland in the Eastern Cape. To tick or not to tick? — that was often the question.

My route plan for the day was set to take on a north-easterly trajectory via Steynsburg and Burgersdorp, with the day's journey ending in Aliwal North. This meant that I would also pass fairly close to Lesotho with its surrounding Stormberg Subgroup of rocks, which contain a number of comparatively younger fossil treasures. Today's riding distance was around 260 kilometres, which at my average speed made good, with stops, of about 40 kilometres per hour, was about six-and-a-half hours travelling time. My general plan for the trip was to try and leave early in the morning and get to my destination around three in the afternoon; the idea being that I would then have some time to explore the area before having to set off early the next morning. It also meant I would be able to avoid the majority of afternoon thunderstorms as well — in theory, anyway.

Thinking of the unavoidable tar section I had to cover later on, I was more than a little peeved; the prospect of having to share my journey with other conventional voyagers shattered the illusion that I was a lone explorer of the timeless wilderness that surrounded me. Over the 350 kilometres I'd travelled so far, I'd only seen one car outside town limits. It was a surreal experience and I was thriving on it; besides, who needs other people's reality anyway?

Something long and orange slithered by my peripheral vision. Shooting a look back over my left shoulder, I noticed a large snake making its way off the road into the sheltering scrub. I turned around and raced back, eager to get a closer look. As I got to the spot, the snake was heading over open ground towards an eroded ditch. It was incredibly fast, but there was no doubt: I'd had a close encounter with the deadly Cape cobra. Although the fearsome orange and brown reptile had now disappeared completely, I'd seen it for long enough to estimate its length to be at least one and a half metres. Yet, as with most other snakes, the Cape cobra won't attack unless provoked or cornered, but I was sure it wouldn't take too kindly to having the tip of its tail run over by a day-dreaming motorcyclist either. This snake is synonymous with the Karoo region, and many of the early pioneers told tales of their having to share their living spaces with these shy and sometimes deadly reptiles. In Eve Palmer's classic account of farm life in the Karoo, *The Plains of Camdeboo*, she reminds us to "Consider the Cobras":

> For eighty years a colony of cobras has lived under Cranemere house. Perhaps they have lived there even longer, for their sleek and ghostly ancestors may have frequented the reed-roofed cottage more than a century ago.
>
> Lying in bed of a night, I used often as a child to think of them moving below me with only a row of flooring boards between us, and strained my ears to hear their sounds. The naturalist W.H. Hudson used as a boy in his home on the plains of South America to lie awake on summer evenings and listen to the snakes below his floor holding a ghostly hissing conversation, "death-watch and flutter and hiss", and would listen and tremble. But although I waited to hear them I never did.
>
> They are there, however, and perhaps in numbers. They fear us as much as we fear them, but they cannot do without us or the joys we offer: the broad stoep with its warm glow, a reptilian delight on a chilly day; those foundations with the lovely cracks and holes, those sheltering floorboards; and

above all the dim high rooms forty degrees cooler than the summer world without. Not for food but for these comforts our cobras bear with us."[9]

Smug at coming away from my close encounter, enriched but unscathed, I blundered too fast into a right-angled corner. It was another one of those "Oh fuck, here goes" moments. I made it about a third of the way through the bend when I knew that if I leant over any further I'd have about as much traction as a giraffe on ice. So I went straight. It's at times like these that you hang on and hope for the best and simply wait for the crash. You take stock of the pretty good life that you've had without the encumbrance of a wheelchair and bolts in your neck, and thank God that today you're actually on speaking terms with your wife. And then after being hurled about like a puppet strapped to a bucking bronco, you come to rest in a cloud of dust with your heart wedged firmly in your throat. Somebody was watching over me — again. And he or she certainly had a sense of humour; all I needed now was to survive being hit head-on by a Mack truck and then I could tear up my route map and sign up with the nearest chapter of the "Immortals".

The T-junction with the main road to Steynsburg signalled the end of the glorious dirt track shortly after my last close encounter; the tar asserting its dominance like a stubborn oil slick spreading across the desert. Cobras are also known to abhor tar — something to do with how hot and sticky it gets in summer, a wandering mongoose once told me. The fresh air was starting to get to me and my face seemed to be on fire. The ram air effect of an open-face helmet meant that my already tangential mind was being over-supplied with unpolluted, highly oxygenated air. Who needs LSD? my friends in my head chorused as I accelerated onto the boring black pathway, en route to the small town in the distance.

Then there they were. Teebus (Teapot) and Koffiebus (Coffeepot) side by side — well, almost, just a short expanse of Karoo veld separating their ancient affair. I remembered a similar picture of these two koppies from Guy Butler's *Karoo Morning*, so I stopped at a conveniently sited picnic spot to take a better look. At that moment a horseman rode into view through the dancing leaves of a giant bluegum. He sat with practised regal grace. Fumbling for my camera, I quickly forgot about the koppies and tried to focus on the fleeting photo opportunity riding swiftly across the veld. I waved, hoping he'd come closer, but he rode south with purpose. I gave up the chase and looked ahead once more. I was convinced that these were the same koppies that were shown to be on the Torr's farm in *Karoo Morning*, just seen from the other side. Lost in someone else's nostalgia, it took me a while to realise that a horse was breathing down my neck. I turned around and there was the horseman astride his glistening chestnut mare. While my knowledge of horses is not particularly thorough, I probably know just enough to recognise a beautiful animal when I see one. Yet beauty and poise were not the most alluring traits of this animal; she had a huge heart, you could see it in her eyes.

"*Sawubona, madoda,*" I greeted him in Xhosa.

"*Sawubona, baba,*" he returned with respect.

With my knowledge of Xhosa mostly limited to greetings and salutations, I asked him what other languages he spoke and he replied: "*Net Afrikaans en Kaffirtaal.*"

I was a bit shocked to hear him use the dreaded "K" word, and then I realised it was my guilt and not his. Yet even in a purely historical context, it's still a tainted reminder of the arrogant frontier days, when the land north and east of the Great Fish River was known as "Caffre" (Kaffir) territory — the land of the "nonbelievers". But out here in the remote countryside, its derogatory connotations, founded in colonial ignorance and religious arrogance, were seemingly unimportant to him. His name was Michael and he told me he worked as a herder on a nearby cattle farm. With some difficulty, I managed to ascertain that he was the sixth generation of his family to live and work there and also that the area had long been his family's homeland. Pointing to a copse of cypress trees in the shadow of the "Teebus" koppie, he proudly showed me where his own house and stables were; he was clearly a man of some means and standing in the local community. We were from two such different worlds and the added handicap of second and third language communication unfortunately lengthened the divide. After a few more polite exchanges he rode off with a wave and a warm, white-toothed smile. Annoyed that I'd only been able to take one year of Xhosa at school, I now wondered who his ancestors were and how many of the frontier wars they'd been involved in. There was a proud, aristocratic attitude in his somewhat reticent and aloof demeanour. If he wasn't of royal lineage, I felt sure that he came from a long line of implacable warriors.

CS

I decided to fill up at Steynsburg and stopped at a dilapidated petrol station on the outskirts of town. Supervising the rustic forecourt was an old-timer with a battered felt hat and a pipe clenched firmly between tobacco-stained teeth. His eyes were clear and sparkling blue. They contained such a youthful glint of mischief that they contemptuously defied the other lines of age engraved on his leathery old face. He looked like a misplaced Oom Schalk Lourens, the beguiling Boer from the Groot Marico region of Herman Charles Bosman's imagination. At any moment I expected him to begin telling me of the latest scandal revealed in Willem Prinsloo's *voorkamer*. But before he could get started, I asked him to tell me something about the town instead.

"*Ja nee*, everybody thinks Steynsburg is just a small wool depot on the way to Aliwal North. But do they know that one of the fathers of our culture had links with this town? You think I'm joking?" he asked with a smile in his eyes.

"No, no," I said politely, trying to stifle my humorous appreciation of this enigmatic character from spilling over onto my face.

"*Nou ja*. President Paul Kruger's grandfather, Meneer Douw Steyn, was born on a farm just outside of town. President Kruger himself was born somewhere near Colesburg, I think, but we at least know that his parents brought him here to see his *oupa* on a number of occasions."

"Were there any big Anglo-Boer War battles around here, o*om?*" I ventured in a more respectful tone.

"Did you never hear how we gave those British the worst surprise of their lives near Stormberg station, there on the Molteno side of Burgersdorp?"

"No, I didn't, but I'll do some research when I get to the next town."

"So what's your hurry; you still got a *langpad* today or what?"

"Ja, I need to still make it to Aliwal today, by way of all the back roads."

"You Englishmen were crazy back then and it seems you are a bit crazy still. *Totsiens seun*," he teased, his wide wry grin almost cracking his gentle old face in two.

Absorbing the backhanded compliment, I waved goodbye to "Oom Schalk" and headed for the dirt track turn-off about five kilometres out of town.

The fact that "Oom Paul", as Paul Kruger was affectionately known by his followers, had probably travelled some of the dirt tracks I was now riding added an unexpected dimension to this leg of the journey. The forces of fate had come to the party, and more than rewarded my lack of too much prior research and pedantic planning.

It seems undisputed that Kruger's grandfather lived in the area, yet what is not clear is whether the charismatic leader, "Oom Paul", was born at Venterstad near Colesberg or Bulhoek, which is actually in the Steynsburg district. That he was born on 10 October 1825 of eminent (yet apparently "landless") farming stock of German origin, however, seems beyond question. He is often quoted as being the "Father of Afrikanerdom", a result of his utter commitment to the creation of a sovereign territory that would allow his policy of "Boer self-determination" to flourish. He was also known to be uncompromising, with a very conservative outlook on life, yet surprisingly, Kruger showed an instinctive skill in the delicate art of negotiation. Against a backdrop of military successes such as defeating the invading British at Laing's Nek, Ingogo and the final battle of the Transvaal War, Majuba Hill, in the early 1880s, Kruger's most significant political success was arguably his achievement of negotiating independence from Britain for the South African Republic in 1884. He had finally shaken off the British yoke of suzerainty, the chief remaining condition being that the South African Republic was not allowed to enter into any agreements with any "foreign" power, including native tribes (except for its neighbours, the Orange Free State) without the approval of the British. It was again another shrewd, if not disingenuous, move on behalf of the British to promote their future interests for a British-controlled confederation of states. Besides these aspirations, they exercised this condition for two more pressing reasons: Britain still needed to protect her precious trading route to the north, while also maintaining a veto power on Pretoria's desire to negotiate with the Portuguese, who held the key to an independent sea port at Delagoa Bay in Mozambique. So while Britain had, on the face of it, redressed her wrongful annexation of the South African Republic in April 1877, President Kruger's government was still not absolutely free to exercise its full independence without the hindrance of some British intervention.

While Kruger was involved in many battles from a very young age, his first being the battle of Vegkop against the impis of Mzilikazi when he was only 11, he did not fight in the battle of Stormberg towards the beginning of the Anglo-Boer War in 1899.

The battle of Stormberg is probably one that the British would like to forget altogether. They were literally caught napping, considerably more embarrassing in the military milieu than being caught with your pants down. But Lieutenant-General Gatacre, who was trying to surprise and drive out the Boer forces dug in at the strategic rail junction of Stormberg, might well have disagreed. The story goes that Gatacre had departed with 3,000 men from Molteno in the east, and the column had marched all night to surprise the Boers with a dawn raid the next morning. Somehow, the directions to the proposed battle site were confused by the attacking force's guide, and the column ended up not being quite sure where it was going. Instead of sitting tight until the directions could be confirmed and not taking any unnecessary risks as his commander, General Buller, had seemingly ordered him to do, General Gatacre did what most men would have done in the circumstances: he didn't ask for directions and, relying on the compass in his gut instead, ended up around five kilometres away from his objective. To add insult to injury, the Boers turned the tables on his forces and stunned them with their own surprise attack — at dawn. After some heavy fighting over a few hours, General Gatacre had to order his men to withdraw to a safer position.

At that stage he was still unaware that around 600 of his men, dog-tired from their forced all-night route march, had, prior to the attack, found a large cosy cave some distance away and gone to sleep. The dozy group hadn't felt in an aggressive frame of mind when they woke up and, being pretty peeved because nobody had told them there was a battle on, had promptly surrendered. General Gatacre was already not terribly popular in the field and was now also responsible for the second catastrophic event of several for the British forces in a short period that was soon to be dubbed "Black Week" by the British press. Gatacre's losses of about 700 men (missing, wounded or captured) were nevertheless not the worst in comparison to the losses and humiliation of other British forces in the same week. Methuen's defeat at Magersfontein resulted in over 900 casualties and Buller's "reverse" at Colenso had cost over 1,100 losses, of which more than three-quarters were said to be dead or wounded.

☙

The road to Burgersdorp was long — and about as bumpy as a record-breaking rodeo ride. I'd got off to a bad start after leaving Steynsburg when I mistrusted the first turn-off, as it looked like it went to a derelict station and then stopped. Some distance on I saw that it had unravelled itself from a series of rusty old train sheds and was racing off into the distant brown veld — just where I needed to be. Following my resolution of trying to cover a maximum of about 200 kilometres (about five hours in the saddle) a day, set during my initial trial run to Willowmore, I found myself often faced with daily targets well over this. This was not entirely due to memory lapses from smoking too much marijuana in my youth, or simply having forgotten just how numb your backside can get travelling over prolonged distances on a motorbike, but was because of certain practical requirements as well. The distance between my designated stopover towns was often inconveniently just that bit further than I wanted to go in a single day. After my first day, which was well over the desired average, day 2's ride at 260 kilometres was also starting to feel like a long haul. The corrugations of the hardened mud road felt like they were going to shake the bike and me to pieces. When I finally got to Burgersdorp about an hour and a half later, I had to pacify a shaken body and soul with some medicated refreshment. I swallowed the painkillers resting in the shady aura of one of the giant plane trees lining the main road into town. My condition may have had something to do with a number of beverages I'd consumed while wallowing in the bath last night, but I wasn't entirely convinced. I resolved just in case, though, to find the elixir known to alleviate the energy sapping effects of all hangovers. This was, of course, the "black aspirin" remedy referred to by Sean Condon in his Australian travelogue *Sean and David's Long Drive*, otherwise known as Coca-Cola.

I didn't spend too long in Burgersdorp, but it struck me as a neatly laid out and very well-kept small town. A quick chat to some of the locals revealed that tourists to the town would probably be most interested in the monument to the Afrikaans language, as well as the "blockhouse" (small English fort) nearby. Consulting my travelling folio of notes over a long "black aspirin" at the petrol station, I made some interesting discoveries. In the protracted struggle to have the Afrikaans language protected and recognised, one of the chief drivers of the first language movement, J.H. Hofmeyr, had achieved an important compromise in the Cape in 1884. The Afrikaans "parent" language, Dutch, was finally accepted as the second language of the Cape parliament and for all other official government communications as well. This milestone along the long road of the Afrikaans language struggle was celebrated with the erection of the "Taalmonument" (Language Monument) in Burgersdorp in 1893. Apparently British forces during the Anglo-Boer War removed the original statue, which was then replaced with a replica by the Afrikaans townsfolk after the war. More than 30 years later, the original statue was discovered in King Williams Town, but had unfortunately lost its head. Only too glad to have most of the original statue back, the townsfolk resurrected the decapitated icon next to the replica. In another interesting aside, I read that when the Boer citizens (known as burghers) were in the process of establishing the town, they had for some sound or otherwise politically expedient reason decided to name the town after the incumbent Cape governor of the time, Sir Peregrine Maitland. He unfortunately refused this honour, and in a display of defiance, the burghers simply decided to name the town after themselves.

I left town after finally suppressing my hangover with another big can of Coke. Before hitting the road I'd managed to take a quick peek at the Anglo-Boer War "blockhouse", and was all the time reminded of General Christiaan de Wet's mocking nickname for Lord Kitchener's pet programme, which he termed the "blockhead" policy. De Wet claimed that the huge cost of the programme (to build, staff and maintain) would far outweigh its efficacy in being able to contain the shrewd and highly mobile Boer commandos. And, between himself and other Boer commanders like Smuts and Steyn, he more than proved his assertions correct. Under cover of darkness and armed with a few pairs of wire cutters, these wily Boers virtually crossed in and out of the blockhouse system pretty much as they pleased. Kitchener had hoped that his blockhouse cordon would not only stop Boer incursions into the Cape Colony, but that it would also serve as a type of net against which his mass columns of skirmishers could trap the enemy. He didn't only rely on the forts and the barbed-wire fences linking them to do this, he had upped the number of regular troops and African auxiliaries guarding them as well. In Thomas Pakenham's brilliant account, *The Boer War*, he lists three of Kitchener's major drives that took place in the "new colonies" of the Orange River and Transvaal to "clear" areas of Boers within the confines of the expanded net. In all three drives, using more than 9,000 men over vast areas of terrain, Kitchener only succeeded in netting under 1,000 prisoners, around 25,000 cattle, 2,000 horses and 200 wagons. But although the British had little success in capturing the Boer fighters themselves, there was no doubt that Kitchener's "drives" put the Boers' capacity to wage war under some pressure, particularly as much of their logistical capacity had been captured. Yet if one takes cognisance of the massive outlay in human and monetary capital required to set up the blockhouse system, its cost-to-benefit ratio would seem not to have offered quite the return expected. Thomas Pakenham tells us more about the enormous extent of the system by the time it was completed: "By May 1902, there would be over 8 000 blockhouses, covering 3 700 miles, guarded by at least 50 000 white troops and 16 000 African scouts."[10]

☙

The countryside had shed its singular and sparse coat of grey-green Karoo bush, which had now made way for islands of mixed grasses, presenting a rippling sea of tan and suede. After leaving Steynsburg, I had ridden up onto the temperate eastern plateau, a region that experiences generally cooler and much wetter summers than the "pure Karoo" I'd left behind. Once I crossed the Gariep (Orange) River I would technically be out of the Karoo proper and be heading into the mixed-grass veld of the eastern Free State. But I was really more interested in staying within the footprint of the Karoo Supergroup of rocks (besides the Drakensberg Subgroup) than complying with the more modern human-made boundaries. Besides, in the course of my journey I planned to cross the misleading "Gariep-Karoo" boundary at least four times, as well as to run parallel to it for many hundreds of kilometres.

I stopped to have a drink close to a lone windmill and marvelled at this naturally driven pump clanking up crystal clear water from a supply deep underground. Until these iconic masterpieces of ingenious simplicity were introduced in around 1870 in the Graaff-Reinet area, little use could be made of the Karoo or any of the other parched regions in South Africa. The system I witnessed was pumping water into a small adjacent reservoir, which, in turn, fed a chain of water troughs. By using an automatic cistern mechanism, these troughs are able to "demand" water from the reservoir when the liquid falls below a certain level.

It struck me just how unusual it was for such an old invention to have lasted so long, and especially to have survived the dumping ground of "outdated" technology that was the 21st century. There was something strangely comforting knowing that my godchildren's children would probably still witness these gangly silver monsters in action one day.

Having appeased the Luddite in me, I rode determinedly towards a cold beer in nearby Aliwal North, not sorry though that I was on a motorbike instead of a horse.

3

Across the Gariep into the Highveld Karoo

(Aliwal North to Trompsburg: 197 kilometres)

No man is wise enough by himself.

Plautus

*T*he beer plumbed new depths in my timeless admiration for the icy amber fluid, and reminded me that there is simply no better drink than your first one. Especially when the mercury is pushing 35º C and your throat is caked with layered deposits of talcum powder-like dust. When I'd seen Aliwal in the distance, I'd made a beeline for the nearest built-up area and had come to a weary stop outside a budget hotel. Sitting on a roughly hewn bench seat, I took in my tatty surroundings. Dark stains on the carpets were partnered with the dank, rank remnants of spilt booze and cigarette ash. A tough-looking waitress gave me a cheery smile and asked if I wanted anything to eat with my drink. I was starving, but I wasn't sure if I trusted the kitchen in a place that so clearly needed a good wash.

I sat there in a hedonistic daze for about half an hour, staring at the fine little bubbles rising to the top of yet another glass of beer. I was slowly becoming "comfortably numb".

"You gonna stay the night?" boomed the waitress behind me.

"Oh, I didn't know you had rooms too," I lied easily.

"Ja, of course, we get many bikers and backpackers here by us."

"What do you charge per night?"

"What me or the room?" she said with a flirtatious grin.

"Well, I ...."

"No, man, I'm only pulling your legs; keep your pants on."

I had every intention of doing just that, and as I retreated to my bike in the parking area a little while later, I suddenly realised what the British war expression "to suffer a reverse" was all about. I felt a new-found empathy for General Buller, who suffered more than his fair share of reverses in Natal during the early stages of the Anglo-Boer War.

Before I'd escaped from the horny waitress, I'd managed to

extract from her that the room prices were under R100 per night, but that meant sharing a bathroom. When she'd said "And you don't mind a bit of sharing do you?" she'd winked at me in such exaggerated fashion that I thought her false eyelashes were going to lock horns for good. But I suppose I was quite lucky though, because unlike the unfortunate Buller, no one else had been around to witness my personal "reverse" that day.

I found a drove of self-catering units virtually around the corner, almost opposite the well-known mineral spa complex. Besides needing to do some shopping and wanting to have a general look around in Aliwal, I'd only planned one essential visit, and that was a swim in the fizzing and restorative waters of the naturally heated spa pools across the road.

I suddenly realised that I had no idea how far the business centre was from my present position, and this was important to me as I wanted to park the bike and get a bit of a leg-stretch into town. The lady with the tower-bun hairstyle at reception assured me that it was less than two kilometres, which would make the return journey around four — perfect.

After dropping my things off at my compact yet clean little apartment, I headed off with a daypack and towel for my fix at the spa. From what I'd read about this once much-vaunted holiday and health resort having deteriorated so badly, I wasn't expecting much at all. So I paid my money, looked past the indifferent service, shabby buildings and overgrown lawns, and headed straight for the giant outdoor pool. There was only one other family there and they appeared to be really enjoying themselves in the acres of peat-coloured water, so I took the plunge. The water was slightly aerated from the various gases that reached the surface from deep underground and had a mildly sulphurous smell to it. Ignoring my nasal senses, I luxuriated in the warm viscous fluid that now surrounded my body. I drifted around the large pool with intermittent propulsion from lazy toes, enjoying my altered state

— just floating in liquid space. After a timeless measure I bumped gently into the side and slowly came back to earth. Getting out wasn't easy, but I had some shopping to do, and the thought of a good meal in the making soon got me going.

On the walk into town I recalled T.V. Bulpin's notes from his classic book, *Discovering Southern Africa*. Among other things, he recorded that when the original farmer discovered the mineral springs on his farm Buffelsvlei in 1828, the content of various gases such as methane, nitrogen and carbon dioxide was so concentrated that a funnel placed over these gases was able to adequately run the large cooking fire of the first restaurant built at the site.

Now don't get me wrong, I love a good walk and I was feeling particularly well-rested after my dunk in the mineral spa, but I had been walking for well over half an hour and I couldn't even see the town yet. The avenue I was walking down was very wide and gave me the expectation of a really grand town to come, *if it ever gets me there*, I thought. The homes on my left were obviously the grander part of suburbia; they nestled smugly beneath leafy plane trees and were surrounded by well-tended gardens and lawns — with what appeared to be the obligatory bird bath that took pride of place in each one. The town had been named for the then governor of the Cape Colony, Sir Harry Smith and his famous victory over the Sikhs at Aliwal, India in 1846. The "North" descriptor was added to distinguish the settlement from Aliwal South — the name of Mossel Bay at the time. At the time of its founding in 1849, Aliwal North was a strategically placed frontier town on the north-eastern edge of the rapidly expanding Cape Colony. Apart from being a health resort, its importance as a transport centre, and later a railhead on the line from East London, developed towards the last quarter of the 1800s. The strong flowing Orange (now Gariep) River was a natural barrier to the further advancement of the railway line, which meant that travellers had to detrain here and proceed on their extended ways by alternative means. But passengers being delayed in Aliwal, often overnight, meant good business for hoteliers and all manner of supply stores. Because of this, the town flourished for many years, but when the railway line eventually surged north over the Orange River, most passengers no longer had a reason to stop there, and Aliwal North's economy suffered the consequences.

Fifty minutes, and at least five kilometres later, I arrived at a T-junction with a road that headed into the main business district. Naturally, the shops I wanted were at the distant end of town, but thanking the toil-police for small mercies, I noticed that at least the road towards them was downhill. My first stop was the chemist. I was tired of being asked by everybody if I'd been snow skiing in Lesotho recently — and those were the polite ones. I sensed that most people thought that my red face, and particularly my red nose, were a result of some seriously contagious rash or, at the very least, an over-developed relationship with the bottle. And having just had a hot spa bath and walked upwards of five kilometres in sweltering heat, my throbbing visage really did look like a toffee apple on heat. Thankfully, the pharmacist was more of a gentleman. Looking down at me from under his glasses, he diagnosed windburn of a fairly serious nature. My open-faced MX-style helmet and goggles set-up was probably not going to win me any awards with the skin care profession, but I preferred the wind in my face and the subtle smells of the landscape to being cocooned in an airtight, full-face capsule. Besides, the mega sunblock cream I'd just purchased would arrest the moisture being leached from my face and warn off the attentions of the ever-thirsty wind for good. Or so I was promised.

As with many present-day South African country towns with predominant Victorian roots, Aliwal North has a large number of classic heritage buildings which sit awkwardly between more modern buildings of the questionable 1960s' and 1970s' architectural style. The juxtaposition in style is particularly noticeable when a soulless government building of that era squats next to a delicate wood and stone Victorian one. Let's be honest, the apartheid government was never revered for its aesthetic sensibilities, and was also by design the creator of many overpowering structures that cowed you into submission long before you crossed the threshold.

My architectural musings were cut short by a colourful sea of African roadside traders. Their vibrant market lifestyle has become an attainable goal for many entry-level entrepreneurs all over the continent, encouraging economic advancement in a uniquely African way. Yet it never ceases to amaze me, though, how so many of them, seemingly bent on supporting the hegemony of Chinese-made knick-knacks, make a living selling almost identical merchandise: sunglasses, peak caps, tiger balms, cell phone chargers, cheap batteries and the ever present car sun-shades. Of course, there are other kinds of vendors that market edible merchandise, but they often sell the same things too: potatoes, onions, cabbage, gaudy packets of coloured crisps, cheap sucking sweets, bubble gum and illegal "loose" cigarettes. And they too seemed to be surviving — even if only barely.

I did the rest of my grocery shopping and other chores in record time and prepared myself for the long trudge home. On the way back I popped into a motor spares outlet to buy some top-up oil and duct tape. Since Johnny's overhaul, the bike was simply purring along, and I bought the oil more as a back-up for later on in the trip than anything else. The duct tape, though, was a last-ditch attempt to try and persuade my rear number plate to continue its meaningful relationship with the back mudguard. Bumbling around the shop, intrigued as ever with the latest car and bike accessories, I witnessed a true indication of "New South African" tolerance. An obviously drunk black African man was trying to enter the shop's turnstile from the wrong side. In his frustration he was now ordering the white Afrikaans man behind the "Parts" counter to serve him at the door. The "Parts" guy was more than a little frustrated by the experience, but he held his tongue and helped the drunk to locate what he needed — and then the swaying customer was on his way. Ten years ago that scenario would have played out very differently, even in the so-called liberal parts of cities such as Cape Town, let alone a conservative backwater like Aliwal North used to be. When you witness such things, you know there is much hope for South Africa's future.

On the way back to my apartment I remembered reading about how Aliwal North had been exposed to such a great variety of South Africa's rich and colourful past. The site of the present-day town and its neighbouring vicinities has borne witness to the passing of Bushmen, Hottentots, roving Barolong, Griqua, Basotho, Xhosa, early Dutch explorers, Trekboers and Voortrekkers, as well as various contingents of British and Afrikaans settlers and colonists. It has seen British and Boer rule, as well as a number of frontier clashes between both the British and the Orange Free State's Boers in wide-ranging border disputes with their neighbour, the astute Basotho ruler Moshoeshoe. In addition, Aliwal North, in its role as a frontier town, also played the part of a staging post for further exploration by colonists and missionaries on their way north. Its strategic positioning on the railway line to Bloemfontein meant that it was keenly sought after as a key town during the Anglo-Boer War, and, as a result, was occupied by both sides at different stages. But the tragic deaths of over 700 prisoners of war (many of whom were children) in the British concentration camp that was situated here is surely the town's most tragic, and probably its best remembered, link with the war.

Yet Aliwal North has also played its role in trying to promote peace as well. Two treaties concerning the proposed settlements for the frontier wars that raged to the north-east of the town were signed here, the first during 1858 and the second around 1869. Unfortunately, neither was completely successful in curbing the ingrained enmity that arose from the recurring border disputes between the Boers and the Basotho. The newly independent Orange Freestaters were in expansive mood, but the resourceful Moshoeshoe was not easily intimidated. Moshoeshoe was undoubtedly one of the greatest early African rulers and he was revered and respected by Africans, Afrikaners and British alike. He established the Basotho nation by uniting many of the vanquished tribes and clans resulting from the Lifaqane ("the crushing" of most other tribes surrounding Shaka's imperious Zulu empire) during the 1820s. Yet Moshoeshoe didn't only rely on building his nation by providing refuge to the defeated and destitute; he also displayed remarkable ingenuity in being able to inveigle his way into the loyalties and respect of the surrounding clans and their chiefdoms. He did this by, among other things, marrying many women within these clans and always making conciliatory gestures to his defeated enemies. As a young boy, Moshoeshoe was known as Lepoqo and was, by most accounts, arrogant, aggressive and obsessed with becoming a great chief one day.

In his book, *Of Warriors, Lovers and Prophets*, Max du Preez gives us insights into some of the lessons Lepoqo eventually learnt from an extremely wise distant relation of his, known as Mohlomi:

> Lepoqo then begged Mohlomi to give him a talisman or medicine that would enable him to become a powerful chief. Mohlomi answered: "Power is not acquired by medicine: the heart is the medicine."
>
> It was a pity Lepoqo could not accompany him on his travels, he said.
>
> "You would then learn how men are won by truth and justice and not by the use of spears. If you were to go around with me, you would find where, by justice alone, I established

peace; and by genuine and effective healing, love abounds where hatred and suspicion reigned before."

Then, according to Mokhehle's interviews with the elders, he spoke the words that became the basis of Moshoeshoe's building of the Basotho nation:

> "You must be a friend and helper to all those who are in tribulation, the poor and the needy. Travellers of all types should be fully protected throughout the areas of your chiefdom. Fugitives escaping death and persecution in their own homelands should find a ready sanctuary in your land. You should protect them. The land you rule should be a home to travellers and fugitives."[11]

It seems that the young Moshoeshoe took these words to heart and, as a result, was always able to listen to others and take heed of good counsel. But Moshoeshoe also knew that there were times when he would need to defend his territories and, when necessary, he used all the military force he could muster to do so. Not only had he developed an impregnable mountain fortress at Thaba Bosiu (which was never to be conquered), he had the foresight to set about a systematic strategy of creating wealth through trade and bartering, in order to purchase the guns he required to match the colonists' firepower. Ironically, much of his nation's wealth to purchase these weapons came from food sales to the Boer and English colonists he fought against. Over a number of years, Moshoeshoe built up a formidable force of around 10,000 mounted warriors, the majority of whom were armed with muzzle-loading muskets, although some of this number were reported to carry the more modern Lee-Enfield rifles.

Moshoeshoe, like many other African chiefs, greatly respected the bravery displayed by warriors in the face of the enemy. According to another excerpt from Du Preez's book, this reverence for bravery extended to his bitterest enemies as well. While some may think it a rather distasteful way to show it, Du Preez tells us that after the courageous Boer leader, Louw Wepener, was shot and killed by the Basotho when attempting to scale Thaba Bosiu, such was Moshoeshoe's admiration for his displays of bravery and courage that he ordered the dead man's heart to be cut out "and told each of his young commanders to eat a piece of it so that they could become as brave as Wepener was."[12]

Moshoeshoe also realised that in order to negotiate more favourably with the colonists, he needed to understand more of their culture, religion and protocols. It seems that this need influenced his inviting of three French missionaries to reside at his mountain stronghold, where he allowed them to preach the gospel to his people. While Moshoeshoe himself was never converted to Christianity, the missionaries' influence on the outlawing of certain tribal customs and the way in which Moshoeshoe conducted himself at meetings with the colonists was extensive.

Yet Moshoeshoe was also mindful of keeping many of his nation's binding customs and traditions intact. Perhaps no evidence of this is greater than the accepted duty he had to bury his grandfather, Motsuane (also known as Peete), in the proper, traditional fashion. As Du Preez indicates in his book, Moshoeshoe faced a real dilemma regarding the carrying out of these burial promises when his grandfather was abducted and eaten by cannibals:

> The elders of his clan, egged on by Peete's son Mokhachane, had no doubt about what had to be done: Rakotsoane and his men had to be captured, brought to Thaba Bosiu, and killed.
>
> As soon as things had settled down at Thaba Bosiu, Moshoeshoe had Rakotsoane and his cannibals brought there. And then he informed his subjects that he wasn't going to kill them. The cannibals, he declared — somewhat

like the biblical Solomon — had consumed Peete's flesh and had thus become the living graves of his grandfather. To kill them would be to desecrate Peete's grave.

Moshoeshoe told Rakotsoane and his men to undress and lie down in a row. He then took the ritual purification offal from a specially slaughtered ox and rubbed it over their bodies, so purifying Peete's grave. He sent Rakotsoane and his men away. Later he sent them two oxen as a gift.[13]

Moshoeshoe also had a talent for doing the right thing at the right time. He knew when to put the knife in, he knew when it was expedient to play the Boers off against the British, and he even knew that if he dressed in Western attire (he sometimes wore the uniform of a French general) his colonial adversaries might take him more seriously — and they did.

After fighting the Boers over frontier disputes for more than ten years and in spite of the second treaty of Aliwal North signed in 1869, he still felt that he needed to be protected by the British. He proved to be right again and after much haggling between the Natal and the Cape Colonies, the Basotho were eventually incorporated into the Cape Colony in 1871. Unfortunately, Moshoeshoe never lived to see his wish come true; he died a year before his final vision could be realised.

ಆ

Looking decidedly like a red-faced European tourist, I made it home with my wallet intact. It wasn't as though there were a lot of muggers about, it was just that I'd drawn a substantial amount of cash at the auto-teller earlier and I'd felt a little vulnerable on the long, lonely road back to my apartment. I took advantage of the warm weather and did a bit of laundry and then fussed around the bike for a while, tinkering with things that were in perfect order. I made peace with my underlying obsessive compulsive nature by placating it with inane rationalisations like *It's no use discovering a loose wheel nut at 80 kilometres per hour.* Yet, I suppose there is also some solace in knowing that you've done your part and that the rest is then surely up to the gods. When all is said and done, though, I'm probably just a bit of tinkerer. But when your knowledge of mechanics is as limited as mine, the act of tinkering can often have unforeseen consequences. Minutes before the start of the only enduro race I've ever ridden in, I was making last minute checks to my dirt-bike. Quite why I needed to take a spanner anywhere near the bike after it had been "race prepared" for the first time in its life is still a mystery to me. Having retightened all the nuts within range of my hungry spanner, I took to the starting grid with misguided confidence. I probably would have got stuck in that first river anyway, but as I was gearing down my clutch lever came off in my hand and I coasted to a sticky stop in the middle of the stream. *Lesson number one: Never over-tighten a nut on an aluminium bracket, lest it breaks off some time in the near future.*

On an overland safari through the desolate expanses of the Kalahari years after the enduro, I remember making last minute checks to my old army surplus Land Rover, just when everybody else was good and ready to leave. Understandably, this annoyed some of the party intensely. Others rubbed it in with caustic humour, and for the rest of the trip, one or another of the group would sidle up to me when I was finally ready to go and ask, "Nick are you absolutely certain you don't want to tighten that radiator hose just one more time?"

A long ocean crossing on a small yacht makes one appreciate the many remarkable, and even more unremarkable, dishes that can be conjured up by throwing an assortment of canned foods together. It was one of those sorts of dishes I endured while watching the weather on TV. *Why is it that so many hotels and self-catering units in South Africa insist on making you gaze at a TV that roosts near the ceiling?* With your neck bent into the most unnatural and painful position, one is unlikely to enjoy anything that's served up by the

SABC, let alone reports of bad weather that look set to stay for the next three or four days. It seemed that an unusual weather system pushing in fronts from the north-west of the country was due to cause numerous thunderstorms all along my planned route west. I consoled my aching neck with some more of my Chateau de Co-Op box wine, and by the time I climbed into bed I thought little of any of the wet and windy challenges that were forecast to lie ahead.

こ3

The noise of cocks crowing clashed with the banter of children on their way to school. I collected my laundry off the washing line and received a few disapproving stares from some ladies climbing into a microbus outside my apartment. Clad only in a towel the size of a dish-cloth, I suppose I shouldn't have been surprised, but then who expects a bus full of women on your doorstep before 7 a.m.?

Unpacking my kit last night, I'd discovered that my much-treasured box wine had blown a gasket and was leaking alarmingly into the protective plastic shopping bag I'd put around it. Fortunately, not too much had been lost, and I decanted the wine into some empty plastic mineral water bottles that I was about to throw away.

(As it turned out, these handy 500 millilitre bottles proved perfectly resilient and watertight throughout my trip, and were also just about the right measure for a nightly liver tonic. The discovery also meant that I was not only limited to box wine because whatever I bought I needed to decant anyway. Everything happens for a reason.)

I had around 200 kilometres (about five hours on the bike) to do today. My proposed route was to take me over the mighty Gariep River, where I would turn left, running parallel to it for about an hour and then turn north-east for the run into Smithfield. I was hoping to say hello to some family friends who ran a successful guesthouse there, and then turn west for the first time on the journey and head via Breipaal towards Trompsburg. With the expected afternoon thunderstorms chasing me, I was suited up and ready to leave by 8 a.m.

For the second morning in a row I stopped on a bridge and looked down on an impressive river. The Gariep River takes its name from the aboriginal word "!Garib", which is said to mean "Great River". And a great river it certainly is as the Gariep is South Africa's largest river by a long stretch. From its source high in Lesotho's Maluti Mountains in the east, it flows west, growing in volume as it races across the dry central plateau for about 2,250 kilometres until it empties into the cold Atlantic Ocean, between Alexander Bay and Oranjemund. A large amount of its water comes from various corners of the Lesotho mountains with a good measure entering from its main tributary, the Vaal River, about a third of the way downstream. Yet, with the Gariep effectively draining about half the country's surface water, the intensity of its flow is also greatly dependent on seasonal rains as well.

I gazed west down the river in the direction of the enormous Gariep dam and calculated that its closest shoreline was around 60 kilometres from where I was standing. Very close to this distant point, one of the Cape's most prolific and important early European explorers, Colonel Robert Jacob Gordon, came upon this same river in the late 1700s. From the maps he drew of his journeys, it appears that he intercepted the Gariep River almost due south of present-day Bethulie. But Gordon, for reasons of deep loyalty, was to honour the river with another name, the background to which is interesting to reflect upon.

Of Scottish descent, Gordon was born and raised in the Netherlands and joined the Scots Brigade of the Dutch army at the age of ten. This proud brigade, made up largely of Scottish expatriates, actively encouraged the sons of its officers to enter the service early so that they could be trained by their kin. Patrick Cullinan, author of *Robert Jacob Gordon: The Man and His Travels at the Cape*, says the following of Gordon's enlistment: "Just by joining the Scots Brigade dual loyalty was immediately implied. Was this double allegiance now reinforced? The question will recur when we consider the suicide that ended Robert Gordon's life."[14]

It appears that this once highly respected military man and explorer met his final nemesis through an elaborate plan of deception propagated by the invading British forces that arrived in False Bay near Cape Town on 11 June 1795. Gordon and the ruling Council of Policy were fed information that the British were in the Cape to protect it from the French who had recently conquered Holland and who, in turn, had forced the Prince of Orange to take refuge in Great Britain. The British did not reveal to Gordon that in fact most of the Dutch "patriots" had welcomed the French invaders as liberators from the House of Orange's "Stadholdership", and had already happily set up an alternative form of national government. The Prince of Orange's rule and consequent authority over Gordon was therefore non-existent at the time of the British forces' arrival in the Cape; yet Gordon was completely unaware of this development. Believing what the British had told him about their wanting to take over the Cape in the name of the House of Orange, but also trying to appease the Dutch "patriot" element within his own burgher forces, it is said that Gordon virtually let the British into the Cape, with only token displays of resistance at Muizenburg and elsewhere. When the British flag was raised instead of the House of Orange's on the day of the official surrender, Gordon realised that he had been duped. Being already despised by his own forces for capitulating to the British without a real fight and having then been cheated by the British as well, Gordon's lifelong loyalties to both the Prince of Orange and the British (through his long association with the Scots Brigade) had now been betrayed. Because of this, and probably due to the fact that he saw no other honourable way out, he ended his own life by shooting himself in the garden of his house on the morning of 25 October 1795.

But Gordon's first years at the Cape appear to have been a lot happier than his last. He undertook three main journeys of exploration into the interior: north to the Gariep River (1777–78), across the Roggeveld to the Hantam (1778–79) and then via a different route with the naturalist William Paterson to the Gariep once more. He is recognised as the most important European explorer in 18th century South Africa and he left behind many detailed and accurate studies of the natural phenomena he encountered in the journals of his travels.

It had not been my original intention, yet I realised as I read more detail of Gordon's first trip to the Gariep that we had followed reasonably similar paths to get to the river, and that I had crossed his path at least three times, also coming close on another occasion near Cradock.

For obvious reasons, the wagon trains used on these early expeditions followed as many flowing river courses as the general direction of their travels would allow. In moving towards present-day Cradock, Gordon followed the Great Fish River in a north-westerly direction and then branched north-east up its tributaries, the Tarka and Vlekpoort Rivers, towards the site where the town of Steynsburg stands today. After these rivers had run their courses, they had two brief encounters with two small tributaries of the Groot Brak River and finally met with two tributaries of the Gariep, first the Broekspruit and then the Brandspruit, before meeting with the Great River itself. All along the way it appears that Gordon was keen to meet with the elusive Bushmen (San), but until this point had not been successful. It seems he was of the conviction that if he could meet with the Bushmen he would be able promote a truce between them and the white colonists. Cullinan reports on excerpts taken from *Gordon's Journals* as follows: "Because these wild people are at war with us we are very much on our guard. I shall do all I can to confer with some of them and see if this savage war cannot be brought to an end."[15]

The day that Gordon "discovered" the Great River, Cullinan records the following characteristically unemotional excerpt from his journal, dated 23 December 1777:

> we came upon the steep bank of a great river. It flowed from the east, a good hour to the west, through a gateway in the mountains. At its narrowest here it is about 225 paces wide as we saw from the flight of a bullet. In addition it flowed as strongly as the Meuse at Maastricht. The southern bank was about 40 feet high and steep, though it was possible to get to the water. There was reed growing in the direction of the gateway in places and there were high thorn-trees. The northern bank was lower, with reed and many willow and some thorn-trees. This bank had stony ridges and coarse, shining sand but the soil in the river itself was clayey and vegetal. There were reefs here and there stretching mostly from one bank to the other over which the stream rustled loudly. We called this river the Orange River; it is the same, we believe, that flows out at the Namacquas, the Garie or Great River.[16]

> In his naming of the "Great River" after the House of Orange, Gordon once again displayed his absolute loyalty to the country and rulers he'd sworn allegiance to from such an early age. It is tragic that, in the end, one so loyal should have been betrayed by the cherished and noble ideals he stood for his whole life.

☙

I was flying along parallel to the Gariep River on an unexpected — and undesired — stretch of tar. With the pharmacist's windburn muti warding off the increased attention of the moisture-sapping wind, I took in the lushly watered farmlands on the banks of the great river without a worry in the world. As per the forecast, the weather was overcast and fresh, with the cloud build-up now gaining on me from behind. The brisk early morning air made me glad that I'd decided to wear my old foul-weather gear. Designed to stave off thick sheets of sea water coming over the bow of a yacht plunging through the Atlantic, it functioned efficiently as both a weatherproof and protective outer skin. Like the pneumatically suited Michelin man, I hunted the distant horizon, ready for just about anything the weather gods could throw at me.

Deliberately trying to spoil my day, a friendly family of suricates (meerkats) decided to make a dash across the road, playing chicken with my front wheel. The temptation to swerve was huge, but in the end a bit of sharp braking fortunately averted a minor extinction event. In looks, the suricate is a kind of cross between a mongoose and a ground squirrel. Like the ground squirrel, the suricate also has the endearing habit of standing on its hind legs to survey its surroundings for food, as well as danger. And all three of these animals live in burrows underground, which they often share to their mutual advantage.

The physical resemblance of these three animals to reconstructions of the earliest true mammals of the Upper Triassic and Lower Jurassic periods (about 200 million years ago), is uncanny. And from my notes, it appeared that they shared a number of similar behavioural habits as well, such as living in burrows and a diet that included insects. Yet, while they may have shared some similarities in appearance, the megazostrodon was at least four to five times smaller than any of these modern-day look-alikes. This smallness of size, as well as their reclusive and nocturnal behaviour, is thought to be one of the many important factors that allowed them to escape predation by the carnivorous dinosaurs that lived on their doorstep. Yet, strangely, if one looks at megazostrodon's earlier ancestors, they were reportedly:

> meerkat-sized therapsids whose bodies were probably covered by hair and were mammalian in many respects. But, from a biological point of view, they were not yet mammals. They had not yet developed the three small bones of the middle ear — the hammer, anvil and stirrup — which are characteristic of mammals; and they still retained the reptilian jaw joint.[17]

One such forerunner to the megazostrodon was the trirachodon, a meerkat-sized cynodont that also lived and raised its offspring in burrows. As McCarthy and Rubidge continue:

> This is not only evidence of communal living, it also suggests parental care of young and raises the question of warm- or cold-bloodedness in these animals. Perhaps the driving force for the changes that occurred in mammals from reptiles might have been the ability to maintain a constant body temperature, and refining the ability to do this.[18]

Having just turned west for the first time on the trip, I was mindful of leaving the region of fertile fossil beds that make up that part of the Stormberg Subgroup of rocks that surrounds Lesotho. In particular, I thought of the so called "Red Beds" of the Elliot formations where fossils of megazostrodon, as well as a number of early dinosaur species, were found. These layers of red sedimentation are said to represent the final strata of fossil-laden rock of the Karoo Supergroup. They showcase a very important time in the development of the Karoo's mammalian and reptilian fauna and will be considered in a bit more detail later in the book.

I continued to ride the smooth black tar through a sea of green. Although the scenery had been pleasant enough, the last half an hour's riding had been relatively boring: too straight, too smooth and just altogether too predictable for a dirt track junkie, so when the dirt road turn-off suddenly appeared on the right, I welcomed it with a loud "Yes please!" The appealing-looking dirt road wound its camouflaged way over a series of low-lying rocky ridges in the distance. At any moment, I half expected to come under sniping Mauser fire from De Wet's Boer forces lying in ambush there, but as I crested the rise a huge herd of gemsbok met me instead. Being so far from their dry, open plains habitat, they were the last sort of antelope I expected to see here. Normally when one sees these statuesque animals in the Kalahari, they are often on their own or in small groups of between five and ten. So to see a hundred or so in flight over the stubble-grass plains in the early morning light of the southern Free State was a real treat.

A little further on I decided to stop for a rest and a stretch. Had I still been smoking my pipe, this would have been an epic time and place to do so. Instead I sucked virtuously on a red berry "Sparkle" and noticed the sun making a determined effort to break through the ceiling of layered clouds overhead. Every now and then a shaft of light would throw blonde highlights on sections of the darkened veld, giving depth and contrast to the brooding scene and the multilayered horizon in the distance. The silver-grey clouds flickered with light and activity, as if indicating some sort of meeting between angels and spirits — and the gods beyond them.

On my journey there were a number of routes that made me feel as though I were the first non-farming member of the public ever to experience them, and the dirt track between Goedmoed and the tar road to Smithfield was one of them. On this stretch, I passed a number of well-kept uninhabited farmhouses. This signalled to me that a viable farm of today needed to be a lot bigger than those started in the early years of the previous century. I spent some time looking at these places from the road and trying to drum up their pioneering ghosts in my head. They came to me as people with an ambition to live simply from the earth; God-fearing people who lived for their families, their livestock and their crops. In part existentialist, they were determined to walk to the beat of their own drums — a freedom we have witnessed through history that they are prepared to propagate, defend and pay for with their lives. There was a part of me that remained behind at these places, a part that dreamed of one day owning a farm again — not to grow anything, except perhaps the silence and solitude around me.

I rode over a high ridge and then descended through a narrow poort lined with poplar trees. And then an enormous pan-like depression opened up in front of me. In the middle distance, a large herd of springbok were bunched together and as the bike got closer they moved off at speed, many performing their stiff-backed aerial jumps known as *pronking*. As I moved further west, especially between Trompsburg and Prieska, I hoped to see thousands more of these nimble buck dotted over the course of my journey. The stories of massive herds of springbok sweeping across similar pans and plains less than 150 years ago are now well known. The colourful 19th-century hunter, Gordon Cumming, reported that: "some hundreds of thousands were within the compass of my vision."[19]

This was an impressive amount of springbok by any stretch of the imagination, yet another witness, who had apparently seen the same herd but had followed it on horseback all day, suggested that the final number was closer to a million. These great seas of springbok on the move were often targeted by the Boers and other hunters as easy pickings. There are numerous historical accounts of greedy hunters who took part in the indiscriminate shooting and wholesale slaughter of these once plentiful animals. What is not as well known, though, is just how threatening "millions" of migrating springbok could also be to virtually anything in their path.

☙

I'd crossed the Caledon River soon after turning onto the tar road joining Rouxville and Smithfield. This tributary of the Gariep is only second in size to the Vaal River and it journeys from the mountains of Lesotho through towns like Ficksburg, Ladybrand and Wepener for nearly 500 kilometres, before joining the Gariep close to Bethulie.

When sent on a mission of inquiry by the governor of the Cape, Lord Caledon, to investigate the nature and condition of the various Xhosa tribes in the north-eastern reaches of the colony, Lieutenant-Colonel Collins struck out north from Graaff-Reinet towards the Orange River around the end of January 1809. Theal tells us more:

> They then traced the stream upward, and on the 3rd of February saw a river of considerable size pour its waters into the Orange on the side opposite to that on which they were. Colonel Collins named it the Caledon in honour of the governor.[20]

Some 32 years before, Gordon had named this river "Wilhelmina" after the House of Orange's princess, but the British subjects clearly had their own loyalties and the river still bears this

name today. Yet, with the current name changing frenzy taking hold in the "New South Africa", it is surely only a matter of time before the name changes once more.

It was around 11 a.m. when I pulled into the sleepy village of Smithfield. The relatively busy tar road I'd been forced to take to reach the town had clashed with my back-roads preferences, yet certain short sections such as this were sometimes unavoidable. I decided to fill up the bike with petrol before I headed off to Pula House for a quick cup of tea with the Von Ahlefeldts.

Barbara and John von Ahlefeldt are longstanding friends of the family, and my wife and I have stayed in their authentically decorated Victorian guesthouse on a number of occasions when en route from Johannesburg to Hermanus. Barbara is also a gourmet cook, and after sipping sherry in the warm glow of the fire in their lounge, we have often enjoyed her innovative and freshly prepared dishes in their cosy dining room, always accompanied by fine wines and husband John's unobtrusive, yet attentive service.

(At time of publishing, I learnt that Pula House has since changed hands.)

It had been a few years since I'd seen them, and as I knocked on the door in my dust-caked motorbike outfit, I wondered if they'd even recognise me, let alone offer me a cup of tea. There was no reply, and I eventually learnt from the gardener that unfortunately they were in Bloemfontein for the day. But with the weather closing in, it was probably time to move on to Trompsburg anyway. I had at least another two hours of dirt tracking ahead of me, so I left the thoughts of a genteel stopover behind and headed west out of town.

4

Battlefields and Diamonds

(Trompsburg to Witput, between Belmont and Hopetown: 250 kilometres)

*Life can only be understood backwards,
but it must be lived forwards.*

Soren Kierkegaard

"So you're from Bredasdorp? Long way on a scrambler, hey."

After the lack of refreshment I'd found in Smithfield, I was loathe to divert my attention from the simple enjoyment of hot marmite toast and a large pot of steaming rooibos tea.

"Actually, I'm now living in Aberdeen; just haven't changed my number plate yet," I replied reluctantly.

He had me cornered on the stoep of the "Wegneem Etes" (Take-away Foods) in Trompsburg where I was soaking up the patchy sunlight and the passing parade of chattering schoolchildren. With his hooked nose jutting out below his battered tweed cap, he denied my display of disinterest and prodded me for more conversation. There was no way out.

"It's a pity the old number plate system has been phased out of the rest of the country; it was always nice to know where your fellow travellers came from," I said, resigning myself to making some small talk.

"Don't you find Aberdeen's too hot and dry after being quite near the sea in Bredasdorp?"

"It took a bit of getting used to, but I'm able to follow a newly chosen career path there, and in Napier I was still figuring out what that career path was."

"I sometimes think of getting out of this *dorp* too, but I'm on a railway pension; where will I go? Besides, it's not such a bad little place and Bloem's *mos* only an hour away."

"Do you need to go to Bloemfontein for supplies, or is it just a *lekker* outing?

"I need to go to the hospital there once a month; damaged my leg in a shunting accident in De Aar, in the days when De Aar was still *mos* a major railway junction. Now half the station has closed down and there's no more jobs for old *spoories* like me."

Warming to the old man, I chatted with him a while longer, talking of the days when the South African Railways (SAR) passenger service was a relatively elegant and safe way to travel. The Trans-Karoo express, for instance: long trains of sleeper coaches with an air-conditioned lounge cum bar coach and separate dining car, where waiters in sparkling white uniforms served up predictable, yet tasty dishes from a table d'hôte menu: stiff green pea soup, fish with "remoulade" sauce, Karoo lamb with vegetables in season, cabinet pudding with custard. And of course that stove-boiled *'moer'* coffee that only the SAR knew how to make. As you took your coffee after dinner, you watched the setting sun dim its golden summer light over the brown stubble landscape. And then to the bar for a nightcap and perhaps a round of cards; at other times you just sat in the '70s swivel chairs, lulled by the train's rhythmic swaying, with your mind transfixed by the dreamy tourist photographs in their perspex frames. Back in your compartment you could stare blankly out the window into the night, settling into a soothing seance with the blackness on the other side, with the sound of coal grit hitting the aluminium window frame and the lilt of the train spiriting you away — to wherever you wanted to be.

"Anything else for you, *meneer*?"

"Uh, ja please. The same again, thanks."

I felt like I wanted to own this little section of stoep for a while longer. Lots of school kids had gathered around the bike and were pointing excitedly at it, making loud motorbike noises and then revelling in their reverberations. The two-hour ride in from Smithfield had been very pleasant. At first the dirt track had twisted all over the place, designed as it was to deliver distantly spaced farmers close to their houses and not to usher travellers into Trompsburg in the shortest time possible. And then, just as the rain had started to come down, the road straightened out onto an enormous pan-like plain and I raced away from the pursuing wetness, head down all the way to Trompsburg. When I got to town the rain had stopped, but the long-held image of steaming tea and hot toast had lingered on.

☙

While the Afrikaans railways pensioner I'd been chatting to may well have got his job entirely on merit, he had reminded me how the old Afrikaner Nationalists had long fostered employment for many of their own. And many of these "protected" jobs were indeed offered by the SAR of old.

From the time Hertzog's Nationalist Party came to power in 1924 until the election of a truly democratic government in the landmark elections of 1994, the white Afrikaner had always enjoyed a certain degree of "job reservation" in a number of state-run enterprises. After the Anglo-Boer War, the financial position of the Boer fighters (which included a significant number of black African people) was desperate. Between Kitchener's "scorched-earth" and "blockhouse-netting" initiatives, the impact on the Boers' domestic fortunes had been catastrophic. In his book, *The Afrikaners*, John Fisher gives us an idea of the poverty they had to endure: "Out in the country the cattle population had fallen to less than half the pre-war numbers, and there were 3.6 million fewer sheep. Some 30,000 farms had been burnt to the ground."

As Herman Charles Bosman, the great South African storyteller, put it in his writings:

> I was in the veld until they made peace. Then we laid down our rifles and went home. What I knew my farm by was the hole under the *koppie* where I quarried slate stones for the threshing floor. That was about all that remained as I had left it. Everything else was gone. My home was burnt down. My lands were laid waste. My cattle and sheep were slaughtered. Even the stones I had for the kraals were pulled down. My wife came out of the concentration camp, and we

went together to look at the old farm. My wife had gone into the concentration camp with our two children, and she came out alone. And when I saw her again, and noticed the way she had changed, I knew that I, who had been all the way through the fighting, had not seen the Boer War.[21]

The British government, while not directly admitting liability for damages, paid out around seven million pounds in "gifts" to assist in rectifying "war damage". Even though this was more than double the original amount promised in the negotiated terms of surrender signed on 31 May 1902, it was obviously still not enough. With their farms and livelihoods destroyed, thousands of Afrikaners flooded into the cities. Such was the known level of poverty among them that they were forced to communicate in English to both disguise their desperation and to enter a business world that, up until that point, was dominated by English speakers. They were also poorly equipped to find jobs in most commercial enterprises: the majority of them were only skilled in farming activities and their other talents, like carpentry and leather making, only appealed to a limited market. Until the outbreak of the First World War in 1914, some of these "exiled" farmers made meagre wages doing whatever work they could lay their hands on, others making it more difficult for themselves by not wanting to accept jobs as unskilled labourers.

It wasn't until the early 1920s that three organisations in particular began the fight against the rising tide of "poor-whiteism". The Nationalists and the recently founded Broederbond shared more or less the same objectives for the social, political and economic upliftment of the Afrikaner community, while the Labour Party also assisted their cause through opposing the "capitalists" demands for an uncontested supply of cheap labour. In trying to attain job security for the "elite" Afrikaner labourer, Hertzog's government started a number of state-controlled businesses, of which ISCOR (1928), the giant Iron and Steel Corporation, is probably the best known.

Yet in pursuing this exclusive and exclusionist policy, the persecuted Boers became the persecutors, and the war victims became the victimisers. The creation of jobs for the Afrikaner indigents such as "wheel tappers" and even "assistant wheel tappers" on the railways, or "elevator drivers" in office blocks and department stores, would have arguably done more good than harm, were it not for the blatant exclusion of all other blue-collar workers from different language and ethnic groups. And this policy was especially severe for black Africans, who were apparently thought to be of a "lesser" class compared to Afrikaners. While predominantly in a logistical support role or working as servants, many thousands of black Africans had assisted the Boer cause in the South African War, and many had died in the field. Even more had died in the concentration camps, and now, not long after the war, black South Africans were being persecuted by blatant job preference in favour of white Afrikaners to whom many had been loyal. Yet sadly, in post-apartheid South Africa, the tables have been turned — the shoe is now firmly on the other foot. White is the old black.

ଓଃ

I noticed him get out the car with stiff, unbending legs. I was standing at the bar talking to one of the Midway Hotel's assistants when Alberto hobbled into the room. We introduced ourselves, chatted about room prices and meals, and soon he was showing me an en suite room at the back of the hotel. Somehow he'd sensed that I liked privacy. The room still needed to be cleaned, but I managed to look past the unappetising remains of a half-eaten room service dinner and told him I'd take it. While the room was being cleaned, I took a walk around the town.

What struck me most about this northern Karoo town was its extremely wide and dusty streets. While most of the old Karoo towns have streets wide enough to turn an ox wagon in, these were wide even by those standards. The storm clouds that had been dogging me since Smithfield now formed a dramatic backdrop to a particularly striking building — a beautiful yet rundown Victorian house. It had a long stoep and small domed tower at one end. It was a renovator's dream, but I quickly shelved the thought before it could take hold of my penchant for restoring old buildings and moved on. Still in the residential area, "Hendrikz Begrafnisdiens" (Undertakers) was boldly advertised on the wall of a badly restored Victorian cottage. I imagined the lounge converted to an embalming chamber and stacked coffins doubling as a reception counter in the hallway. It was when I heard the faint strains of organ music that I decided that I'd tarried too long with the dead and moved purposefully towards the bustle of the town's somewhat livelier main street.

When I'd enquired about the town's history and of any surrounding fossil sites, Alberto had suggested I talk to the librarian at the municipal library. Emmy van den Bergh was born to share information. The local *dominee's* wife, she was obviously used to assisting people in need; be it to comfort them during traumatic times or simply to provide information to wandering writers on motorbikes. I'd not expected to uncover such a wealth of historical and other interesting material here, but Emmy had me captivated for nearly an hour. She also gave me a hardcover book entitled *Geliefde Dorp Oorspoel met Genade* (Beloved Town Overflowing with Mercy) written by a previous *dominee*, Dr Gedrie van der Merwe. It was published by the N.G. Church council for Trompsburg's centenary celebrations in 1998.

Back in my hotel room and reading the *dominee's* book, I was soon into another one of the many side journeys of my trip, time travelling through the Karoo's recent and ancient past.

08

The decisive skirmish between the combined British and Griqua forces and the Boers at nearby Swartkoppies (about 60 kilometres south-west of Trompsburg) in May 1845, appears to have had its roots in the policies propagated by an astute superintendent of the London Missionary Society, Dr John Phillip. It seems that Phillip believed that the various "native tribes" north of the Orange (Gariep) River required protection from encroachment by emigrant white farmers. He suggested that this would best be achieved through the ordered establishment of a continuous band of "native states" along the entire northern border of the Cape Colony. The influential Dr Phillip lobbied the then governor of the Cape, Sir George Napier, to institute this plan for the "natives" protection, particularly for the Bushmen (San), whom Phillip was especially concerned about. The band of states he proposed stretched from the Griquas under Andries Waterboer in the west (the western boundary of which is close to modern-day Upington) and the territory occupied by the Tembus and Xhosas in the east (an area not far north of present-day Port Elizabeth). Napier and the British secretary of state liked the idea of chosen paramount chiefs policing their own states against incursions from the Boers, and were even prepared to provide some financial and armed support where they thought it necessary. The other option, of simply annexing the northern territories and subjecting all the inhabitants to British law and protection, was not deemed desirable at that stage. To understand the enmity that later existed between the Griquas and the Boers, it is helpful to review some of the events that led up to their clash at Swartkoppies.

After the death of his father, Adam Kok (the third) won the leadership contest over his brother Abraham and became chief of the Philippolis Griquas. It was during his period of "protection" that the Philippolis district saw progressively more Boers start to take up permanent residence in the area. While they had no right to alienate their allotted tracts of land, it appears that individual

Griquas were eager to sell or lease the land to the immigrant Boers at bargain prices. Clearly not able to control the actions of his people, or the land-hungry Boers, Adam Kok sought to stop the wholesale redistribution of land and approached the magistrate at Colesberg for assistance. His plan paid off, as Napier, the governor of the Cape, reacted by sending back-up troops to Colesberg and then signed a treaty of alliance with him in October of 1843. The treaty gave Adam Kok control of the area between the Modder River in the north, the Orange River in the south, Waterboer's Ramah district in the west and Moroko's territory in the east. As with the original treaty signed with Waterboer back in 1834, the colonial authorities granted Adam Kok virtually the same benefits: a yearly stipend as well as arms and ammunition.

To complicate the problem of the emigrant farmers further, this collection of Boers were not all part of one group. They were divided into two distinct factions and their political ideologies were greatly at odds with each other. The first group, under a man called Mocke, wanted an independent Boer republic north of the Orange, and the other group from Natal, led by Michael Oberholster, were content to be ruled by the British, but not by the Griquas. Yet both of them seemed to agree on one thing: to strongly resist any attempts by Adam Kok to stamp his authority on the region. Adding to the tension was a certain Commandant Kock who, in an alliance with the government of Potchefstroom, was actively trying to deliver the territory north of the Orange River into the latter's control. His large group of militant followers put a lot of pressure on those opposed to this idea, often telling them, in no uncertain terms, to move back to the Cape Colony if they disagreed.

The new governor of the Cape, Sir Peregrine Maitland, soon realised that he was going to have to back up the land treaties in the area with a show of force. While Maitland was ruminating over his next move, petty squabbles and posturing between the Griquas and the Boers began to escalate. It was finally a disagreement over punishment metered out to two black farm workers by Commandant Kock that seemed to push Adam Kok over the edge. He believed that offenders of the law were under his jurisdiction and that any punishment should only be handed out by the resident magistrate in Colesberg. The Boers had other ideas and the two offenders, who had allegedly threatened the farmer with their assegais, were "sentenced" to a severe flogging. Adam Kok decided that he and his followers would arrest the farmer (who had suffered the alleged "assault") and present him for trial in Colesberg for taking the law into his own hands. When they got to his farm house, the farmer was not there, yet instead of coming back later, Adam Kok was said to have verbally abused the farmer's wife and also stolen three guns and some ammunition. Understandably, this action did not go down very well with the Boers. The incident sparked off skirmishes between the assembled armed groups on either side, and then it appears that both Boer and Griqua went on a mission to steal as much cattle from each other as possible. The calls for peace between the warring parties by the special magistrate of the area, Mr Rawstorne, went unheeded.

With the fighting continuing, Major Campbell, Rawstorne and 200 soldiers crossed the Orange River from Colesberg and proceeded to Philippolis on 22 April 1845. A meeting was called between the colonial military contingent and the Boer leaders, and the Boers were asked to desist from engaging in any further hostilities with Britain's empowered ally, Adam Kok. The Boers replied that they were not answerable to the British government, but to the government of Potchefstroom, and also needed to be recognised as a "free people" like the Griquas. These and other concessions could not be met by Rawstorne. In the meantime, British reinforcements from the eastern frontier had arrived, and with no agreement being possible between the parties, the Boers were ordered to surrender to the British forces. The Boers ignored this order, and Theal summarises the decisive skirmish of Swartkoppies that followed:

> On the night of the 1st of May Colonel Ricardson left Philippolis with one hundred and eighteen cavalry, one hundred and sixty infantry, and the bulk of Adam Kok's Griquas, and made a forced march towards Touwfontein with a view of surprising the Emigrant camp. A body of Griquas was sent in advance to draw out the farmers. They succeeded in doing this, and then pretended to run away. Some two hundred and fifty farmers under Commandants J.G. Mocke, Jan Kock, Hermanus Steyn, and J. Du Plooy, pursued them to a patch of broken ground called the Zwart Kopjes, about five miles from Touwfontein. The cavalry then under cover of some hills got unobserved in the rear of the farmers, who suddenly and unexpectedly found themselves in front of British troops. The action that followed is not deserving of the name of a battle, for the farmers did not even attempt to make a stand. On the side of the Emigrants one farmer and a French adventurer were killed, and another farmer was mortally wounded. Fifteen prisoners were taken, among whom were two deserters from the British army. These men were subsequently brought to trial before a court martial, when one was sentenced to death and the other to fourteen years' imprisonment with hard labour.[22]

After the Swartkoppies engagement, the "republicans" under Mocke and Kock set off for Winburg, while the other half of the emigrant Boers, under Oberholster, swore future allegiance to the British Crown and remained on their farms in the district. Denying Adam Kok the sweeping new powers he demanded, the British installed a resident "agent" of the colonial authority at Philippolis. This official was accorded magistrate-like powers and was to collect rents and taxes due from the farmers, half of which would be handed over to Adam Kok in exchange for his continued "protection" of the area with a minimum force of at least 300 of his troops.

The events of Swartkoppies are more important than they first seem. They reflect a microcosm of the greater colonial border strife that continued to give the British headaches, which simply wouldn't go away. In February of 1848, having had enough of these ongoing disputes, Sir Harry Smith eventually decided to annex "the whole country between the Orange and the Vaal eastward to the Kathlamba Mountains."[23]

And this act eventually led to the significant battle of Boomplaats, just west of Trompsburg — and not far off my intended route plan for the next day of my journey.

☙

The thunderstorms that had threatened earlier flashed and boomed overhead. The damp floral scent of rain rising up from the previously parched earth flowed into my room through the big open windows. It was a sensory call to life from an afternoon slumber that came after the history book had fallen on my head — and it coincided timeously with my plans for a drink at the bar before dinner.

Percival was born to be behind a bar. Although generously built, he swivelled and turned between fridge and bar counter with the nimbleness of a ballet dancer in point shoes. His swift, deft movements between fixing drinks and returning to chat with the customers had set his small baseball cap slightly askew, giving his already humorous disposition added comic appeal.

Percival also acted as the legs that Alberto could no longer use with confidence. An immensely successful sheep farmer with numerous merino champions to his name, Alberto had somehow contracted a rare virus that had virtually struck him lame. When he'd spoken of this episode to me earlier in the day, his face had been engraved with the deep lines of pain that the tragedy had caused him. Yet looking at the smiling face behind the bar now, it was clear that with the help of his many friends Alberto was in the process of moving on from an agonising past into a more accepting future — not an easy point to contemplate, let alone arrive at.

Two smartly dressed black businessmen appeared over the rim of my beer glass.

"Howzit, *meneer*, where are you from?" asked the more gregarious of the two.

"Far, far away; I'm on a long motorbike journey around the Karoo; and yourself?"

"Nah, I'm from Jozi, got a financial consultancy and my partner and I are busy auditing the local municipality's books, so not everybody in town digs us."

"Why, have you discovered some money missing there?"

"Can't really say, bru; but hey, let me buy you a drink and you can tell me about your journey instead."

Vusi was the face of the new emerging black elite; the vanguard of the "Black Diamonds". Brimming with confidence and a zest for life, there seemed to be no end to his business exploits and network of contacts. Politicians, musicians and top businessmen all cosied up together in his busy world of commerce, and all were somehow instrumental in securing the future deals for one of his many companies. And these ranged from music promotion to advertising consultancies and, of course, finance. I was exhausted just by watching his energy flow. Normally I'm a little suspicious of anybody I've just met who tells me of their overly successful life, but with Vusi it was different. His energy and sincerity were of such power that you'd have to be a block of concrete not to be swept along with his tide.

The man on my left, also from Jo'burg, but white this time, had his own bullet-proof glass company. He was in town on some or other installation for the local BP garage. Coming from the capital of violent crime in the north, his business was apparently doing famously. Brushing off his success modestly, he turned to me with a dead-pan face and said in a low conspiratorial whisper: "What can I say, *boet?* Crime pays."

"Nick, can you smell something funny around here?" Alberto asked tapping his empty glass on the counter.

"No, not really," I said with some trepidation as to what was to follow.

"No, man, are you sure?"

"Yes, quite sure."

"No, man, I'm sure I can smell something. Isn't it maybe a dead barman?"

The penny eventually dropped and the pirouetting Percival refilled Alberto's glass.

Dinner was ready and I moved off towards a steaming veg platter in the vast dining-room next door. The glass of red wine I poured from my inelegant, yet practical, plastic "decanter" showed absolutely no sign of bottle shock, and I silently toasted the characters I'd already met that day, and those that I was hoping still lay in ambush ahead.

I popped back into the bar for a nightcap later. Vusi and his business partner, Rendani, were having an animated discussion with the bullet-proof glass man. The gist of the conversation revolved around white racial stereotypes in South Africa, and the current topic was Vusi's perception of the differences between English- and Afrikaans-speaking white folk.

"Ja, but you can't say that the English-speaking population are all whingers on the strength of Tony Leon's nasal whine," countered the glass man.

"Look, bru, the thing is I just find it easier to do business with Afrikaners. They just seem more straight-forward. There's less subtlety with them, less guesswork. Maybe they're just more on the surface," said Vusi, rolling his big brown eyes skyward, his baby face nodding backwards and forwards to emphasise his point.

"What amazes me is that you okes are prepared to cosy up to the people who were largely responsible for apartheid and who never gave the voting rights of blacks a second thought, especially since Hertzog's Nationalists came to power in the 1920s," said the bullet-proof glass man.

"It may seem strange to you, but perhaps it's because we're similar tribal people. I mean, we're both strict followers of fundamental family values and other cultural traditions. And both of our groups came together as tribes in South Africa, while the English-speaking whites brought their traditions with them when they settled here."

My head had been swivelling left and right like an umpire at a tennis match. I grabbed my chance to say something when the debate paused for a moment.

"You know what, guys, there's a lot of truth in what you're both saying, but I need to set the record straight on one thing. The root stock of most English-speaking South African families arrived in this country almost 200 years ago. When they decided to settle in South Africa they made a conscious decision to make their new country their home. So maybe they don't have an easily identifiable culture that's radically different to the Brits, and yes, most of them still enjoy a number of Eurocentric pursuits, but I can promise you one thing, you offer the descendants of any of those early families a one-way ticket back to Britain and you'll have very few takers — because they simply wouldn't fit in there anymore."

"Ja, that's only because you've got it so good here, bru," sparred Vusi.

"Granted we have it good here, yet our forefathers spilt no less of their sweat and blood than your average Afrikaner — or any other South African group for that matter. Perhaps we're more individualistic than other cultural groups and often stand divided on issues of common concern, but that doesn't mean that we should be made to feel less important or welcome as citizens," I returned.

The conversation see-sawed back and forth and on some small, yet still significant level, the cultural complexities of the "New South Africa" seemed better understood by the time we tottered off to bed.

ೞ

Breakfast was a solid country hotel buffet affair. Our well-lubricated political and cultural debate in the bar the previous night had left me with a mildly throbbing sinus hangover. It was too early for the "black aspirin" treatment, so I swallowed two Panado with my fresh orange juice instead. By the time I fetched my luggage in the room after breakfast, I was feeling a lot better and ready to hit the road.

The morning air was fresh and the veld sparkled with moisture from the previous day's rain. I'd left the mixed grassveld behind me somewhere between Smithfield and Trompsburg and was currently travelling through a narrow band of vegetation known as the sweet grassveld. Soon after leaving Trompsburg I would be moving out of the temperate eastern plateau, firstly into a desert succulent area for a while and then back into the Karoo shrub and grasses for most of the remaining journey. Both of these latter biomes occur largely within the vast semi-arid plateau that encompasses the bulk of the Great Karoo's far-reaching boundaries. The day's route plan was a substantial 250 kilometres — about six-and-a-half hours on the road — and would take me through the old diamond-mining town of Jagersfontein, the nearby railhead of Fauresmith and then onto Luckhoff, with my final destination being Hopetown.

I passed the farm Tweefontein about ten minutes out of town. Emmy had told me that various fossils had been discovered there and had kindly given me the owner's name and telephone number. Yet on speaking to him, I'd learned that the finds had in fact taken place a little further down the road at an adjoining farm called Platfontein. I'd unfortunately been unable to raise the owner before leaving town and resolved to try and contact him at a later stage.

The battleground of Boomplaats was only about five minutes ride off the main dirt road to Jagersfontein, so I decided to take a look. On the way into the site I saw two statuesque secretary birds strutting purposefully through the spindly brown grass. Their awkward, stiff-legged gait made them look as if they were on stilts, their stooped postures and stern dispositions giving them the appearance of two Dickensian schoolmasters comparing notes on a field trip. The claimed evolution of birds from dinosaurs can be readily recognised when comparing reconstructions of archaeopteryx, (the earliest known bird ancestor, which lived around 150 million years ago) with the modern secretary bird. Whilst archaeopteryx was only about the size of today's crow, its stature and general appearance closely resembled that of the secretary bird, the most obvious differences were its reptilian teeth and long bony tail inherited from its dinosaur ancestors. Yet, even with this evidence, it took palaeontologists many years to reach accord on the evolutionary pathway linking dinosaurs to birds.

Standing in the thick silence under the blue gums at the site commemorating the battle of Boomplaats, I felt the strange presence of peace often left behind on old battlegrounds. And then an anecdote I remembered about another departed soul, from the slightly more recent Anglo-Boer War, gave me reason for a more light-hearted moment. Having lost his preferred horse in an engagement with British forces near Edenburg in 1901, Denys Reitz (of *Commando* fame) had ridden hard to escape the enemy and had somehow managed to outrun them on a shetland pony. The image of this battle-hardened Boer bouncing into the Boomplaats battle site on a diminutive horse brought a bright smile to my face. But jokes aside, the nearby Boomplaats cemetery had nearly caused the Reitz family their own tragedy as well:

> This graveyard was of some personal interest to me, because it had almost caused my father the loss of his position as President of the Free State when I was a boy. The British government many years before had erected headstones over the fallen soldiers inscribed with the words: "Killed in action against the Rebel Boers." Many of these stones, in course of time, fell to pieces, so my father ordered replicas with the original inscription faithfully copied. This gave rise to much ill-feeling, for there were indignant patriots who considered the epithet "rebel" an insult to the Boers, and my father very nearly lost the next presidential election in consequence."[24]

The Battle of Boomplaats (29 August 1848) was largely the result of emigrant farmers from the Cape Colony wanting independence from British colonial rule — and the British refusing. Sir Harry Smith, recently appointed governor of the Cape, was of the opinion that all emigrant farmers who took up arms against the British forces were "rebels". He held this view as the vast majority of the forces now mustered against him under Commandant-General Pretorius were still considered citizens of the Cape Colony and, because of this, he believed them still to be accountable to the laws of that sovereignty. In addition to this, whether legally enforceable or not, the Cape of Good Hope Punishment Act of 1836 also gave the governor the opportunity to prosecute any of its citizens for offences committed south of 25° of latitude, close to present-day Bela-Bela. Yet, the border situation only reached boiling point when Sir Harry Smith proclaimed the Queen's full sovereignty over a vast new area to the north of the Cape Colony, described as that bounded by the Orange River in the south, the Vaal River in the north and the Drakensberg (then known as the Quathlamba — "piled-up rocks") in the east.

When asked by Commandant-General Pretorius to withdraw this proclamation, Sir Harry Smith refused to back down and finally crossed the Orange River with his assorted force of around 800 men on 26 August 1848. His ranks swelled when the Boers' old adversaries, the Griquas (under Waterboer and Kok), as well as a number of pro-British emigrant farmers, added about 300 fighting men to his cause. En route to meet the forces of the Boer emigrants, it appears that Smith tried to dissuade several Boer commandants from siding with "Pretorius's uprising". Adding to the enmity between himself and the British was the fact that Pretorius felt that they had not honoured an earlier agreement with him. He believed they had promised him that if he could prove that the majority of emigrant farmers were against British rule of the area, the British would then not impose themselves on the region. Pretorius had then drummed up the necessary support for independence among the Boers, but the British had still gone ahead and proclaimed sovereignty over the disputed territory. Smith, countering this argument, intimated that the agreement Pretorius was alluding to referred to emigrant farmers' opinions north of the Vaal River — and not to the south. The truth of the matter will probably never be known.

Yet, regardless of the road that led them there, the opposing sides seemed set for a confrontation. Smith was, however, still hoping that his considerable force (somewhere between 1,100 and 1,400 strong) would give him the required leverage to get Pretorius to change his mind and back down from engaging in battle. In search of Pretorius, Smith made his way through Philippolis and Visser's Hoek, and then halted at Touwfontein on the morning of 29 August 1848. Intelligence gathered from a shepherd revealed that the Boer forces had spent the night at Boomplaats, and further scouting uncovered them in a range of hills not far from their overnight position. It appears that Pretorius was hoping to lure the British forces deep into the hills where his army of around 500 lay in ambush. But with Smith a tantalising target in the vanguard of his column, it seems that some of the Boer fighters opened fire too soon, thus warning the bulk of the British forces behind.

The battle that ensued saw much fierce fighting, with the British forces slowly edging forward by systematically dislodging the gauntlet of Boers from their defensive line of hills. After defending the last ridge and realising they had no chance of overcoming the superior numbers and firepower of the British, the Boers finally fled to the east. But as Theal tells us:

> Sir Harry Smith, who had grown old fighting in the Spanish peninsula, in Kaffirland, and in India, in his next despatch to the secretary of state described the battle of Boomplaats as "one of the most severe skirmishes that had ever, he believed, been witnessed." There were no cowards on either side of the engagement.[25]

The estimates of the fatalities on both sides are a matter of some dispute. The British losses were somewhere between 17 and 22 killed and 38 wounded, whereas the Boers insisted that only nine of their number were killed; Sir Harry Smith originally reported that 49 burghers were found dead in the field, and five wounded. The disparity in the number of losses seems to be mainly due to the Boers being concealed among boulders in the hills and acting as sharpshooters, compared to the British forces who had to storm the hills over open ground. Whatever the final tallies, the Boers suffered a decisive defeat at Boomplaats and after this show of strength, the colonial government was able to govern the newly proclaimed Orange

River sovereignty for several years with little threat of military opposition.

಄

With my mind still on the battlefield, I coasted towards the old diamond mining town of Jagersfontein. The open grassland was punctuated with the occasional herd of blesbok, while ranges of crusty sugar-lump hills floated above the indistinct horizon in the distance. Flotillas of centipedes diced unwittingly with death as they tried stubbornly to herd me off the road. A fiscal shrike sat in plump contentment on a fence post as I passed, its well-stocked larder of newly harvested centipedes wiggling defiantly on barbed-wire spikes.

After about half an hour of smooth dirt riding, I reached the old mining village and industrial compounds on the outskirts of Jagersfontein. The town gets its name from a farm (originally owned by Jacobus Jagers, a Griqua) where the area's first diamond was discovered by a Mr J.J. de Klerk in 1870. Not very well known by the broader South African public, this quaint old mining town boasts a hand-dug "big hole" (vertical open mine) significantly bigger than Kimberley's. The town also held the record for the biggest single diamond found (the 971 carat Excelsior stone) until the famous Cullinan diamond was discovered close to Pretoria in 1905. Diamonds from Jagersfontein are affectionately known as "Jagger" diamonds and the quality of the blue-white stones, in particular, are still used as an international benchmark.

I parked the bike in the quiet main road and took in the delightful old buildings. The general architectural ambience made the village feel like a crossover between a typical Karoo *dorpie* (small town) and the gold-rush town of Pilgrim's Rest in Mpumalanga. When the initial settlement was proclaimed as public diggings on 29 August 1870, it had little to offer in terms of public facilities. To remedy this, the original Jagersfontein farmstead was bought by the government to function as an administrative centre, and a big eucalyptus tree served as an unconventional jail, a solid base to which prisoners could be tethered.

Looking around at some of the Herbert Baker-designed buildings — a number of which are run down and empty — I thought of them as memorials to the town's more prosperous years of the late 1800s. Although it is common for most travellers to think of Karoo *dorpies* as being unnaturally quiet and empty, especially on a week day in the middle of the month, Jagersfontein looked decidedly deserted. Perhaps the buildings marking the obvious grandeur of the past made me expect to see flashes of commercial opulence. Instead, I was greeted by scenes of a few poverty-stricken people in the doorways of tatty "General Dealer" stores, housed in beautiful, but decaying Victorian buildings. I was saddened by the seemingly wasted tourist potential of the town itself, yet, not too far off the main street, the Open Mine museum does allow one to get a sense of the boomtown frenzy of a bygone era. But what it lacks in obvious high-street tourist appeal, Jagersfontein certainly makes up for in authenticity — just a little imagination is required.

Moving a little further down the road, I was quite surprised when I came upon a promising-looking coffee-shop. A compact, neatly dressed woman was busy getting the shop ready for the day's business.

"Is your coffee on the boil yet?" I asked.

"Will be in just a couple of minutes; take a seat so long."

I was surprised by her fluent English, probably because I'd expected to be served by a conservative Afrikaner *tannie* in such an Afrikaans dominated town. But, as I came to learn on my travels, in many of these small country towns, a number of the nouveau *dorp* dwellers are worldlier city folk who've opted out of the rat race, yet brought their city sophistication and multilingualism with them. And by her style and obvious efficiency, my hostess certainly appeared to be one of them.

Sitting on the veranda of the coffee-shop, I noticed another enterprising-looking business called "Stagedor Productions" across the road. The name suggested a theatre company of some kind, and, piqued at this incongruous promise of thespian delights, I crossed the street to take a look. It is difficult to describe the multitude of office support services that this little shop offers the public, but of theatre productions there was no visible evidence. It turned out that the owner, a fairly recent immigrant to the town, was also the editor of the local free newspaper, the secretary cum treasurer of the business chamber and a knowledgeable provider of tourist information as well. It always amazes me how so often, especially in these small struggling towns, the local people who have been in the town for many years are generally so slow to get involved to uplift the broader community. And then so much is left to be done by so few, and most of them are *inkomers* (foreigners). Pondering over this phenomenon, I crossed back over the road to my steaming cup of black filter coffee. I'd noticed earlier that the coffee-shop lady was unpacking a tray of freshly baked bran muffins and was pleased that I'd ordered one. It sat like an island of indulgence among a sea of jams and cheeses — what bliss.

Paging through the local free newssheet, I wondered whether the conservative wisdoms it contained were indicative of the mindset of the town as a whole, or just the contributors themselves. The most interesting titbit I gleaned between its covers was the fact that the Jagersfontein Mine rugby team had beaten a touring Transvaal XV by 6 points to 4, a much talked-about and historic victory way back in 1914.

I could have easily sat there all morning, but I'd only done a fifth of my planned day's journey and I needed to get on my way.

I thanked my efficient hostess and set out on the road to nearby Fauresmith, only some 12 kilometres away.

Quite how I missed the turn-off into Fauresmith is still a mystery to me. For some reason I'd not been focussing on my odometer and was convinced that the town sign I saw pointed south and not east as I'd expected it to. About 15 minutes later I came upon a sign to Philippolis, which I knew with some certainty was not on the way to Fauresmith, so I turned around and headed back into the teeth of a mounting gale. The trouble with an old scrambler with a smallish engine is that it generally does not like to compete with strong headwinds, so when I finally found the town, I had already lost so much time that I didn't have too long to spend there.

Fauresmith's most striking feature is unquestionably the railway line (the old railhead for Jagersfontein) that runs down the centre of the town's main street. Apparently, it was necessary to lay the track in this position due to the town being almost encircled by koppies on three sides. According to various sources, this enchanting feature is only shared with four other towns in the world: two in the United States, one in Australia and the last in Mozambique. Reflecting on this unusual feature, I came to the conclusion that it was probably not the safest place to be wandering about on foot after visiting the local pub, but then again, useful if your rugby team has lost and you just want to end it all.

A number of archaeological sites were also excavated in the vicinity of the town, and the cumulative effect of the findings gave rise to the term "Fauresmith Culture". The items uncovered included numerous stone artefacts and implements that were apparently used by early and middle Stone Age people to hunt large-sized game between 35,000 and 50,000 years ago. Yet, when similar findings were discovered at other diggings in the adjacent Northern Cape, the defining term "Fauresmith Culture" was, of course, no longer singly relevant and it lost its previous importance.

Yet, when Denys Reitz rode through Fauresmith during 1901 on his way to locate General Hertzog, as well as a horse with longer legs, he may well have thought that Stone Age men still lived there:

> As we went up the main street a number of unkempt individuals rushed at us, rifle in hand, and ordered us to halt. They crowded round threateningly, with shouts of "*Maak dood die verdomde spioene*" ("Kill the damn spies"), although they must have known that we were nothing of the sort, and only wanted a pretext to rob us. We sat our horses, uncertain what to do with such ugly customers, and it looked as if we were in for serious trouble, for already greedy hands were clutching at our wallets, and trying to pull us from our saddles. Just then two gaunt, famished-looking women rushed from a neighbouring house, and shrilly ordered them off. They had so much influence over the rabble, that they stood aside growlingly, and allowed us to accompany our forbidding guardian angels to their home.[26]

Noting the town's plentiful Victorian architecture and neatly kept sidewalks, and having said hello to a number of friendly locals, I felt reasonably confident that the "rabble" had moved on and made a mental note to come back again.

Winding my way through a series of hills outside Fauresmith, I looked up to check on the mood of the weather gods. Things looked ominous, and it seemed like the power of the dry-weather halo I'd been wearing was about to be tested. Then the bike spluttered to a juddering halt. Now fixing a motorbike in the rain on a deserted Karoo road has never been my idea of a fun day out, yet I tried my best not to upset the surrounding fauna by keeping my profanities to a muffled minimum. Having extricated myself from my foul-weather gear and opened up the tool bag I carried around my waist, I felt like an unqualified surgeon attempting to perform a double bypass. Cannily, I decided to look at the spark-plug cap first; it looked very healthy, so I pushed it expertly back into place. After tapping this and that, I looked accusingly at the fuel filter, half expecting a large piece of grit to be blocking the fuel's passage. Instead, my keen mechanical eye was drawn immediately to the nub of the problem. The fuel lever was off.

Red-faced yet somewhat relieved, I resumed my ride west. One of the only downfalls of old four-stroke motorcycles is their propensity to become flooded. This is why, when I stop for any length of time, as I did in Fauresmith, I always switch the petrol off, but then, clearly, sometimes forget to switch it back on again. Being mechanically challenged, I'm always amazed at how my wife (who, thank God, had a very practical father) and I managed to overcome various engine troubles while sailing around Brazil in our small 30-foot Miura. Quite how we managed to disassemble a water pump and then more incredibly, reassemble the unit, in 35º C heat and 80 per cent humidity — all the while squashed between the cabin sole and the chart table like a pair of sweaty, and swearing, sardines — I will never know. What I do know, though, is that the feeling of satisfaction (coupled with sheer incredulity) at being able to overcome the seemingly impossible was immense. Our joy, however, was short-lived. Some floating rope wrapped itself around our propeller not long after we got under way. Our forward progress was severely hampered as we entered a narrow channel between two large rocks that experienced a strong tidal race. Back to our mooring we hobbled, and after diving into the filthy and murky waters of Guanabara Bay, I managed to disentangle the rope and we made it out to sea without further incident — for the rest of that day anyway.

Thinking of my need to invest in a workshop manual and some quality time getting to know the "art of motorcycle maintenance", I set off in the direction of Luckhoff — some 48 kilometres distant.

The flat plains stretched languidly to the low-slung ridges on the darkening horizon. I expected to see vast herds of springbok, yet there was just no sign of them. Even the occasional sheep had disappeared. Just emptiness, seemingly devoid of life, yet I knew the landscape was masking the little creatures that chose to remain camouflaged and inconspicuous: the meerkats, mongooses, tortoises, lizards, agamas, skinks, geckos, snakes — and thousands of insects such as beetles, termites and ants. The wind was building up to storm strength and it slowed me down significantly, the old 250 cc engine battling to maintain cruising speed against the strong gusts. And with the weather worsening, I decided to look for overnight accommodation in Luckhoff.

In many of the small towns I was passing through the municipalities often doubled as their tourist information centres, and Luckhoff was no exception. I rode slowly through the town's streets and, passing a number of interesting looking stone buildings, I reached the municipality's offices. The Afrikaans lady behind the counter was overly helpful — I got the feeling that she didn't see many tourists, and as such, I was quite a novelty — and she plied me with heaps of information on the town and the surrounding area. I sat there a while reading the material, deciding on my next move. She'd also given me the telephone number of the Barnards, who host guests on their farm Koffiekuil. But after trying their number a couple of times and receiving no reply, I felt that something was telling me to push on. I decided to have a quick look around the town before I left and threaded my way through the burgeoning throng of farm labourers doing their Friday shopping.

From a historical and tourist perspective, there wasn't a whole lot that held any interest, and I surmised that most tourists passed through Luckhoff en route to the more picturesque and popular resort at Vanderkloof Dam, some 35 kilometres away.

A stone gunpowder magazine bore testimony to the town's participation in the Anglo-Boer War and a gas streetlamp marked the romantic lighting of a bygone era. I'd bought a photostat copy of the town's history from the municipality, and besides learning that the town was named after the N.G. *dominee*, H.J. Luckhoff, as well as a few other inconsequential facts, I found the poems and anecdotal writings of one of the town's prominent Afrikaans writers most entertaining. With apologies to the writer, Mr Pieter Fourie, for any nuances that may be lost in translation, the anecdote that follows depicts the turning on of the gas lamps around the turn of the 20th century:

> Luckhoff is getting street lights. Not the type of light bulbs fed by a Lister engine from a power station somewhere. No, gas lights. The last town in Africa with gas lights!
>
> Wow, what an occasion that was! Our family sat on the stoep at the bottom end of Rabie Street awaiting the darkness in eager anticipation not even rivalled by Christmas Eve. Then with the light of one match *Blokman* propelled the entire town into the twentieth century with a showering of light. Suddenly, out of the blue, a large scrub-hare was caught in the beam of the street light … sitting bold upright like the late Uncle Piet Burger atop his saddle-horse. And sit he did … just like Blanc Bosman sits at the very well known high wooden counter not so far away from church! And for this "scrub hare" his "sit" was also a refreshing one.

After filling up the bike with petrol I set off in search of the elusive dirt track to Wanda. Most people I'd spoken to had tried to direct me through Orania — that conservative "whites only" enclave to the south-west — en route to my day's destination of Hopetown. But I was doing my best to stick to the dirt tracks, besides I'd been through Orania once before and had no desire to revisit the foolhardiness of segregation that the vast majority of white South Africans had gladly left behind after 1994.

The wind and rain started its relentless pummelling. My desire for fresh air, provided by my open-faced MX helmet, was soon tempered by the stinging rain. Anyone who has ridden a motorbike in the rain wearing a helmet such as mine will tell you that it's the new improved version of Chinese water torture. It's uncanny how the hard liquid missiles manage unerringly to find the small area of soft cheek skin between your goggles and the lower part of your helmet — not to mention your naked nose, which is totally exposed to their stinging assault. As a result, I looked forward to Wanda as though she was a long-lost protective aunt with rain-proof skirts. Through my blurred vision I caught glimpses of the changing landscape — there seemed to be more sand and less vegetation — and I wondered just how long ago it was since this increasingly desolate region had last seen rain.

After a tortuous hour, a lone building presented itself on the horizon. It turned out to be a police station, and it was the only building I ever saw in Wanda. Not feeling like cheering myself up in a dry but probably humourless charge office, I pressed on towards Witput, close to the junction with the N12, where I planned to turn left onto a short stretch of tar and head towards Hopetown.

The last three-quarters of an hour's riding before Witput reminded me of helming a yacht into an oncoming gale. In these conditions, depending on how fine a windward course you are steering, it's necessary to fight the boat's natural desire to go sideways on to the wind. This phenomenon is known as "weather-helm", and I was experiencing almost exactly the same difficulty on the bike, except my margin for error was even smaller. I had to steer very precisely so as not to trip myself up on the high sand ridges on either side of my chosen metre-wide track; I focussed hard on getting it right as I was reasonably keen to avoid making a lasting impression in the sand. But by surrendering to the difficulty, a kind of Zen meditative concentration eventually took over, something I've found that often results from repetitive, yet challenging tasks. Despite being in a trance-like state I noticed a railway line about to cross my track. And then a deserted station and a cluster of old railway houses rose to partner it through the slanting rain.

I'd arrived in Witput, from whose village well some dark myths were about to unfold.

5

Railways, River Ways and a Well Full of Laxatives

(Witput via Belmont to Prieska: 221 kilometres)

*Till we feel the far track humming,
And we see her headlight plain,
And we gather and wait her coming –
The wonderful northbound train.*

Last verse of "The Little Karoo" by Rudyard Kipling

I got off the bike and walked over to the station. From a distance the building still looked neat and functional, but when I got closer the decay became obvious. Weeds were pushing through the platform and a broken counter window marked where the ticket office had once stood. The passengers and parcels being long gone, the pigeons had taken over — I saw two male birds squabbling over a patch of territory near an old fireplace — and the pages of an outdated timetable turned in the wind.

Jumping onto the tracks, I placed my ear on the line to hear if there were a train coming. But all I could hear was my own breathing, and then the distant echo of a child's voice from long ago. On our way home from boarding school on a Sunday, my friend Douglas and I used to listen for trains like this, and then bet each other Star toffees on how many seconds would pass before the next train would arrive. He usually won, as he would keep his ear on the line much longer than I dared — but then he regularly got his arse kicked by the station master as well.

No matter what "advances" are made by science, there are some forms of existing technology that are just too good to be pushed out the way by the newcomers. Take a book, for example. With the advent of the canny digital storage systems of the modern PC, many computer pundits predicted the complete disappearance of paper. They were more confident of these assertions when PCs became smaller — and even portable. Yet, even with the advent of "digital book readers" like the Kindle, conventional book sales in South Africa are still going strong. This is because a book is a form of technology that simply can't be improved on: it's organic, pliable and can even screen out the sun while feeding you information — and it doesn't need batteries as it's powered by your mind.

The concept of passenger train travel is in much the same league.

In terms of transporting people, it's a hundred times more space- and fuel-efficient than the motor car. And running on "clean" electrical power, it's a thousand times more environmentally friendly as well. But apart from its practical benefits, rail travel also does something for the soul. My late Aunty Sheila used to catch the 6.35 a.m. train from Fish Hoek to Cape Town every day of her life. In addition to a healthy four kilometre walk to the station and back, she knew she had three-quarters of an hour to herself every day: to read the paper, do the crossword or just stare blankly out of the window. With train travel, the choice is yours; do the same journey in a car and you're liable to become hypertensive in the traffic. There's no doubt in my mind, Aunty Sheila's positive and philosophical outlook on life was definitely influenced by the many meditative journeys she'd taken. So why then do so many people in Cape Town prefer using roads over railways? Is it because of a perceived boost in status, a bad metro service, time-saving, convenience, safety or just plain ignorance? Apart from generally poor and crime-ridden metro rail services all over South Africa, perhaps some other contributory factors are the perceived need for "personal space" in a commuter's "private time" — as well as speed of transfer, particularly on long journeys. But if the South African railway authorities — and government initiatives — had been more proactive in developing the high-speed rail technology that's been on the table since 1984, speed of transfer would certainly not still be a handicap today. And when it comes to the more affluent commuters not wanting to share their physical space with others, surely the environment is worth sacrificing something for? Of course, assuring passengers of an efficient service and safety from crime needs to be a given.

Back on the old teak-slatted concrete bench at Witput's deserted station, I heard a nostalgic high-pitched "zing" rise from the rails. A bright orange electric locomotive appeared through the veil of soft rain and was coming on at a steady speed. As it drew abreast of me, the electric hum of its many thousands of horsepower reverberated through the platform and pulsed through my body. The driver waved at my captivated form from his cabin in the sky, and the assorted rolling stock and its jumble of freight thundered majestically by.

 ⋘

The railway line first reached nearby Hopetown from Cape Town in November 1884. Contrary to a number of opinions, it appears that the discovery of diamonds in the area during the late 1860s was not the only motivator for this progression. From its humble beginnings in 1862 with only 34 kilometres of track (Cape Town to Eerste Rivier) to its name, the Cape Colony steadily expanded its network into the rural hinterland, where its main purpose was to facilitate the transport of farm produce, such as wool, to various local and international markets. The line eventually reached Kimberley in November 1885, and with it came the decline of the many well-established coach services on the Kimberley route. One of the best known of these services was Gibson's "Red Star Line", which operated from the railhead at Wellington, and while it took twice as long as the rail service that surpassed it, it had conveyed travellers efficiently and in reasonable comfort for many years.

On the new train to Hopetown, journeying towards the Kalahari in June 1885, was the controversial adventurer-explorer G.A. Farini. Although often accused of being given to exaggeration, Farini's accounts of his trip still offer some valuable first impressions. After seeing the parched landscape and being told by people along the way that certain areas of the Karoo had not experienced rain for many years, Farini commented: "Ah! I felt sure, all the time, that Hell could not be a great way off this place," and then he went on to say: "and as for those who are obliged to spend their lives here, they need have no fear of a future punishment."

Yet, thankfully, he was slightly more polite about the train ride itself:

> Indeed, the only good thing I saw on the whole journey to Hope Town — 600 miles — was the railway. Well built and ballasted, and kept in thoroughly good order, it "rode" easily, and admitted of a good rate of speed being kept up. The whole distance was traversed in thirty-two hours, including stoppages — not at all a bad pace, considering the gradients in many cases were as much as one in forty.[27]

Being on the main Cape Town–Johannesburg line, the small station at Witput has witnessed its fair share of South African railway history as well, and surely no period was greater than the glorious days of steam. In order for steam engines to be economical through the hot and dry Karoo and to obviate the need for numerous expensive water replenishment points, British engineers developed a system whereby the steam expelled from the boilers could be recycled and converted back to water. Using this system where necessary, steam traction worked efficiently in South Africa for well over 100 years, but was largely replaced by diesel power in the mid-1980s. Yet many steam-engine drivers and other steam enthusiasts were determined not to let go of the "old technology" without a fight. One such person was A.E. Durrant, a leading SAR expert who reported on an experiment to judge the comparative efficacy of one Class 26, 4-8-4 steam locomotive against the pulling power and acceleration of two Class 34 diesels. Patrick Whitehouse, in his book *Steam Railways of the World*, summarises the details:

> After a dead stop at Modderrivier from signals caused by errant freight, the [steam] train bounded along at 110–120 km/h compared with the official road limit of 100 km/h and at Witput, where signals were again at danger, it restarted from a dead stand to 80 km/h in four train lengths.

Unfortunately the experiment, though successful, has been to no avail as the CME hierarchy of the SAR have now decided to dispose of steam traction.[28]

☙

After getting back on the bike, I crossed the tracks and noticed a wonky, hand-painted signboard in a driveway that read: "Welcome to Witput Country Lodge in the land of milk and honey — just bring your own cows and bees!!!" The sign made me think of the "Fawlty Towers" hotel from the famous British TV comedy series, and it was really tempting to change my plans and book in. It was only another 25 kilometres to Hopetown, but the rain was starting to come down harder and I was also pretty pooped from riding into the teeth of a gale for the last few hours. Besides, overnighting at a quirky looking "Country Lodge" in a tiny rail-side hamlet was surely reason enough to stay on its own.

I made my way to the old lodge's front door through giant cobwebs of mist. There was no sign of life anywhere, not the clink of a distant glass nor the smell of wood smoke — nor any kind of activity whatsoever. After knocking and waiting a long while, the door suddenly creaked a little way open and a petite form with a husky voice was framed against the blackness inside. I was suddenly lost in wild imaginings: I had taken a wrong turn somewhere and — never mind having to face the nutty hosts of "Fawlty Towers"— I was about to be abducted by the Adams family.

"Yes, can I help you, sir?" the petite woman asked, bemusement softening her pointed features.

"Uh, ja, sorry, I was day-dreaming when you opened the door. I thought maybe the place was closed — there seemed to be nobody about."

"We don't get too many visitors this time of year, only really in the season when the Jo'burg people head down to the coast via

Kimberley. My husband and I were just outside in the garden, our daughter is visiting from George."

"I see; well, that probably means you've got a room for me. May I have a look?"

She walked me down a long, dimly-lit corridor and opened up a door to the last room on the right. It was enormous, with an en suite bathroom, simply furnished and although a little threadbare here and there, wonderfully clean and bright. And at R75 per night I thought I might stay for a week, especially since I seemed to have the entire lodge to myself. To top it all, if I kept a casual watch from my bed I was bound to get a glimpse of the old Trans-Karoo (now called the Shosoloza Meyl) passenger train trundling past. What a find!

Thinking about a walk around the lush green garden outside my window, I fell asleep on the big double bed. I awoke some hours later to the noise of *bakkies* and birdsong. Bleary-eyed, I opened the curtains and saw some farmers pulling into the car park. Well, it's after work on Friday and a few of the local farmers are probably just coming for a drink, I thought. I couldn't have been more wrong. It was the regional Farmers Association and they had arrived en masse for their annual general meeting — so much for having the place to myself! To avoid conversations about this year's locust plague and anti-worm preparations for sick sheep, I decided to seek refuge in the garden.

It was during my dodder around the lodge's grounds that I discovered a sign attached to an old well that was to expose some dark myths from another age:

> This is a historical well from which, according to folklore, the British North Lancashires' Regiment drank on the evening of 22 Nov. 1899 prior to the battle of Belmont. This well was discovered on 12/04/96 during the building of the front entrance wall.

According to folklore, unbeknown to the British, canny Boer scouts in the vicinity of Witteputs doctored the water with a laxative distilled from a plant called *Khakibos*. The troops as might have been expected, literally shat themselves the following day and could therefore not participate in the battle with the Boer forces at Belmont.

According to Major Bullshiter of the third Med. Regiment, this gave rise to the well known Afrikaans expression, "*ALTYD DEUR DIE KHAKI*".

Various artefacts e.g. a Cannon ball, Horse shoe, Pieces of Cast iron cooking utensils and (1 Doz.) "Long Johns", recovered from the well and vicinity, can be viewed in the lobby.

As I made my way to the bar through the lobby, I was pleased to discover that these "artefacts", particularly the undergarments, were no longer displayed there. The bar was crowded with large farmers and their small children; all were freshly showered and wearing their trendiest, yet somwhat stiff-looking, casual outfits. Broad grins and backslapping were the precursors to an evening where the formalities were to be short-lived, and the *kuiering* (chatting) with *dop en tjop* (drink and chop) at the braai was hoped to take up most of the night. Holed up in my corner of the bar, I returned half-nods of acknowledgement to my presence until curiosity got the better of one of the farmers.

"Are you a new farmer in the area?" he asked me in Afrikaans, eying my colourful scarf as if it were the serpent that caused all the trouble in Eden.

"No, I'm just passing through. Travelling around the Great Karoo on my old scrambler and writing about my journey," I replied nonchalantly.

"Oh, I see; I thought you were here for the AGM. Must be a

long way on an old scrambler hey, but then my grandparents used to ride everywhere on horseback I suppose. *Jong*, their backsides in those days were as tough as Oom Mannie's kudu biltong."

The farmer looked somewhat relieved that there wasn't an unknown quantity — especially an English speaker with an eccentric dress sense — joining the meeting and moved along the bar in high spirits, slapping backs as he went. I sat watching the good-natured ribbing and general camaraderie of the group, and then noticed how one of them spoke condescendingly to the barman as he ordered another brandy and coke.

Although Beyers was a big man, his rounded shoulders and stooped disposition imbued him with an aura of inferiority. The wounded eyes that looked out on the world from behind the bar spoke of a man out of sync with his environment. But before I could chat to him for any length of time, I was unfortunately called to dinner.

꼿

"Ja, this place was built just before the Boer War broke out I think. It used to be quite a well-known country inn in the days when Kimberley was still prosperous," said Beyers, warming to his role as a tourist guide.

I'd popped back into the bar for a nightcap. The crush of conservatives had left for their own gathering in an outside courtyard and we were able to chat for a bit.

"I was looking through the collection of visitors' books at dinner, hoping to find names of some famous old guests, but I went back all the way to the 1940s and couldn't flush out a single celebrity."

"They say the heyday of this place was soon after it opened until the outbreak of the war, and then after the war again to the late 1920s. Think of all those mining magnates and smugglers from Kimberley with pockets full of money. No such thing as buying a single drink then: you bought a bottle and you finished it before you staggered off to your room."

It turned out that Beyers used to be the station master at Belmont, about 15 kilometres up the road towards Kimberley. After 12 years in charge of boosting sagging freight revenues, he'd had a minor stroke and took up permanent residence in the old Belmont Hotel, which he'd bought some years previously. He told me that he now ran a small off-sales and also took in occasional guests that stopped over to visit the Anglo-Boer War battle site there.

He insisted that I come and visit him in the morning and promised that if I did, he would take me on a tour of the old station. I was tempted, but I needed to first see if I could fit it into my riding schedule, as there was a lot of ground to cover to Prieska the next day.

෮෨

I was incredulous of the amount when I got my bill after breakfast. My stay at Witput Country Lodge had cost me all of R125 for dinner, bed and breakfast. After leaving them an appreciative tip, I headed up the "Diamond Way" to Belmont station.

More than a hundred years before me, a group of around 8,000 British soldiers — without those, of course, who'd drunk from the well at Witput — were also on their way to Belmont. In charge was Lord Methuen, on his way to rescue Kimberley from the Boers that were laying siege to it. Although Methuen had seen action with General Warren in Bechuanaland (Botswana) in 1885–86 and, because of this, had some experience of the challenging veld that lay between his Orange (Gariep) River camp and Kimberley, it was the unenthusiastic opinions of his ability, voiced by some of his superiors, that cast doubt on whether he was the best man for the job. One such opinion came from the man General Buller had just succeeded as British commander-in-chief, Sir Garnet Wolseley, who is quoted by Pakenham as saying: "Paul Methuen is a great friend of mine and I have always regarded him as an able ... soldier." Summarising Wolseley's sentiments on the matter, Pakenham further reported that "[h]e doubted, however, if he was 'man enough ... to "run the show" in the Cape' during Buller's absence in Natal."[29]

Methuen was probably unaware of these slanderous sentiments at the time; but in any event, he had other more pressing problems of his own. For one, as he had half the number of mule wagons originally promised him, and no oxen, he was too reliant on the railway to propel his army northwards. This meant that the "invisible" Boers, with their new "smokeless" gunpowder, could dig themselves in at strategic points along the railway and Methuen's forces had little option but to run the gauntlet they laid down. Methuen's other major handicap was that of gathering intelligence. Even his veld-adept and camouflaged "Rimington's Tigers" were kept at bay by the long-range accuracy of dug-in Mauser firepower that blazed, seemingly without trace, over the vast stretches of flat land they had to reconnoitre.

Working only with field maps without contour lines and a rough sketch of the Boers' positions in a series of eastward hills running parallel to the railway line, Methuen drew up his Belmont battle plan as best he could. The Boers were mainly positioned on two lines of hills at different elevations: Table Mountain and Gun Hill were part of the first line of lower-lying hills while the Mont Blanc range behind them was about double their elevation at around 65 metres high. Even though these ridges were not very high, their slopes were steepest on the side facing the British line of attack and they afforded the excellent Boer marksmen great advantage over the lengths of open ground they commanded.

Facing a well-ensconced enemy of around 2,300 Boers under

Jacobus Prinsloo, Methuen decided that his various companies would advance on the first line of hills at 3 a.m. on 24 November 1899. His strategy was to take these positions first and then for a large force, which would be supported by firepower from the first line of captured hills, to attack the higher Mont Blanc range from the less steep — and less exposed — northern slopes. Yet, as with most battle plans, events in the field necessitated some tactical changes.

It took the British far longer to achieve their first objective than they'd anticipated. The Boers held onto their positions on Table Mountain with great determination, and a good number of them waited to face the charge of bayonets before finally giving way. But it was two battalions of Coldstream Guards, diverted from their supportive role of the Grenadier and Scots Guards' attack on Gun Hill, that gave Methuen the greatest cause for concern during the battle. The Guards were thrown off course by strong Boer fire coming from two koppies to the south of Mont Blanc, and they decided in the heat of the moment to go forward and meet their attackers head-on. Their commander, Major-General Colvile, realising that if they crossed the large expanse of exposed ground they could suffer heavy losses, sent his brigade-major to recall them to Gun Hill. He was only able to turn about a quarter of the committed Guards around and, assisted by the artillery that was rallied in support of their cause, the Guards overcame their tormentors and eventually captured the two koppies. Thinking on his feet, Methuen changed his original plan of trying to take Mont Blanc from the north and threw the bulk of his forces into a frontal attack of its main ridge, in support of the Guards.

By 10 a.m., only seven hours after it started, the short yet fierce battle was over. The British had lost 54 men and the Boers around 80. Although many British soldiers were wounded in the frontal assault on Mont Blanc, the battle was still a decisive victory for Methuen, who, in the first significant engagement of the war on

The wide open plains leading up the Bruintjieshoogte near Somerset East on Day 1.

Nick the 'pie-man' - my breakfast companion in Cradock.

One of the many farm gates opened and closed on the trip - entering the Grootrivierhoogte's poort near Steytlerville on the trial run before the main journey.

At the top of Swaershoek Pass about half an hour out of Cradock.

Michael the horseman outside Steynsburg.

The sun dancing behind a patchwork of clouds near Smithfield.

Vusi and Rendani relaxing after being on the auditing trail in Trompsburg.

Alberto making noises about the 'dead barman' – Trompsburg.

the western front, had defied his detractors and shown that he was able to react with clear resolve when faced with grave decisions in the heat of battle. He was very pleased with the way his men had fought, and was quoted as saying: "With troops like you no general can fear the result of his plans." In tackling whatever obstacle was in front of them, the Coldstream Guards came up for special praise from their commander, Major-General Colvile, who said that his men had "done for themselves what no general would have dared to ask of them."[30]

༄

Beyers was a different man that morning. When he'd welcomed me to the Belmont station a short while earlier, I could see why he appeared out of place behind the bar last night. Stations, trains and all their related paraphernalia were his life; being a barman was obviously just a way to earn some much needed extra income.

"Did you manage to sleep with all those happy farmers making a noise last night?" enquired Beyers with a wry smile.

"Ja, no problem. I was so tired that not even a freight train crashing through my room would have woken me up."

"For me, the sound of trains is actually very comforting. When I was station master here and we used to have trains coming and going at all hours, I found their arrivals and departures were built into a hidden clock in my head. If a train didn't arrive at its usual time, only then would I wake up, but otherwise not."

"You must miss the old heyday of the railways, then?"

"Ja, I tell you, when I was still a youngster with the *spoorwee* (railways) in the '60s, the South African Railways was tops. People took a real pride in their work, and keeping a train running on time was what really challenged us. But ja, man, that's enough about me; let me show you around a bit."

Even though Beyers had officially retired way back in 1993, Belmont station was still, unofficially, his pride and joy. Living in his old hotel within spitting distance of the station, it was obvious from its well-kept condition that he visited it daily to keep it tidy and also to spare it from being ruined by squatters and vandals. There were even some flowers in the beds, and the grass had been trimmed recently. As further proof of his concern for the station's continued upkeep, I learned from him during our visit that he'd already put a number of "care-taking" proposals to the new "regime" in charge of the railways. Another of his proposals concerned setting up a guesthouse for battle site visitors in the old station building — apparently a national monument — but all his efforts thus far had failed. And although on current evidence it seems unlikely, perhaps Transnet will still come up with a plan to save these valuable monuments to our past.

"You see this little room here," Beyers said pointing to a tiny cubicle off the main ticket office. "I had this room built on as a nursery for a staff member's premature baby. The poor little thing was born so early and had to spend so much time in an incubator that she couldn't just leave it at home with someone else."

"Talking of nursing frail humans back to health, didn't the British use part of this station as a sanatorium for their wounded soldiers?" I asked.

"Ja, it was in fact partly in this building and the mortuary was right next door. But come, I'll show you something very interesting."

We walked to the northern side of the building and he pointed to a number of scars gouged into the dressed stonework surrounding a doorway. They were apparently the marks left by bullets from Boer Mausers.

"Do you think those happened during the battle of Belmont itself or did they occur in later attacks on the British garrison stationed here?" I asked, instantly transported back to that fierce battle more than a hundred years ago.

"Can't really say, you know, but there was a fair amount of action in these parts. Even though the Boers were defeated here, they never gave up trying to harass the British."

He was certainly right. In fact, to try and ensure that the British retained the ascendancy in the area, as well as to protect the vital railway line, a Lieutenant-Colonel Pilcher arrived at Belmont on Christmas Day 1899 and took command of the garrison. His forces were soon strengthened by two companies of the 2nd Duke of Cornwall's Light Infantry, and later two companies of Australians joined the Canadian regiment already stationed there. From the old accounts it's evident that the Canadians and Australians threw themselves into their training exercises with characteristic vigour and were not short on enthusiasm for active engagements either. And not long after they arrived, the Australians got their chance: a Boer laager had been reported about 30 miles west of Belmont station.

Showing a canny instinct for the tactics required for success against the Boers, Pilcher had dispatched soldiers to surround the "native" settlements in the area to ensure that their presence could not be divulged to the enemy in the field. The strategy was a complete success and the Boers at Sunnyside were caught so by surprise that they took flight and even left their gin behind:

> So cleverly had the proceedings been contrived, and so ingeniously were the orders interpreted by one and all, that the Boers were completely non-plussed. There was a hurried stampede, and the Federals bolted, leaving their laager with all its luxuries, its boiling soup, its gin and water bottles, &c., at the mercy of the invaders.[31]

Having been decimated by the Boers in their trenches at Magersfontein, the British forces on the western front were in dire need of a few morale-boosting victories, and the Boers' humiliating defeat at Sunnyside must have gone some way to achieving this.

⚜

After being shown the workings of the old manual signal controls and their various fail-safe methods of engagement, I said goodbye to Beyers and climbed onto the bike. Just as I was about to leave, a lady I'd chatted to in the bar at the Country Lodge the previous evening arrived with a slow puncture. Beyers was her chosen samaritan, but the odd thing was that I could see no evidence of the tyre in question having lost any air. Not thinking much of it at the time, I set off for Hopetown. It was when I was filling the bike up with petrol and she pulled up behind me, with her tyre still intact, that I saw the loneliness in her eyes. And when a lonely, middle-aged woman has you in her sights, it's time to go — and fast.

Caught up in my own wild imaginings of being pursued across the flats by an attentive admirer, I missed the dirt-road turn-off that would have taken me to the old wagon bridge I was planning to visit. Some ten kilometres out of town, on what I assumed was the wrong road to Prieska, I stopped to take stock of the situation. In the shade of the only acacia tree in miles I sat down and chuckled. I mean, maybe she didn't want a casual fling with a wandering motorcyclist, perhaps she just wanted to chat, but I'd enjoyed the melodrama anyway.

The map indicated that even though I wasn't on my originally chosen path, I was on one of the main dirt tracks to Prieska. Having settled that, I got out my faithful photocopies of Bulpin's *Discovering Southern Africa* and unpacked some of what I'd missed by racing through Hopetown:

The origin of the name Hopetown, is odd. It is said locally

that the widow of the first owner of the farm, Michiel van Niekerk, wore a necklace to which was attached a small anchor. One of her servants admired this anchor and was very impressed when told that it represented hope. The servant made an ingenious imitation from tin which was nailed above the entrance to the farmhouse. When the house was demolished, the symbol of hope was preserved and eventually fixed above the door of another house by a local farmer's wife, Mrs Curry. The little token was considered to be the good luck emblem of Hopetown, which became a municipality in September 1858.

Of course, the thing that brought the greatest hope to the town was the discovery of a shiny little pebble. The story goes that a child, Erasmus Jacobs, was found playing with a "glittering" stone by a neighbouring farmer, Schalk van Niekerk, in 1866. He was so clearly impressed with the stone that it was reported that the boy's mother persuaded her son to give it to Mr van Niekerk. After travelling halfway around the Cape Colony and it being proved to be a diamond of 21.25 carats by a Dr Atherstone in Grahamstown, it was eventually bought by the governor of the Cape, Sir Phillip Wodehouse, for 500 pounds.

> There might have been more excitement about the diamond's discovery if it could have been established exactly where the boy had found it, yet nobody could be sure. But not long afterwards, another magnificent stone was found in the region and the rush was on. A Griqua "witch doctor" called Booi had stumbled across the diamond that weighed in at 83.5 carats and was to become known as the "Star of Africa". [32]

When rich finds were made a few years later at the Colesberg koppie site in present-day Kimberley, Hopetown was also well situated to supply the new settlement with provisions. But when the railway line arrived from Cape Town in 1884, 15 kilometres to the east of Hopetown, the town was virtually cut out of the Kimberley supply chain altogether. Eventually, things got so bad for Hopetown's businessmen that in 1897 an unscrupulous local conjured up a big new "diamond find" on the farm Rooidam. Having disguised diamond-studded soil in fodder and grain bags, the fraudster dumped the phoney pickings at strategic points around the site. With the bait set, one of the fake finds was "discovered" and the rumour mill went into top gear. Around 10,000 prospectors hurried to Hopetown and the town's economy boomed once more. But the hoax was eventually revealed and, disgusted by the treachery, the prospectors left town as quickly as they'd arrived. The scandal was to sabotage Hopetown's prospects for many years to come.

Sitting on the side of the road gazing over the flat brown veld stretching far into the north, I thought of the small boy's plaything that had begun Hopetown's diamond rush. I wondered if he or his mother ever saw any of the money that Schalk van Niekerk got for that "glittering" stone, or even if they were ever apprised of the significance of the find; a find that eventually gave rise to a diamond mining industry that boosted the Cape Colony's economy to previously unimaginable levels.

From being virtually unpopulated, the dry plains around Hopetown, Barkly West and, later, Kimberley were suddenly crammed with thousands of people from all over the world, their eyes sparkling with the riches they'd always dreamed about. But life in the original tent towns was tough. Following the sweet stench of good fortune, assorted rogues and ruffians came from all directions, and the pickings were good. Tsunamis of rags to riches stories erupted from this epicentre of the nouveau riche, and while many of them were true, for most, the reality was far less rewarding. Only about one in five of the diggers were able to fund their expenses from their small, 32-foot-square claims, and it was mainly the early prospectors with a number of claims, like

Cecil Rhodes and Barney Barnato, who made handsome returns. Reflecting on early town life in Kimberley, Bulpin wrote:

> Life was uproarious, with rumours, rows, bad smells from non-existent sanitary arrangements, dust, heat, shortages of water and a plethora of insects, vermin, loafers, thieves and swindlers. Political squabbles over the ownership of the diamond areas raged between Britain, the Orange Free State, the Griqua and the Tlapin tribe, emphasising the general insecurity of life.[33]

The discovery of diamonds attracted international and local investment as never before. It also gave huge impetus to the development of the road and rail network required to facilitate the greatly increased movement of goods and people. While black labourers worked under dangerous conditions and were mostly restricted to unsanitary and crowded compounds for their three to six month contracts, the wages paid were still the best that could be earned by "unskilled" workers at the time. And it seems for many of them, the sacrifice they made was worth it, as it put them on a more even footing with their white rulers at the end of their contracts. Their wages bought them guns and they ferried these home to the north and east in great numbers, thus eventually helping to reduce the white man's hegemony on superior weaponry.

Yet, despite the monetary investments that were pouring into the country, one of the most significant inflows to South Africa was that of human capital. Great leaders of commerce, industry and politics were born out of the promise of fortunes on the diamond fields, and certain domestic government figures were also seen to rise to meet the increased demands made on civil society. Some of these leaders became great statesmen who left lasting impressions on the South African political landscape. These were men such as the tenacious and indefatigable Cecil John Rhodes, the cock-sure cockney with the Midas touch, Barney Barnato, the highly intellectual and principled politician, John X. Merriman, and a diamond buyer who was sent to Kimberley by his principles in London and never looked back, Ernest Oppenheimer — the founder of the mining giant Anglo-American. Every one of these men were legends in their respective fields and together they were hugely influential in shaping the South Africa of the 20th century and beyond.

ଓଃ

A giant rock monitor was sunning itself in the road up ahead. The first summer rains of the season had left huge water-filled craters on the dirt road to Prieska, and I'd been so absorbed in the muddy enduro-riding that it was lucky for the prehistoric-looking lizard that I'd not ridden over him. But I was really pleased to have come across the monitor, as it was an important reminder of the many reptiles that used to wander the more fertile alluvial plains of the Karoo hundreds of millions of years ago. The rock monitor is a distant descendant of the youngina group from the Upper Permian period, the ancestral roots of which gave rise to all modern-day lizards and snakes. And going even further down the evolutionary chain, it is interesting to note that these and all other reptiles originally evolved from amphibians that occurred during the Carboniferous period, some 350 million years ago.

It was stalemate. As I would advance a few paces to get a better look at the creature, it would retreat a few paces sideways, always keeping a constant distance between us. I was quite surprised at its behaviour, because when I've approached these monitors in the wild before, they've usually scurried away quite quickly, as they can be pretty agile when they want to be. Yet this one was determined to stay near the verge of the road. And then I observed why. A steady stream of large centipedes was attempting to cross the road at that particular point and the monitor was happily stocking up on protein.

The intermittent grassveld dotted with the occasional acacia tree around Hopetown now gave way to coarse Karoo scrub anchored on stony soil. I had been travelling within the semi-arid climatic zone from round about the time I'd left Fauresmith, and would remain in this region until I got home. Although the vegetation of this area is broadly classified as "semi-desert, Karoo shrub and grass", it can still vary significantly, the degree of change largely dependent on the topography and the resultant presence of a number of micro-climatic influences.

Moving westwards, the land became even more parched, and the increasing distances between the farmhouses accentuated the starkness of the landscape and my sense of being totally alone. When travelling through a similar landscape about 100 kilometres to the north-east in the mid-1940s, travel writer H.V. Morton dropped in on a farmer to try and gauge how they extracted life from the drought-stricken and "bleached country":

> I explained myself in detail, and he relaxed. Perching himself on the tiny harmonium stool, he sat there like someone in a Greek tragedy, with his huge hands on his knees and his eyes every now and then gazing out of the open door to the brassy heat which sat as firmly on the land as a lid on a saucepan.
>
> Ja, it was a terrible drought! *Verskriklik*! All the *mielies* were withered, and there was some kind of worm in them as well. All the cattle had gone on trek. Some farmers had been forced to sell up and go to town to look for work. He moved uneasily and unhappily on the stool.

After saying goodbye to the hospitable farmer and his family, Morton remarked to himself: "I went on my way reflecting that with many people farming in South Africa seems to be not a way of earning a living, but an hereditary habit."[34]

A pair of white-quilled korhaans erupted from some low-lying scrub as I continued towards Prieska; due to their raucous and alarmist tendencies, these birds often scared the daylights out of me when they suddenly appeared out of nowhere. The early explorers knew them as "scolding-cocks", an apt epithet if ever there were one. Watching their frantic flight into the south-west, I noticed a large build-up of storm clouds in the background, and as I still had about an hour's ride to travel in the storm's general direction, I watched its progress with interest — and some trepidation.

By the time I reached the T-junction with the main tar road from Douglas, the storm was putting on a spectacular show. Thick fingers of lightning were jumping from the black dome overhead and stabbing the brown landscape with their pent-up flashes of magnesium blue. I sat there for a while, gripped by fear and indecision, deciding on whether to run the gauntlet on my exposed transport or head north until it passed.

I decided to make a run for it, sealed up my valuables and rode like hell for the horizon. Thankfully, it turned out to be the right decision. Just as I was about to head straight into the centre of the violent storm, the road veered out of its path to the west. After crossing the Gariep River, I sat on the bike looking at a billboard advertising overnight accommodation and saw clusters of wraithlike vapour trails rising off the tarmac, a fitting finale to the awesome storm that had just passed. And with the cool and fragrant dampness filling my helmet, I set off in search of Riverview Lodge.

6

From the Place of the Lost Goat to a Dam of Peace

(Prieska to Boegoeberg Dam: 150 kilometres)

All orators are dumb when beauty pleadeth.

William Shakespeare

"*E*r, uh, I'll have a Windhoek Light please," I stuttered, trying not to stare at the youthful cleavage bursting out of the tight white T-shirt in front of me.

She was a younger version of Britney Spears, but with real sex appeal — and the untainted innocence of youth. Her movements were being shadowed by every male eye in the house and the articulate pout of her lips indicated to me that she didn't mind the attention.

Contrary to my plan of driving around and evaluating a few options, I'd gone straight to the Riverview Lodge after seeing their advert, and taken the first room that was offered. And "Britney" wasn't even featured in the ad. When the owner had nonchalantly told me that there was a little pub and restaurant upstairs, I'd smiled politely and thought that maybe I'd just make something to eat in my room. It wasn't that the place didn't feel upmarket or clean because it was both those things, but what sort of pub and restaurant service could he be providing from this fairly ordinary looking domestic dwelling? I'd thought. As I looked around the well-appointed bar and crowded restaurant, I regretted jumping to conclusions earlier.

Just before I left for my table in the restaurant next-door, I saw another enchanted patron bumble his order to the siren behind the bar; "Britney's" allure had claimed yet another victim's tongue.

03

The first thing that got my attention when I walked around the town earlier in the day was the imposing Dutch Reformed church. It wasn't its strategic position perched up on the hill that intrigued me, but its seemingly unusual blend of gothic revival and Middle Eastern architecture. The church's bell tower was capped with the closest thing I'd seen to a minaret for a long time. I imagined the Dutch Reformed *dominee* sharing keys with the Muslim imam — and then I imagined a perfect world as well.

From my research on Prieska prior to the trip, I'd learnt that the ancient ford used by the Khoi and San peoples close to the modern-day town was named "Prieschap", which, depending on your source, means either "place of the lost goat" or "place of the lost she-goat". What is undisputed in all the literature I read, though, was that the predominant commercial activities are sheep farming, the cultivation of a number of river-irrigated crops such as vegetables, maize, fruit and lucerne, the harvesting of salt from enormous salt pans to the south and, of course, the mining of copper, zinc and, in the days when it was still in demand, asbestos.

I'm not sure what I was expecting from the medium-sized town of Prieska, but I was certainly quite impressed with its range of shops and services. Even though there are some Victorian buildings that hint at the town's 125-year-old history, the general architectural impression is more of humble modern dwellings linked to the upsurge in mining activities that occurred around the 1970s.

Heading off to the municipality in search of tourism information, I was trailed by a few persistent and thirsty beggars. Thankfully, I eventually managed to persuade them that despite my red nose and generally dishevelled appearance, I wasn't the patron saint of alcoholics and sent them on their way. An antiquated and dilapidated display of gemstones, plus a few other historical titbits in the municipality's foyer, set the tone for the dearth of information on any of the town's current or past attractions. I later discovered that the only person able to impart any knowledge to passing tourists was on sick leave, and nobody else had been briefed to help in her absence. Luckily my pack of photocopied pages from Bulpin's *Discovering Southern Africa* was close at hand, and I decided to walk to "the riverside resort known as Die Bos". When I'd first arrived in the town I was tempted to label Prieska as a mini-Upington: both are positioned right on the Gariep River and exude similar auras of oases in an otherwise parched wilderness. But walking to "Die Bos" I was convinced that the main difference between the two, besides size, was in fact the variation in topography — my legs had soon noticed that Prieska was not flat.

I spent a pleasant half an hour wandering through the shady roads of this old family resort, spotting a number of interesting riverine birds along the way. The Gariep's fast-flowing, dun-coloured waters looked nostalgically refreshing from the riverbank and I regretted that I hadn't brought a swimming costume. The last time I'd swum in the Gariep had been with my old bush companion Lionel. A couple of days into the Namakwa 4X4 trail from Pella to Vioolsdrift, we had stopped for a relaxed lunch at "Die Groot Melkboom" and then decided to have a swim afterwards. It was then that I discovered that there's no more effective tonic to wash away the lingering malaise that follows a few beers under the African sun than pitting yourself against the torrent of the Gariep. The trick is to somehow find footholds in a submerged rock and lie back at 45° to the stream. Get it right and you get an all-over aquatic massage that makes the average spa-bath seem ineffectual by comparison, but lose your footing, and you'll soon find yourself many long kilometres downstream. After that particular swim, I fondly remembered one of my stepbrother's favourite earthy gems of wisdom: "If there's one thing I know, you'll never regret a swim."

I could have dawdled about the peaceful resort a while longer but I still wanted to visit the old British fort on top of the Prieska koppie, so I left a bit sooner than I'd wanted to. And although I enjoyed my short visit to "Die Bos", my overall impression of its facilities, from the unmanned and broken down entrance booth to the tired-looking rondawels, was unfortunately that they were well passed their prime and in dire need of modernisation.

Looking around at the well-dressed and well-fed patrons in the restaurant, I sensed a definite aura of prosperity emanating from the assembled townsfolk. But then it was Saturday night and perhaps the town's more affluent residents had few other choices open to them.

"Can I get you some wine with your meal?" "Britney" asked with a doe-eyed smile.

"Yes please; can you recommend something from the region?"

"I really like the pinotage from Douglas, but they've got a lovely shiraz too."

"Well, I'm sure you've got good taste, so I'll go with the pinotage."

I probably would have bought crude oil from her and liked it, but I have to say the pinotage showed a lot of promise, and if I'd given it a bit more time to breathe, it possibly would have been even better. Whatever the case, it certainly made a pleasant change from the Chateau de Co-op I'd been subsisting on for the last few days. The waiter who brought my chicken kebab and chips must have been all of 12 years old, but judging by his slick professionalism, he was already an old hand. Thoroughly enjoying my meal and thankful that I'd saved myself from another "yacht-chow", I spared a thought for the testing conditions faced by the small British garrison that manned the old fort I'd visited earlier in the day.

Protected only by a corrugated roof overhead, not only did they have to withstand the searing heat of the relentless Prieska sun, but I was sure that being such a distant outpost, they would've needed to be really careful with their meagre rations as well. And the person responsible for the British being often so thinly spread over the vast South African landscape, in an almost futile attempt to check the marauding Boer guerrilla fighters, was the new commander-in-chief of the British armed forces, Lord Roberts. Roberts had been called upon some months earlier to replace the unfortunate General Buller after a spate of misfortunes brought about the latter's downfall.

Besides the horrors of "Black Week", which had sullied Buller's reputation during his first few months of command, it was seemingly a telegram sent by himself to the secretary of state for war, Lord Lansdowne that finally undid him. After the "serious reverse" experienced by Buller at Colenso, he was of the opinion that the bulk of the British forces should be sent to the western front of the war, and by engaging a large part of the Boer forces along the way, he would indirectly take the pressure off Ladysmith. Allied to this plan was the strategy to send a significant part of the British army back to predetermined defensive positions south-east of Ladysmith, to protect southern Natal from further Boer attacks. Unfortunately, the plans in Buller's head were not very well articulated in his telegrammed response to Lansdowne, who had just cabled him to "sack both Gatacre and Methuen":

> No. 87 Cipher. 15 December. 11.15 p.m. My failure today raises a serious question. I do not think that I am now (that is, since the apparent diversion of the 5th Division) strong enough to relieve White. Colenso is a fortress, which I think, if not taken on the rush, could only be taken by a siege.... I do not think either a Boer or a gun was seen by us all day .... My view is that I ought to let Ladysmith go, and occupy good positions for the defence of South Natal, and let time help us ....

Buller's detractors in the cabinet, led by Lansdowne and Balfour, managed to twist the balance of the decision makers to support the belief that "Buller had lost his nerve." Their telegrammed response to Buller indicated the severity with which the cabinet ended up viewing his much misunderstood telegram: "The abandonment of

White's force and its consequent surrender is regarded as a national disaster of the greatest magnitude."[35]

And that was the end of Buller as commander-in-chief. He was relegated to the position of commander of the army in Natal and replaced by the veteran of the Indian wars, Lord Roberts. While Buller could have arguably handled things differently in the early stages of the war, it seems doubtful whether any British commander, with the same resources at his disposal, could have resisted and successfully repulsed the well-executed attacks that characterised the Boers' early efforts in Natal.

Buller believed that in order to successfully conquer the Boers and their territories, any advancing army would have to first defeat all the Boer fighters in a particular region before moving on to attack the next. If all the Boers were not killed or captured, they would simply rise up again once the British army had passed. Lord Roberts, on the other hand, believed that if he could capture Bloemfontein and Pretoria, he would then be able to force a general surrender. Although Roberts' juggernaut managed to overcome Bloemfontein without too much trouble and was in Pretoria by June 1900, as Buller had predicted, the Boers were far from defeated and their guerrilla tactics, under astute generals such as De Wet and Smuts, went on unabated.

One of the outcomes of these highly mobile bands of Boers roaming the countryside was the stirring up of Boer loyalists within the Cape Colony's borders. Even though many "Cape Afrikaners" had seemingly got on with their lives while the war raged to the north, it didn't take much to get a number of them to unleash their latent dislike for British rule and join the Boer cause. And there was no stronger rallying cry for the Boer patriot than being exposed to a commando of his countrymen. It was one such commando under General Liebenberg and the "Cape rebel", Steenkamp, that inflamed the situation in and around Prieska and started the rebellion among the region's Afrikaners.

According to the author C.J. Strydom Scheepers, in his book *Kaapland en die Tweede Vryheidsoorlog*, an expeditionary force of about 200 men under Steenkamp and Liebenberg was sent to Prieska to stretch the British front line, and on 16 February 1900, they proclaimed the district as part of the Orange Free State Republic. The commando managed to stir up around 700 Boers to join their cause, and soon the unprotected regions of Kenhardt and Gordonia joined Prieska as Boer conquests. But, according to Strydom Scheepers, the British relief of Kimberley and the fact that Lord Roberts' forces were well on their way to Bloemfontein meant that the "Prieska commando" had to pull back to the Free State to assist in the defence of Bloemfontein. Although it is not reported where the battle actually took place, General Liebenberg's commando apparently defeated a British force under Adye on 6 March, but the relief forces that were approaching Prieska under Lord Kitchener were deemed too large to be stopped. As a result, on 18 March 1900 Prieska was occupied by the British, with Kenhardt and Upington falling into their hands soon afterwards as well.[36]

While the uprising of the surrounding farmers and townsfolk was severely dealt with by the British, Lord Milner was still convinced that despite the strong preventative measures being taken, the Cape's rural Afrikaners were ripe for a mass revolt. And because of this, in strategic towns additional measures were instituted, such as those the British took in Prieska, namely the building of the small fort and other defensive positions on the Prieska koppie overlooking the town. The fort's walls were made of the local Tiger's Eye stone and it was fitted with a large water tank inside as well as an escape tunnel that led to the side of the koppie; probably installed as a way out if the garrison found themselves besieged. The exact size of the British garrison stationed there is not known, but from the graves of British soldiers in the Memorial Garden that died between 18 December 1900 and 2 October 1901

— long after the "Prieska revolt" itself had been quelled — it is probable that the soldiers stationed there had some contact with returning Boer raiding parties — but it is more likely that most died from disease, which caused far more deaths in the ranks of the British than Boer bullets ever did.

⁂

After a strangely fitful sleep, during which something I'd eaten, or drunk, had been punching me in the gut all night, I awoke to the sound of my neighbours making love next door. The sounds of their rampant passion conjured up alluring images of "Britney" — she'd arrived offering "room service" wearing a coquettish smile and little else — and although it was still too early to get up, I thought a shower would be helpful all round.

Talking to my host, Dana, at breakfast, I mentioned to him that after taking my scheduled detour towards the old asbestos mine at Koegas, I was thinking of staying the night at Marydale. He concurred with my route plan, but suggested that I should rather continue for another 40 kilometres and then stay at the self-catering chalets at Boegoeberg Dam instead. I had only planned to take a rest day in Kenhardt on day 8 of the journey, but it was my sixth straight day in the saddle, and I decided that if Boegoeberg proved to be as likely a resting place as it sounded, I would take my break a day early.

Once again on my lone journey I found myself stopping on a bridge over the Gariep River. It made me think of all the travellers, including the ancient Khoi and San peoples, early missionaries, colonial explorers and others who had forded the river near this point. On his way north in 1811 with two of the London Missionary Society's most stoical emissaries, Anderson and Kramer, was the famous traveller, naturalist, writer and artist, William Burchell. Looking over the river to the east, towards the spot where he crossed, I read his account of his first sighting of the Gariep in this vicinity, nearly 200 years ago:

> The water glinting under a fervid sun, caught my eye through the leafy screen; and a few steps lower, opened as enchanting a view as could be possible for fancy to imagine. Whether the feelings of an enthusiastic lover of scenes of nature, may have influenced my judgement, I cannot say; but still I think that, whoever shall visit the banks of the Gariep, and not feel both delight and admiration, must be cold indeed, and very deficient in taste or sensibility.

According to the map that accompanies Burchell's two-volume travel classic, *Travels in the Interior of Southern Africa*, the ford, known to him as "Shallow Ford", was about five kilometres east of Prieska. Sitting on my bike atop a modern iron and concrete bridge, I counted myself lucky that I wasn't going to even get my shoes wet — let alone face the probability of falling into a hippopotamus hole as the early explorers did — to cross the swirling muddy waters beneath me. Burchell's describes their crossing as follows:

> The waggons being all assembled, several men, some on horse-back, and some on oxen, were the first to enter the river, not only for pointing out where the water was shallowest, they having been twice across during the morning; but to give warning to those who were behind, if by chance a hippopotamus hole should be found in their way. They were followed immediately by the train of waggons, each with a steady leader at the head of the team, to restrain the oxen from turning down with the current, which they are very inclined to do, when left to themselves …. The bottom was found to be full of large pebbles, and the greatest depth no more than two feet and eight inches; but the current was therefore very rapid and strong …. Each waggon took a quarter of an hour to perform the passage, which might be

estimated at a little more than a quarter of a mile. The oxen were driven through by about a dozen Hottentots; and as many as were required to swim the sheep and goats over in safety.[37]

☙

Soon after I got off the short stretch of tar leading towards Niekerkshoop, the dirt track started to wind up a steep pass cut into the surrounding range of hills. Riding through a narrow poort, I scraped past hard ridges of coffee-coloured rock that jutted out into the road at odd angles, and then I noticed a huge sociable weavers' nest that lay dead ahead. It was attached to an old telephone pole and its weight had caused the pole to lean over in Dali-esque fashion. Watching these gregarious birds darting about and chattering away, I remembered that they were not only sociable among themselves; these friendly weavers happily co-exist with other bird species — such as the pygmy falcon — as well.

I'd deliberately designed my route plan to take me well off the path of the quickest way to Marydale, and powering my way up the curving dirt roads of the narrow pass, I knew I'd made the right choice. It was Zen dirt all the way. Stretching my legs in the strong wind at the top of the pass, I studied the foreground of twiggy bushes that were interspersed with clumps of spindly grass and noted that the colour of the earth between the brittle vegetation had changed to a burnt sienna — and the soil was dry as dust. And then the expanse of veld led my gaze over the concave valley that stretched towards the lumpy brown ridges in the distance. Without a fence in my line of sight, I felt sure the view was little different to that Burchell would have seen nearly two hundred years before. Yet putting the view aside, I had to admit that there was in fact at least one major difference: the almost complete absence of wild animals. Yes there were a few buck here and there, and many other smaller mammals and reptiles that were not plain to see, but of the bigger species, such as rhinoceros, elephant and giraffe, there were, of course, none. Lions, zebra, eland and even the now extinct quaggas were also commonplace during Burchell's travels — not to mention the throngs of springbok that used to gather in herds as far as the eye could see. With their local habitat under threat from encroaching farmers, as well as being hunted by the colonial Europeans and Afrikaners with such fervour, these once plentiful animals were pushed ever northwards and eastwards, beyond the rapidly expanding borders of the Cape Colony during the 1800s.

I first noticed Jan and his family coming over a rise when they were still far in the distance. And by the looks of his homemade donkey cart, which rode at an awkward angle behind three skittish donkeys, it was going to take him a long time to get to wherever he was going.

"Hello there; where are you travelling to?" I asked him in his native Afrikaans.

"We're on our way to Prieska to do some shopping," replied Jan, his gnarled and pliable features writhing expressively beneath his old stained hat.

"*Sjoe*, but that's about forty kilos from here; how long will that take you?"

"Ag, only about four hours, but coming back when we loaded and we've got to get over the pass, it'll take a little longer; the donkeys *sommer* take it a bit slower then."

"Tell me, Jan, do you still get some wild animals like leopards in these parts?"

"Man, my Uncle Petrus once saw a leopard in the hills not far from here. But my family are not sure whether he really saw it or he had just visited too long with Oom Tas that day," he said jerking his thumb towards his mouth, "but we still have a problem here with jackal and lynx, especially the jackal — they are terrible, really."

"So how do you protect the sheep and goats from them?"

"Well, we put the young sheep and goats in kraals at night, but we still have to try and kill those gluttons with traps or by hunting them with rifles."

I knew he was right, as there were tales all over the Karoo of how jackals were not satisfied with just a lamb or two every now and then. According to a number of farmers, they would often maim a whole flock of sheep in a fit of bloody mindedness by biting their lips and noses off, or even inflicting worse injuries — leaving them to die slow and agonising deaths. Violence begets violence. Suddenly I understood the need for the convoy of Mad Max-like, "vermin hunter" vehicles I'd been shocked to see in Prieska earlier that day.

When raised in the same litter as a domestic bitch's pups, it has been noted just how intelligent the jackal is. It learns quicker than the other dogs and is far more assertive, often scaring the other contenders away from the food bowl — virtually starving the opposition until it can absolutely eat no more. It seems that gluttony may be one of the few chinks in the jackal's armour, because faced with a plentiful supply of food, a jackal will generally stuff itself to bursting point. Yet jackals are able to deal with most adversity they encounter with characteristic verve and cunning. Take the problem of fleas for example, of which Lawrence Green recorded the following:

> Jackals when infested with fleas have a trick which is also known to foxes. They will collect a mouthful of wool from fences and bushes and then stand in a pool of water. Gradually they will allow themselves to sink, tail first, until only the jaws and the wool are visible. By this time the fleas have all taken refuge in the wool. Then the jackal lets go of the wool and swims quickly out of reach of the fleas. Sometimes a piece of wood is used instead of wool.[38]

Jan had been in the district since birth and had moved out to the farm with his wife some ten years ago when the Prieska village life got too noisy for him. During all the time we spoke, his wife kept herself busy paying attention to the toddler that was sitting on the front seat between them. Waving goodbye, I felt a paradoxical kind of kinship with him — we were both travellers on the same dusty road, but our lives were worlds apart.

ಆ

In early November 1779 the explorer Robert Gordon was moving south-eastwards down the Orange (Gariep) River, also towards the modern-day town of Prieska. He was trying to return to the same spot in the river, close to present-day Bethulie, that he'd arrived at heading west during a previous trip; the same journey on which he'd "discovered" the Orange River and loyally named it after his Dutch prince. His current mission was an attempt to complete his mapping of the course of the Orange, yet for reasons unknown, Gordon decided to turn around in the vicinity of modern-day Koegas before he'd reached his destination, at a place called Noekeis Kraal, and then return to the Cape. Historians have commented that Gordon may well have felt that the remaining journey was not necessary, as he presumed the river simply carried on in a similar south-easterly direction until it reached Bethulie. He clearly hadn't expected the river to head off on a north-easterly tangent, as it does when one views the line it takes from Prieska towards Douglas.

Gordon's journals, which are largely laconic, appear to mirror exactly what he saw. While camped at Noekeis Kraal on the eve of their return journey, he observed some interesting antics being performed by the local Briquas (not to be confused with the Griquas): "If the ground is made of clay they make two tubular holes in it, which are made opposite each other. Then they put the tobacco into one hole and suck through the other with their mouth, there being water in the middle."

It seems that many of the Hottentot clans of the time used tobacco as an intoxicant, and even though they appeared to have had the good sense to use water as a filtering device, they would still "gulp themselves drunk on the smoke. When they have gulped most of it down they sit for a while afterwards as though shocked, without being able to speak or stand up."[39]

Reading about these observations reminded me of my own first "tobacco-high" smoking my friend's Navy Cut plains at the age of 14. I felt so drunk, though, then dizzy and sweaty — and eventually sick — that it was certainly not something I would've called a "high" at the time. But then I thought I'd never get used to the taste of beer either. Of course, the "high" Gordon describes sounds remarkably like the "tobacco" they used could have been marijuana; certainly the type of ground pipe the Briqua used to smoke their "tobacco" is a method often favoured by certain modern ganja aficionados on field trips. On his canoe travels down the Gariep, William Dicey met an 87-year-old farm labourer of Koranna descent who concurred that ground pipes were the way his forefathers "smoked themselves senseless". Sensibly, so as not to break with the Koranna tradition, Dicey and his travelling companions decided to re-enact the activity with their small stash of thinking man's tobacco and appeared not to have been too disappointed by the results.

I was pleased I'd brought Dicey's book, *Borderline*, with me. Reading through it as I was propped against the concrete railings of the Koegas Bridge overlooking the Gariep, it let me into another little known occurrence, the Koegas atrocities of 1879. Against a background of great tension between native bands of marauding bandits and the local Boers, there were two incidents that clearly indicated barbarous and racist treatment of the Khoi, San and Xhosa peoples at the hands of the local Afrikaner burghers. Dicey elaborates on the first incident that eventually sparked an outcry from the Cape and abroad:

> In the first incident a group of San and Nama men were arrested in the vicinity of Koegas on the vague suspicion that they had attacked a farmer. En route to Kenhardt jail, the men supposedly freed themselves and attacked their escort. Leonard Blaauw, Oude Rooy, Tisiep and Hans T'Wakiep were shot dead. A fifth man, Piet Blaauw, survived bullets to his head, neck and shoulder. The evidence against the *burghers* Bergmann and Hennik was overwhelming. They had been mounted and armed with both rifle and revolver, while the prisoners were on foot, tied to one another. The inquest, conducted in the veld where the corpses had been left to decompose, found that the position of the bullet-holes in the skulls was more consistent with execution than escape. More damming still was the fact that Piet Blaauw testified against them. And yet, somehow, amid "shouts and shrieks of joy" in the packed courtroom, the accused were acquitted. The Reverend D.P. Faure, the court interpreter, was horrified: "…the verdict was scandalous, and its popularity was a still darker feature."[40]

One of the reasons I had decided to take the Koegas detour was due to a charming tale of a horse called Dragonder. The old story goes that a man bought a horse from a dragoon based with a British cavalry regiment in Cape Town. In memory of the horse's previous owner, the man called the animal Dragonder, the Afrikaans equivalent of dragoon. Some time later he took the horse to the north-western Cape on a hunting trip, but somewhere along the way he lost the horse and had to return home without it. A year later the man returned to the same hunting grounds and found the horse close to where it had strayed previously. Miraculously, Dragonder had used its hooves to dig into a dry river bed and uncovered a spring that had enabled it to survive in the hostile environment. And with the discovery of water, it was then possible for someone to farm the land. In memory of the horse that made the venture possible, the grateful new farmer called his farm Dragonder, but the name later evolved to become Draghoender due to years of incorrect pronunciation by the local Khoi people. It also became the name of the small railway settlement I was about to pass on my way into the tiny old mining town of Marydale.

The ride from Prieska to Koegas had been both illuminating and meditative. The dirt track had spanned one long dry valley after the next and the only human beings I'd encountered were Jan's family in their donkey cart. The red-brown valleys were separated by low-lying ridges that, once crested, repeated much the same ancient landscape you'd just experienced; a kind of monotonous, yet relaxing, sense of déjà vu that just kept repeating itself over and over again.

From the grey asbestos hills of Koegas, a number of them bristling with quiver trees, I set off towards the tiny settlement of Draghoender next to the railway line near Marydale. Leaving the virtual ghost town of Koegas behind me, I spared a thought for all those miners of blue asbestos who had contracted asbestosis in this rich, but potentially deadly, supply centre of the fibrous mineral. Asbestosis is caused by exposure to asbestos dust, composed of needle-like crystals, which, when inhaled, can pierce the lining of the lung and cause painful inflammation — and eventually even cancer. Ironically, in its silicified state, blue asbestos is better known as the beautiful and innocuous Tiger's Eye.

Bouncing along from one sharp ridge to the next, I came to the conclusion that there's only one road surface that can really trouble you on a dirt-bike, and that's a corrugated one. As soon as I left what I came to call the "secondary secondaries", those ideal smooth dirt tracks that only carry the occasional farm vehicle, and got close to a town or major tar road, these teeth-rattling hazards would pop up with great frequency. And frequency is really what it's all about. Because to limit the bone-shaking effects, you either have to go like hell and only try and make contact with the interconnecting ridges of the corrugations, or crawl along at a snail's pace, allowing your wheels to ride up and down the short, steep waves of compacted dirt. I decided to go like hell and arrived in Marydale just as the Sunday churchgoers were quietly emptying onto the town's main street.

I'd already decided to move on to Boegoeberg for the night, and if it looked promising, I would simply move my rest day forward as I'd thought about earlier. So all I really needed from Marydale was food and petrol. Yet, what appeared to be the only petrol station in town, looked decidedly closed for business, so I asked a policeman where else I could fill up.

"Nowhere else, *meneer;* we've only got the one station; but don't worry, you just wait there by the pumps and I'll get the owner to open up for you."

I sat at the petrol pump, incredulous that the policeman felt it was his duty to fetch the owner and sort me out. But then service in these small rural communities is often like that. The owner arrived in his Sunday best, still clutching a bible and a hymn book. I felt a little guilty for getting him to dispense all of 30 rands worth of petrol on his sabbath, but in the end, it was a small price to pay for my own peace of mind on the unknown road ahead. Riding around the town after filling up the bike, I observed it as a flat and dusty matrix of low-slung houses and a few commercial buildings. Its "boom time" during the golden era of the Koegas asbestos mine had clearly passed. And, as it happened, it was lucky that I had decided not to stay over in Marydale, as I couldn't even find the old hotel mentioned in Bulpin's guide. Besides the friendly policeman and duty-bound petrol station owner, I also wasn't overly inspired by the energy of the people I encountered in the village. Perhaps it was just the restless ghosts of miners past — or the town's apparent lack of current purpose and pervading sense of poverty — that put me off a bit.

After stocking up with as much food as I could carry, I escaped the large crowd of hungry-looking school kids and roared down the street to their wide-eyed approval.

ଔ

As I opened the door onto the teak deck overlooking the Boegoeberg Dam, I heard the cry of a fish eagle. Looking over the empty resort from my stone chalet on the edge of the hill, there was absolutely no doubt as to where I'd be spending my rest day. I'd cornered a little piece of Nirvana, African-style — and it looked like I had the entire resort to myself.

After six days on the road, it was good to finally come to rest. Yet strangely, when I woke up on the morning of my first official rest day, I felt a little disappointed that I wouldn't be climbing on the bike. It was hard to push the pause button and stop the liberating landscape from sliding by. I kept myself busy with a number of domestic chores and a bit of bike maintenance, and then took an explorative amble for the remainder of the afternoon. An old road, hugging the contours of the mountains on the river's southern bank, led me towards the west. The irrigation canal below surged and sparkled as it ferried its precious cargo to the farms of Groblershoop, and far beyond. Dassies scattered, vervet monkeys played hide and seek and two troops of baboons barked out their boundaries in a territorial dispute on the ridges above. This was dry and desolate country, a bleached Martian landscape, but that was only when you looked away from the Gariep. The narrow river valley itself bustled with life. Greens, blues and putty-whites were the dominant colours of the fertile swathe that brought promise to an otherwise unpromising-looking land.

After the high road, I opted for the lower riverbank path on my return. I notched up a great number of birds: goliath, squacco and black-crowned herons, darters, cormorants, chats, egrets, kingfishers, bulbuls, larks, white-eyes, hamerkops and a first-time sighting of the vocal diederik cuckoo as well. I also surprised an enormous water monitor (leguaan) eating a large frog on the water's edge. Watching it take to the water and swim swiftly away, I felt incredibly privileged to witness this ancient survivor at such close quarters. This close relation of the rock monitor is Africa's largest lizard (up to 1.6 metres long) and is found predominantly around rivers and waterways in the eastern half of the country, but also occurs along the entire length of the Gariep River, all the way to Alexander Bay.

When I got back to my stone chalet on the ridge I cooled down with a long, cold shower and then made myself comfortable on a deck chair overlooking the dam. It was sometime between the first and last sip of my second cold beer that I started to reflect on my reasons for making the trip.

So what was this journey really all about then? Was it about just getting away from everyone and everything and having an adventure on my dirt-bike in an invigorating wilderness environment — and perhaps proving that I could make it around this hostile semi-desert on a basic old scrambler? Or was it more to do with learning about the history, sociology and cultures that have formed and are still shaping the South African environment today? Was it maybe to do with all those things I'd promised myself I'd read up on one day, "when I had the time"?

It was probably all of these things rolled into one, but ensconced on that small teak deck with the soothing view, I came to realise that the most important dimension of the trip was reacquainting myself with myself. And it was only possible because I had separated myself from all the hundreds of extraneous influences we deal with every day: the noise and clutter of day-to-day life, the trials and tribulations of all our complex relationships and the constant challenge of dealing with an over full mind.

I likened my circular trip around the Great Karoo to a journey through a labyrinth. Because walking through a labyrinth facilitates dialogue with your inner self by virtue of the journey you take into the centre and then out again. It's the medium that's somehow able to connect you with your essence, and the motorbike journey was doing much the same thing for me. It facilitated the stilling of my mind through the meditative concentration of controlling the bike, and thus the messages from my inner self, and from without, were able to reach me unimpeded by the noise and clutter of everyday living. The journey, experienced in the moment, was the medium that conveyed these unsolicited news flashes. There were messages about my vocation, the way I lived, the way I loved and the way I wanted to be. Most importantly, my vocational evolution from city adman to rural writer/photographer was confirmed for me as being the best thing I could be doing right now. Because only once fulfilment finds you can you be truly happy — and then that happiness serves you and others around you as well.

The full moon floated in a shimmering well of diamond-studded black ink. Owls hooted in the intervals between the oscillating roar of the river. Sitting with my legs draped over the deck's railings, I saluted the balmy night with a glass of red wine — and then relaxed and reflected some more.

7

From Cool and Rested to Hot and Bothered

(Boegoeberg to Kenhardt via Groblershoop: 160 kilometres)

... our problem is that of becoming individuals, finding an authentic mode of personal existence.

Bryan Magee on Heidegger

Ancient plains and big horizons – the veld between Fauresmith and Luckhoff.

Beyers pointing out some of the bullet marks on the walls of the Belmont station caused by boer sharpshooters during the Boer War

Jan and his family on their way to do some shopping in Prieska some 40 kilometres away.

Taking a walk along the old high road from Boegoeberg dam to Groblershoop. I got a good view of the river beyond the wall and the irrigation canals next to the new road.

After the wasp attack at the station, Putsonderwater put me in a strange frame of mind.

Windmills on the march – Windmill Museum, Loeriesfontein.

There was something mythological in the way this pattern of stones was laid out. Verneukpan is in the background.

This group of rocks in an otherwise totally bare stretch between Putsonderwater and Kenhardt, gave cause for further enquiry.

I thought I was just arriving in the town, but I was in fact just leaving it. And because of this, my plans to have a long sought after cup of filter coffee were suddenly in disarray. Passing through the small town of Groblershoop left me with a fleeting ten-second movie clip as reference: a couple of loosely gathered shops fronted by dusty parking lots, a forlorn-looking petrol station, a farmers co-op that looked as secure as Guantanamo Bay, an installation of public call-boxes and huddles of reluctant-looking labourers. And then a big, bright Total garage suddenly marked the end of the village; like the last bastion of capitalism, it was bravely staving off the encroaching dry veld that lapped thirstily at its foundations. Realising this was my last shot at getting petrol before Putsonderwater, I decided to take advantage of the life-blood on offer before it evaporated in the searing heat. It was only 9 a.m. and the mercury had already hit 32° C.

The half-hour ride in from Boegoeberg Dam to Groblershoop was a rare treat in these dry climes, as the valley I had followed was crammed with orchards, vines and the incongruous musty-earth smells of water-spoilt soil. When the dam was completed in 1931 it opened up immense opportunities for the irrigation of the whole valley south-east of Upington. And even though I'd not seen much evidence of business activity there, Groblershoop is touted as the commercial centre that supplies the thriving fruit farming industry with most of what it requires. But before I left Boegoeberg Dam, I'd stopped to have a last look at the thick sheets of clear water dropping over the 11-metre-high weir, and it made me think of a near accident that occurred there a few years before. It was a short while before William Dicey and his expedition passed this way that two other marathon paddlers had almost attempted to "shoot" the weir on the strength of bad advice they had been given in Prieska. Fortunately, they were dissuaded from making the suicidal attempt at the last minute by two fishermen who just happened to be there at the time. Yet there are those who believe that there are no accidents — only what is meant to be.

When I'd passed a group of small islands that separated the Gariep into numerous channels on my way in to Groblershoop, it reminded me of the bands of rogues and rebels that had holed up on these natural fortresses centuries before. Defiant men and women of mixed blood under the dissident leadership of colourfully named people like Donker Malgas, Klaas Pofadder, Gamka Windwai, Klaas Lukas and Jacobus Afrikander. They were often being chased for crimes like cattle theft by bands of farmers and the indefatigable men of the Cape Mounted Rifles led by officers such as Captain Sission, Commandant McTaggart and Captain Maclean. In search of Pofadder, Lukas and Malgas, Maclean and his men trailed the fugitives into the Kalahari Desert, where they eventually ran out of water and had to survive on the liquid they extracted from wild tsama melons. But they never gave up the chase. Pofadder was captured first, Malgas was killed trying to escape and only Lukas managed to get away; yet with his band of followers reduced to just seven men, he was no longer considered much of a threat by his pursuers.

When Lawrence Green wrote of these beautiful island refuges found along the lower course of the Gariep, he noted:

> Those who know the islands of the Orange River do not long for island paradises in the Pacific. Here within the borders of the Union you can find beauty and prosperity between the river banks — dream islands with the richest soil in the world.[41]

And as I'd cruised through this panoply of abundance, it was gratifying to realise that the whole narrow river valley — that paints a bright green line for hundreds of kilometres all the way to Upington — was now almost all as fertile as those "dream islands" of yesteryear.

Red sands and ground squirrels came into the frame soon after leaving Groblershoop. It was starting to look like Kalahari country and I thought of the plaintive croaking of barking geckos at dusk, and half-expected to see a lone gemsbok silhouetted against the ridge of some sharply-cut dunes that appeared in the distance. Instead, the wide ash-coloured road led me past some modern-looking farmhouses. Plain whitewash coatings appeared to have given way to trendier dark colours with cream accents; perhaps the result of farmers' wives connecting with the home-decorating styles of the internet and satellite TV, but then some stone kraals, windmills and the musty-molasses scent of farmyard manure re-connected the picture with its more traditional roots.

Although stretches of red sands and the occasional dunes are seen in the dry veld of the Northern Cape, they are not found as frequently as in their true Kalahari habitat north of the Gariep and into Botswana. Yet the sands from both these regions are coloured red for the same reason: the dominating presence of iron oxide, a kind of primordial rust that has intermingled with the earth to add colour to these ancient landscapes. But just north of Groblershoop lies an anomalous patch of red sand that has not only lost its colour, but is said to roar as well. Located at a resort known as Witsand, this large "island" of white sand, two kilometres wide by nine kilometres long, lies in the middle of the more conventional red sands and has apparently been cleansed of its previous colour by a water source that lies beneath it. With the iron oxide gone and having experienced almost constant wind erosion, Witsand's sands contain larger particles, have far fewer fine grains yet are also very smooth. This, combined with the dry atmosphere, causes the sand to "roar" when it is walked on. In his epic study, *Kalahari: Life's Variety in Dune and Delta*, Michael Main observed that:

> The roaring sound, which is loud and not dissimilar to the noise of a passing truck, seems to emanate from deep within the dune and is caused by the dryness and polished nature

of the grains. In good conditions it can be heard over 500 metres away.[42]

A number of years ago, on an island beach west-south-west of Rio, my wife and I experienced a similar phenomenon. As we walked across the pristine white sands of eastern Isla Grandé, it shrieked raucously, complaining as if every footfall had struck it a mortal blow. We'd joked at the time about ill-informed inmates trying to escape from the island's prison, and how they were sure to be discovered if they chose that beach as a secret path to a waiting boat — and freedom. Perhaps that's why there are so few escapees from this exquisite rain forest island. But even without shackles, its unspoilt beauty captivates you — making it a difficult place to leave, whether you're free to or not.

༄

Day 8 marked the start of the southern leg of my journey. I was entering a region that until fairly recently was still officially called Bushmanland after the San hunter-gatherers that had populated it for millennia. The region is made up mainly of hot and dry grasslands and dominates the northern and central sections of the Northern Cape. It is bound by the Gariep River in the north, the Sak and Hart Rivers in the east, Calvinia in the south and Namaqualand in the west. The landscape is predominantly flat and is also home to huge shallow depressions more commonly known as pans, many of which are very rich in salt. Surprisingly for this very dry area (annual rainfall is between 50 and 200 millimetres per annum) some of these pans also conceal water, just metres below the surface.

But Bushmanland has not always been as tranquil as the region I now found myself riding through. As the early colonial farmers pushed north from the Cape, conflict over land usage between themselves and the Bushmen was inevitable. At first, towards the latter half of the 17th century, most farmers only made seasonal journeys into Bushmanland to take advantage of the good summer grazing there. During these visits, they were regularly subjected to attacks by roving bands of Bushmen who would often drive off their cattle as well, but, as numerous commentators have suggested, this was thought to have been inspired more by hunger than malice. And this "hunger" was arguably caused by the Boer incursions into previously exclusive Bushmen territory; their presence had the devastating effect of reducing the available pasturage for the Bushmen's natural quarry: the wild game that used to roam there in great numbers.

As a result of the clashes between Boer and Bushman that followed, the Bushmen clans south of the Gariep were virtually wiped out by the early to middle 1800s. Some records claim that as many as 200,000 Bushmen could have been killed in the first 200 years after Jan van Riebeeck's arrival in 1652. Small numbers of survivors were said to have thrown in their lot with certain Griqua clans, and some were even absorbed by their sworn enemies, the Koranna; others migrated far north to the relative safety of the Kalahari in present-day Botswana.

When Lichtenstein, the German doctor, naturalist and traveller, journeyed through Bushmanland in the early 1800s, he seems not to have been very impressed with the place. His somewhat jaundiced comparison of the Bushmanland region to the Karoo reflects the lack of rain at that time: "The Karroo is at a certain time of the year refreshed with genial rains, it becomes green and lovely to the eye, it is overspread with flowers. But no such happy moments ever bless this deplorable region."[43]

03

Rows of cone-like sociable weavers' nests partnered the telephone poles that stretched to the horizon; they looked like dishevelled thatch umbrellas relocated from a windblown tropical island beach. Dotted all along the way to Putsonderwater, numerous small sidings were kept company by dilapidated houses of railway workers past. I sensed their spirits keeping silent vigil over their old domains, yet with the almost complete demise of railway traffic in these parts, I knew it had to be an extremely boring pastime, even for a ghost.

At Putsonderwater station, a porter's baggage trolley appeared to be waiting patiently for the next train to arrive. A timetable fluttered on the notice board and a suitably pedantic signboard disclaimed responsibility for any baggage losses, "howsoever caused". Yet the advertised amenities clamoured their appeals in vain, as the passengers and freight had seemingly come and gone — for good. It was as though at some particular juncture in time everyone had suddenly taken flight. Walking around the deserted platform, I remembered a similar scene from one of John Wyndham's famous 1950s science-fiction novels and I looked around warily, wondering where the "triffids" might be lurking. My gaze tracked a formation of tumbleweeds rolling across the parking lot, and then it settled on a crow poised on a creaking door swaying in the restless wind. John Wyndham made way for Alfred Hitchcock.

Every glass window pane in the town appeared to be broken, yet there was not a vandal in sight. The town was so bereft of life that I was convinced even the ghosts had left; all that remained were the empty shells of crumbling old buildings — the desiccated carcasses of lives gone by. But to make sure I wasn't missing anything, I walked into the station building to have a last look about. For some strange reason I still had my helmet and jacket on. It turned out to be a blessing, because as I stood in front of the old ticket office window, a squadron of wasps decided to attack my headgear. I ran out of the building like a mental patient at a fly-swatting contest, flailing my arms and cursing my tormentors.

And in my haste and confusion, I very nearly stumbled into the well that I presumed gave the town its name — and, thankfully, it really was without water. I was suddenly relieved I'd decided to fill the bike up in Groblershoop, because not only was Putsonderwater without water, it was without anything at all, and that certainly included petrol. Grateful for my relatively full tank, I hastened to make tracks before the wasps regrouped or the "triffids" decided to mount an assault of their own.

The Bushman grass bowed to the hot dry wind from the east. The dirt road to Kenhardt was about 75 kilometres long and it stretched unhurriedly over the rigid landscape, continually shifting its straight line in the shimmering heat. I'd swapped my thick "foul-weather" jacket for a lighter top some time ago, but the combined heat of the sun and the motorbike's engine was still adding to my rising body temperature. I was starting to see more and more pools of water silvering every naked stretch of the horizon, and my skin started to tingle with the expectation of a swim in a farmer's reservoir along the way; but there was no sign of life, let alone water, anywhere.

When I'd researched the various areas I would be passing through on my journey, I'd read about some intriguing rocky outcrops found in parts of Bushmanland called inselbergs. Even though I was not expecting to come across any of these remnants of ancient erosion processes on my chosen route (they are found more to the north-west of the region, just south of Namibia) I was fascinated by their serendipitous placement in an otherwise unforgiving wilderness. Their flat-topped or dome-like forms are apparently important places of refuge for plants and animals in this mostly harsh and hostile environment. And in this capacity, inselbergs are also said to act as "rest stations" for animals migrating east to west over the inhospitable Bushmanland terrain: a kind of "Ultra City" for itinerant fauna.

I was just lamenting that I was unlikely to see one of these intriguing stony outcrops when another strange formation came into view. The cluster of big boulders in front of me looked like a directional cairn you might find on a mountain trail for giants; perhaps it was an ancient beacon designed to keep prehistoric animals on track as they crossed the predominantly featureless landscape. I got off the bike to take a closer look. Apart from wanting to see this incongruous geological formation up close, I was also hoping to find some petroglyphs: evidence of the Bushmen's passing. At one point I thought I'd discovered a picture of a large bird cut into the rock, but it was the heat playing tricks with my mind again, and there were unfortunately no real Bushman engravings to be found. Yet the boulders themselves proved interesting enough after some research I did later in Kenhardt. And it was their burnt brown colouring, their shape, size, texture and particularly their location that assisted me to explain their origins.

These boulder piles are actually eroded dolerite and were originally formed by intrusions of magma rising up vertical channels in the surrounding rock known as dykes. Depending on the size of these often balloon-like igneous intrusions, they are known either as plutons (smaller) or batholiths (larger). Due to cracking of the original shapes from various forms of erosion over millions of years, the original pluton or batholith is often reduced, in whole or in part, to boulders of varying shapes and sizes. As for the dark brown colour of many of these boulders, it is apparently caused by concentrations of dark minerals contained in the original magma from the Earth's mantle. These haphazard piles of igneous rock can be seen in various shapes, sizes and forms over large tracts of the Northern Cape, from Carnarvon northwards to the Gariep River and westwards towards Springbok.

☙

I'd never been so pleased to see a town as I was to see Kenhardt that day. The hour and a quarter journey from Putsonderwater was a bone-jarring ride of epic proportions. Corrugations didn't half describe the obstacles I'd faced, and, once again, it was one of those dreaded "primary secondary" dirt tracks that carried more traffic than most that had caused all the trouble. The ghost trade between Putsonderwater and Kenhardt was clearly on the up. When I'd looked at the map a little earlier I'd noticed a town just north-east of Kenhardt called Rugseer (back pain) and I now felt I understood its origins. To make matters worse, I'd also had to fight a strong headwind of stifling dragon breath from the west; the frontal system that had been toying with my sensibilities since Smithfield might have moved on, but it had left a vicious hot wind in its wake.

Around 140 years ago another man had also had to battle his way to Kenhardt. He was the new magistrate and his name was Maximillian Jackson. After defeating a band of rustlers en route, Jackson and 50 policemen set up camp under a giant camel-thorn tree and went about trying to restore order to this rebellious frontier region: a place that had become a refuge for those ruffians, rogues and runaways who were trying to escape the Cape Colony's far-reaching laws and punishments. As I rode around the town getting the lie of the land and seeing what sort of B&Bs were on offer, I came across the old camel-thorn and stopped to reflect on the role it had played as a "jail" for some of Kenhardt's early wayward citizens. The tree was definitely showing signs of its great age (it is said to be about 600 years old), and its scant foliage looked like it would certainly struggle to keep any prisoners tethered there today from dying of the heat. Perhaps it was the same back then and a few torturous weeks tied to a tree in the relentless heat was the general idea.

The urgency for a replacement magistrate was exacerbated by the increasing number of new prisoners being captured by Captain Sission and his effective northern border patrol. On one particular occasion, his force was chasing Klaas Lukas in connection with the numerous cattle thefts in the area, and although Lukas himself managed to escape, Sission and his men took 113 prisoners and also recovered most of the stolen animals. But time would show that Jackson, who had arrived to replace the acting special magistrate, Captain Nesbitt, didn't seem to understand the double-crossing nature of the criminals he was dealing with, and as a result, he lasted less than six months in his new post.

His troubles seem to have started with his offer of pardon to some of the chief rabble- rousers of the region: Donker Malgas, Gamka Windwai and Klaas Lukas. And because the terms of his offer were abused and his subsequent attempts to capture them were unsuccessful, he was seen as unable to contain the situation. This "failure" on Jackson's part saw the arrival of the attorney-general, a Mr Upington, from Cape Town. He was accompanied by Commandant McTaggart and a posse of volunteers who proceeded with all haste to the outlaws' hideouts on the Gariep River islands. Embarrassingly for Jackson, the new group not only managed to corner most of the outlaws he'd failed to arrest, it took hundreds of their followers prisoner as well.

In describing the collection of humanity on the northern frontier, with particular reference to Malgas, Pofadder, Afrikaner, Lukas, Windwai and their followers, Theal offers his candid , yet somewhat arrogant, sentiments:

> If all South Africa — possibly all the world — had been searched, a more utterly worthless collection of human beings could not have been got together than these ragamuffin vagabonds who refused to submit to the restraints of law and order, and set the colonial government at defiance. The only grievance that any of them had was that part of the ground they roamed over was being occupied by farms, but the Xhosas, Korannas, and Afrikaner Hottentots would have had

ample locations assigned to them if they had consented, as other members of their tribes had done, to lead settled lives.[44]

☙

A seven-toed footprint led me straight to the Kambro-kind Lodge on Kenhardt's main road. Unfortunately, the lady I wanted to see with regard to this mysterious impression was away for a few days, and I made a note to speak to her another time. But in her absence, Elma le Roux's assistant, Stephanie, guided me through a number of photograph albums that contained a treasure chest of Bushmen engravings, many of which were discovered on the farm Arbeidsvreugd, about 60 kilometres from Kenhardt.

I first saw the "seven-toed footprint" story on SABC 2's "50/50", back in 2002. There were a number of things that troubled me about this "footprint" from the start; for instance, there is no other recorded evidence of the existence of a seven-toed animal; if a footprint were made in igneous rock, it could only have been effected while the magma was still in a molten-hot state, which seems unlikely; and then to complicate matters further, due to its indented shape, the impression does not appear to be consistent with a conventional Bushman engraving either. During the "50/50" programme, Dr David Morris of the Kimberley Museum discounted the idea that the "footprint" belonged to an animal. He put its unconventional shape and homogenous colouring down to a different method of engraving that was done long before any of the others it was being compared to. Adding another dimension to the puzzle, Elma le Roux claimed in her interview on the programme to have seen giant "human" footprints as well, one of which she said measured 32 centimetres long. She went on to compare this finding to rock engravings of "human" footprints discovered in Botswana that were apparently measured at a similarly large 34 centimetres long. But with the conventional scientific wisdom stating that our human ancestors have only walked the Earth for around the last 2,000,000 years, Elma's giant "human" footprint defies an empirical explanation. Yet it was something she tried to shed some more light on when I eventually managed to catch up with her some months later.

Although it turned out that the Kambro-kind Lodge was fully booked, Stephanie kindly managed to set me up in another self-catering house, just a little further up the road. It was also decorated in quaint Bushman style with petroglyphs and a multitude of other old Bushman artworks and curios filling the house, yet I was pleased that the plumbing and other conveniences were somewhat less ancient.

After bringing in my luggage and securing Rebeccasaurus in a garage next door, it was tempting to just sit there and chill in the cool, curtained darkness. The outside temperature was 38° C and was steadily edging out my earlier enthusiasm for a brisk walk around town. Perhaps my sublime respite from the rigours of the journey at Boegoeberg Dam had made me soft. But after a long pause and a really good cup of tea, I managed to separate myself from the couch with the thought of a cold shower on my return and braved the blast-furnace outside.

A shop advertising Bushman curios lured me inside. It turned out to be yet another Chinese "General Dealer" — I'd seen one in every small town I'd been through thus far — in disguise and even if I'd wanted to buy anything, there was little chance of making myself understood. I imagined his customers trying to return faulty electronic equipment and explaining what the product was or wasn't doing; it was bound to end badly. Some commentators are calling them "Africa's new colonialists" and it is surely only the levelling power of their cheap merchandise in bargain-hungry capitalistic societies that allows them to spurn the languages of their host countries. After all, they would probably argue that everyone understands the value of low prices. Chinese economic imperialism is certainly not a new thing, though, their great commercial fleets were plying the world's oceans long before the early European traders and then as now, they always seem to win over the obeisance of other nations by making their technologies or commodities an indispensable part of the host nation's psyche. In fact, the early Chinese "tribute" system was designed to engender such awe among the rulers of the receiving nations that they would immediately recognise China as a superior power and bind their allegiance to it. And in more recent times, think of the mostly positive impact that cheap Chinese merchandise has had on the lifestyles of poverty-stricken Africans; particularly those in the poorer rural areas.

I'd barely walked one block when the thought of a bitterly cold Windhoek kept repeating itself. And then, miraculously on cue, the welcoming vision of the Kenhardt Hotel swam through the rising heat and sucked me into its cool interior. The bar's decor was a fusion of Bushman and Boere baroque: the barstools and chairs were all covered in shiny plastic with yellow paw-prints, the black and yellow walls showcased hunting trophies and Bushmen artefacts, there was a pizza oven in the far corner and the overhead fans seemed to be powered by Rolls-Royce jet engines. Supertramp's *Crime of the Century* was playing at full volume through four old hi-fi speakers, and I felt very much at home.

She brought me a beer that was glistening with condensation. Even the beer mug had been in the freezer to help the liquid hold onto its elusive promise of arctic coolness.

"Where are you on your way to?" she asked in an expectant tone that made me think that people seldom stopped over for longer than they absolutely had to.

"To Loeriesfontein next, but I'm taking the long way around on the dirt road, between the pans."

"So you're not rushing through to Cape Town in one day like most of the people that pass through do. Something about all our open space seems to scare the *dingis* out of them."

"No, the endless horizons and the space are part of why I'm here. But tell me, is there perhaps an official tourism bureau in town that can shed some light on Kenhardt's early history?"

"Well, you can try the municipality; but hang on, I might have something you'll find interesting."

She moved with a gracefulness that belied her fuller figure and there was a mischievous glint in her eye that hinted at a wicked sense of humour: something of a prerequisite for being successful in the hotel trade, I mused — and especially behind a bar counter in a town with a rough reputation like Kenhardt.

Sitting in what I assume was the same bar around 50 years ago, Lawrence Green had been pondering the elusive origins of Kenhardt's name:

> I also heard an ingenious explanation which brought in an aged coloured woman who lived on the site of the village before any white people settled there. She was hospitable to white travellers, giving them a clean hut to sleep in, so that in later years many remembered her. They would say: "*Ek ken haar graf*" (I know her grave). From the Afrikaans words "*Ken haar*" the name of the village is supposed to be derived. It is not a completely satisfying theory. I wish I could find traces of old man Kenhardt. If he ever lived, he must have been an adventurer worthy of that wild frontier district.[45]

Suzette returned with a photocopied document entitled *Kenhardt: Uit Ons Geskiedenis*, an authoritative historical account of the town and the region. It was written by the late headmaster of Kenhardt High School, W.A. Burger, during his retirement years. It was just the type of information I was looking for, and after sinking another cold Windhoek, I made off with my treasure to the municipality to do some photocopying of my own.

Having done my chores and walked around part of the town, I decided to take a trip out to the Rooiberg Dam. The cold shower and the snooze would have to wait; besides, I was kind of hoping the large collection of cool water just might invite me in. The dam was ten kilometres out of town on the dirt track to Van Wyksvlei, and on arriving there, I felt like I was suddenly back in the Kalahari. The bike and I were ploughing through long stretches of deep red sand and we were surrounded by acacia trees on either side. Then the welcoming expanse of water appeared in the desolate surrounds; it was reminiscent of a particular bay I'd visited on Lake Kariba in Zimbabwe many years ago, and it was probably the large collection of dead trees in the shallows that did it. I rode on a little further and came across one of the most serene burial sites I'd ever seen. The tomb was encased in natural stone and enjoyed the joint shade of two magnificent quiver trees; the inscribed cross read "Elizabeth, beloved wife of Percy Ashenden (1854-1898)". Looking at the view over the cross towards the dam, it wasn't hard to see that of all the things they'd shared, a love of the peace brought on by pristine natural surroundings must have been among the most important to them.

Once again, those words from my stepbrother: "You'll never regret a swim," encouraged me to take the plunge. Barry had first said this to me when I was debating whether to dive off our small yacht halfway to Rio. It wasn't so much that I'd just woken up that was putting me off at the time he said it, it was the five kilometres of ocean beneath us that I'd found quite eerie. I went in nevertheless, and the tame dorados that had been following the boat gave me a sense of perspective, as well as a strange sense of security: we were in their domain and our travelling partners were looking out for us. Whatever the case, I was certainly glad I'd dissuaded one of our crew members from hooking them for supper. Looking down into the depths was a surreal "tunnel of light" experience; the clear water caused by the windless calm made it feel like you could see forever.

Fed by the inconsistent trickle of the Hartebeest River, the waters of the Rooiberg Dam are pretty muddy, and the hot wind rippling its surface made it impossible to see more than half a metre underwater. I lay on my back in the shallows, paddling in lazy circles while watching the water lap the stony shoreline, relaxed in the knowledge that crocodiles were no longer part of Bushmanland's ecosystem. Or so I'd heard. Circular ripples in the distance indicated the rise of a fish or frog; a grey heron moved overhead on lazy wings; and a reed cormorant skimmed the water's surface from the other direction. The day's heat and grime had dissolved into the dam. It was time to head back for a snooze.

Not too many explorers ventured through Bushmanland in the early days of the Cape Colony. Most of the travellers heading north to the Gariep and beyond went via the ford at Prieska; others in search of copper (which they originally had hoped was gold) kept closer to the west coast. It wasn't only Bushmen they were afraid of: the almost complete lack of drinking water made them fear dying of thirst even more. Reading the work by Burger that Suzette had given me, I came across the tale of an early *smous* (trader) called George Thompson, who braved a trip through Bushmanland in 1824 "by a route never taken before by any traveller." About 150 kilometres south-west of Kenhardt, it seems that he met a Bushman while searching for water. With apologies to the author for any details that may be lost in translation, this is an extract from his journey:

Thompson took a course from here over Adriaansvlei and a

pan he christened, Commissioner's Pan, to the Katkop River, where he hoped to find water. Here he came across the most attractive Bushman women he'd ever met — "might even be called a beauty". The Bushman explained to them that they would find water about 50 miles away in a north-westerly direction, and after a painful route of about 80 miles without food or water, they eventually reached the Gamka (lion) River after 16 hours, a tributary of the Hartebees, only to find a lion there but no water.[46]

While farmers and families of European origin were exploring the possibility of settling in Bushmanland in the late 1800s, a Bushman shepherd from the Kenhardt district was doing some European "exploring" of his own. His name was Klaas Velletjies, and when he returned from England he had in his possession a bowler hat belonging to the Prince of Wales and a morning coat made by the royal tailor. Lawrence Green tells us more:

> In some way which I have never been able to discover, Klaas Velletjies was sent to England with his wife and child. This queer trio appeared before Queen Victoria, and the Prince of Wales presented Klaas with the clothes I have mentioned. Klaas often related his court experiences round the camp-fire, but the deepest impression he carried away from England with him was of the Smithfield market. He had never imagined that there was so much meat in the world.[47]

I woke up sweating from the heat. It was after 6 p.m., yet the hot air still clung stubbornly to the parched landscape. But after a long, cold shower in the garden, I slowly started to come out of my stupor and made my way to dinner. I took a roundabout route to the hotel, not only because I was after some sunset photographs, but also to have a look at those parts of the town I hadn't covered yet. Besides being badgered by a few youths for "bread money", I couldn't have wished for a better slide show: two farm workers heading back into the veld silhouetted against the sun, the carcass of a 1930s Chevrolet rusting quietly in the burnt-orange light, a mangy mongrel on a chain waiting lovingly for his master to return and an old mission church's white bell-tower contrasting starkly against the darkening horizon.

After a tasty dinner and my daily measure of red wine, I left to finish my preparations for the early start the next day. Day 9 was to be my longest leg yet, nearly 300 kilometres through some of the most desolate, waterless and remote areas in the country, and I needed a good night's sleep to help me tackle it. But as I lay there in the stifling heat, trying to block out the nagging mosquito whines, I knew that any sleep I got was going to be a bonus. Thank goodness for that outside shower.

༺ ༻

It was more than six months later when I caught up with Elma le Roux to discuss the seven-toed footprint and some of the other Bushman rock art she'd uncovered. I met with her in the Kenhardt Museum, where she's the curator. When I shook her hand and looked into her eyes, I was impressed by the raw enthusiasm they contained. She stood behind a huge old table and began shuffling and sorting through the hundreds of photographs of Bushman engravings to show me her best examples. The conversation that followed went something like this:

NY: How do you explain what you call the seven-toed footprint in very old igneous rock?

ELR: I can't explain it, but I'm convinced that it's a genuine impression and hasn't been carved out by man or eroded by nature.

NY: Now this rock would have been hot molten lava at the time that this "impression" was made. Why is it that footprints of other species haven't been captured in similar rocks at other sites around the country?

ELR: Look, I'm not an academic or a scientist, so I can't explain how it came about, but there can be no denying what's there.

NY: You've also discovered some engravings that resemble ancient creatures such as the one you say looks like a pterodactyl; what is the significance of that discovery?

ELR: The San are believed to have had photographic memories. Now if they drew what looks like a pterodactyl, surely this means that they must have seen one?

NY: Many rock art experts believe that Bushman engravings are often the result of their transposing of entoptic phenomena, often in the form of geometric shapes, which they've seen while hallucinating during trance rituals. Do you think this may account for some of the shapes shown in your photographs?

ELR: I'm really more interested in the animals and human activities that they recorded.

NY: Okay, but what about the depiction of half-animal, half-human forms, the so-called therianthropes, such as the well-documented "swallow-shaman" rock painting from the southern Cape? Do you think this sort of depiction of Bushman shamans merging with birds could explain the engraving that you believe looks like a pterodactyl?

ELR: As I said before, I believe the Bushmen drew what they actually saw.

NY: What you're in essence saying is that man may well have walked with dinosaurs and has been around at least 63 million years longer than most palaeontologists think they have. Is that correct?

ELR: I can only show you the evidence that I find; people must make up their own minds.

NY: You've also discovered what you refer to as giant "human" footprints in some of the surrounding rocks. Do these further point to man's having been around when these rocks were being formed, hundreds of millions of years ago?

ELR: Some scientists call these ancient engravings or impressions, created by thousands of years of erosion. Other well-qualified archaeologists disagree and are convinced that these impressions and others found overseas are actual human footprints.

NY: You showed me what you believe are outlines of ancient human fossils lying in the rocks near the Bushman engravings. Why don't you convince archaeologists to excavate these sites and prove your theories correct?

ELR: I would never agree to desecrate these ancient holy sites.

NY: You call yourself a Creationist. Does that mean that in your view, man was created before any of the prehistoric animal species?

ELR: I believe in the word of God, and God does not talk of evolution in the Bible.

8

Across the Land of Begin Again

(Kenhardt via Brandvlei to Loeriesfontein: 295 kilometres)

A life in the desert is certainly most charming with all its drawbacks, for the mind can have unlimited action.

Andrew A. Anderson

The day ahead promised an epic journey: close on 300 kilometres of some of the most inhospitable wilderness South Africa had to offer. In my fitful sleep the previous night I had dreamt of vultures circling above my head. As I lay on my back on the cracked earth staring up at a white-hot sun, one of the vultures said in a high-pitched wheezy voice: *"Leave him for now; he's not quite done yet."* I woke up smiling in a "far side" kind of way and fended off another squadron of mosquitoes; they were determinedly trying to take me back to their nest, drop by drop. Before I left town, I thought it wouldn't hurt to re-check that I had enough provisions and drinking water.

Describing his travels through this region, Lawrence Green noted:

> I was not surprised to hear it called "the land of begin again." Gently it rolls westwards from the main railway line through the Great Karoo, a treeless land with few landmarks, often like an inland ocean. The poet William Charles Scully regarded Bushmanland as one of the most complete solitudes on earth. He loved the empty spaces and found inspiration there.

It seems that many people find a great intellectual and spiritual freedom in stark desert landscapes; a strange irony, almost as though the physical barrenness of the environment fertilises the mind. For me, I find that the brain sparks unbidden and the tongue is loose, a bit like cocaine without the numb nostrils and a dent in your wallet. But not everyone finds emancipation in these wide open and often desolate spaces. For instance, a woman that Green met on his travels complained to him that:

> We live behind invisible bars, imprisoned by limitless space. The earth is so flat that we long for the sight of a mountain.

We are imprisoned by the plains of freedom. The space you admire so much makes us feel petty, and indeed we are small.[48]

The green and yellow grasslands waved in the cool morning breeze. What I saw all around me was definitely not a picture of desolation. In fact, it was easy for me to understand why in the summer months, the early Boer farmers around Williston, Calvinia and Loeriesfontein had made for Bushmanland to graze their livestock there. Of course, the pasturage was dependent on good seasonal rains, and while accessing it, the Boers also had to be constantly on the lookout for marauding bands of thieves and hungry Bushmen. Certainly no walk in the park.

The turn-off to Verneuk Pan, the 50 kilometres long and 15 kilometres wide sandy depression made famous by Malcolm Campbell's world land speed record attempt in 1929, appeared on my left. My good friend, Douglas had shot a number of TV commercials there, and I felt I'd heard and read enough about the place to avoid the long detour; more importantly, I had a bank of shimmering images in my head that I was not yet ready to replace. Yet besides this, the day's riding schedule was very tight, and I also knew I would have a sighting of its lesser known south-western arm a little further on. Instead, I decided to sit on the side of the road for a while and eat some crackers. I was feeling a little melancholy on account of a dassie (hyrax or "rock rabbit") that had decided to run in front of my wheel. I seemed to only strike it a glancing blow, and although it appeared pretty stunned, it had managed to get up and run off into a pile of rocks on the other side of the road. Even though they are known to be remarkably resilient little creatures, I doubted that it would survive the impact. The probability of me hitting that hyrax in these vast reaches of open space must have surely been about the same as winning the Lotto. I tried to console myself with the thought of "trusting the ways of the universe", but all I could see was the pain I'd caused. An agnostic friend of mine who denies any dates with predetermined destiny would probably have called it "just another fragile travelling coincidence". But regardless how it came about, and how I should have viewed the experience, it was still making me very miserable.

But sometimes, misery acknowledged in the moment is not always a bad thing. In that moment I gave thanks for all my blessings, all the "fragile travelling coincidences", synchronicities and predetermined events that had shaped my life to that particular point. Sitting on that rock in the claimed geographical centre of the country, I was joyfully miserable as hell. And to top it all I then started to mumble a kind of love sonnet to my wife — the emotions of love and tragedy were seemingly braided into one chord.

Still in reflective mood, I thought again how this solo journey around the Karoo was without question the single best thing I'd ever done for myself. One seldom has time just to go with the flow of what arrests your interest, and then to linger in the moment, becoming aware of the being that sits behind your persona. Some may relate this "being" or "self" to the equivalent of an eye behind the camera. Talking to my dictaphone, making notes of my various sightings and musings, was also a strangely companionable exercise. I was getting to know myself and even laughing at my own observations and commentaries. *Yes, I know what you're thinking and you may well be right. But the beauty of having a split personality is that you're never truly alone!* In fact, I was enjoying being on my own so much, observing the world, the people and the interplay of everything in between, that I was a little concerned as to how I was going to react when I had to share part of this space with Harvey over the next three days. It had very little to do with anything about him or his personality and everything to do with selfishly wanting to guard this novel and precious time alone.

But there was also some part of me that was greatly looking forward to sharing a small section of this special adventure with somebody; especially when that somebody was one of my best friends, a respected mentor and probably the most enthusiastic person alive. Not taking life too seriously, under threat of jail, and even death, from the apartheid police in his days of being a newspaper editor, Harvey is certainly endowed with a well-developed sense of humour. And it has allowed him to smile his way through many challenging times in his life and to stride ahead, times where others may have grimaced and fallen prey to melancholy and depression instead. He also happens to be my stepfather, a blessing of fate that no amount of appreciation can ever do justice to.

When I'd asked him if he might like to join me somewhere along the route of my circumnavigation, he'd jumped at the chance and decided to meet me at Loeriesfontein. One of his good friends, Dennis, was originally meant to come with him, but had a change of plans at the last moment. For some reason known only to himself, Dennis was in search of the longest straight section of road in the country, and he'd apparently believed it was located on the stretch of tar somewhere between Brandvlei and Kenhardt. Perhaps he'd found his Holy Grail somewhere else.

Over the years, Harvey and I have had some amazing adventures together. We've ridden motorbikes through all sorts of terrain and had innumerable close shaves, been involved in car rallies, climbed many mountains, walked hundreds of paths, hiked many trails, capsized yachts, been on a number of safaris, had black-tie dinners in the desert and visited a host of strange lands. We've also shared a lot of beer, or, should I say, drunk a lot of beer together, as Harvey is not a person to share his beer with anyone, no matter how good a friend you are. It was on an expedition along the cut-lines of Botswana that I first noticed Harvey's markedly protectionist tendencies towards his stash of booze. On that particular trip there was a communal supply of beer and wine kept in the larder tent, and our private stocks of hard tack were stored in our individual luggage. As the trip wore on, the communal supplies of beer and wine became worryingly low, and one's private stock became increasingly important in lubricating the late night chatter around the fire. Towards the end of the journey, both Harvey and Rex regularly claimed to be on their last bottle of Scotch. And when the last drops were poured, both of them would claim they had absolutely no more. But after a short time of abstinence, one or the other would suddenly appear with "a spare bottle they'd forgotten about". It was interesting to see who would appear with yet another "forgotten bottle" first, and while Rex gave Harvey a very good run for his money, I would have to say that Harvey's poker-faced grit, and marginally better staying power, won out in the end.

When my stepbrother, Barry, and I teamed up to start the first yacht race we'd ever entered, Harvey decided to go ahead and wait for us in Rio. It was a tremendous act of faith on his part. Miraculously, his faith in our skill and determination eventually paid off, but that was only some days after the race had officially ended. And as a result of our tardiness, Harvey had to endure the end of race party on his own: "It was a great party. The nubile, feather-bedecked, semi-clad ladies of the Rio Carnival incited the Cape sailors to dance the samba, the rumba and the conga… right there in the middle of the sedate, exclusive, and highly formal yacht club." After jumping into the club's pool with his money belt still on and wetting "five million-odd cruzeiros" in the process, Harvey was a little dejected because he'd had to turn down an invitation from some of the sailors to one of the groovy nightclubs in Rio — his only spending money being soggy and useless:

> Some of the bachelors, after weeks at sea, had found one of Rio's topless nightclubs. It was at the very bottom of all gradings.

"It's terrifying," they told us. "The women come right into the men's toilets and have sex with the poor guys against the wall in there. The young girls are like animals. It's horrible. It's disgusting."

"When are you going back?"

"Well, right now. It's 2 a.m. and should be warming up. Want to join us?"[49]

But even as one of my most respected mentors, Harvey has not always given me the best advice. After persuading the Hermanus yacht club that I would be an asset to their membership base, Harvey and I set off across the lagoon in my new sailing dinghy. Well, to be honest, it wasn't so much a sailing dinghy as a hybrid rubber-duck motorboat with a centreboard and a sail. The problem was that when you were sailing this "hybrid", the tiller took the place of what turned out to be in our case a much needed motor. As we took off from the quay with a gale on our quarter, I knew we were in trouble. We'd not gone two metres when the craft flipped over; "an inauspicious start for a Rio 'veteran'", I thought I heard them muttering from the clubhouse. Once we had righted the boat and were under way again, no matter what I did to adjust the point of sailing, the tiller wouldn't respond and we were fast heading for some rocks on the far side of the lagoon. I mentioned the problem to Harvey, but he seemed characteristically unperturbed. Luckily the yacht club's rescue boat had seen our failed attempts at tacking and raced out towards us in an official froth of white water.

"What ever you do, Nick, don't let them tow us in. Not on your first outing at the club. You'll never live it down."

Bowing to Harvey's experience of fending off years of bar-room jibes in numerous clubs, I waved off the rescue boat with a false smile and a thumbs-up.

Three hours later, after eventually being able to signal the rescue boat from the rocky shores miles away from where the assistance was first offered, the rescue boat towed us back to the club. We decided to give the club pub a miss and rather have a beer at home.

Whatever lay ahead over the next three days, I knew a few things with absolute certainty: we'd drink a fair amount of beer, face more than one misadventure together and laugh like hell.

༃

As it turned out, I only managed to get within about a kilometre of Verneuk Pan's south-western arm. But my view of it from the roadside was enhanced by an installation of slab-like dolerite boulders glinting in the early morning sunlight; the layout of these seven big flat rocks struck me as a likely place for the elders of a Bushman clan of yesteryear to have met to discuss their next hunting expedition, or any other important clan matters. Whatever their purpose, they led my gaze to the great depression in the distance and I thought of the luckless speedster, Malcolm Campbell, who was *verneuked* (cheated) there. If he had attempted the world land speed record just a few months earlier he would have been successful, but in the build-up to his attempt, another racer in Daytona, Seagrave, in his Golden Arrow, had unfortunately pushed the record well out of Campbell's reach. Although Campbell ended up breaking the 207 m.p.h. he'd originally come to conquer by reaching a top speed of 218.45 m.p.h., Seagrave's new record stood at a formidable 231.36 m.p.h., and Campbell had thus been *verneuked*.

I was completely alone in all this emptiness and savouring the freedom of it. With the bigger pans of Grootvloer and Verneuk to the left and right of my track, I was riding through my very own grass-covered depressions that were well off the main tourist route. This was the beauty of the dirt tracks I'd plotted on the journey; they were designed to let me explore what the average tourist wouldn't see, and I was seldom disappointed. There's also something incredibly liberating about "owning" the road that stretches to an impossibly distant horizon; it's so serene, and in today's overcrowded world, even surreal.

I knew that I was meant to detour from my planned south-westerly trajectory and head east for about six kilometres, but when I'd already measured off ten kilometres and there was still no turn-off, I became a bit concerned. I was literally in the middle of nowhere, and besides the angst of thinking I was losing my way, I was also having to watch my petrol consumption pretty carefully. With Rebeccasaurus's range being only around 225 kilometres, my safety margin for getting lost on a long day's journey was not very big. The colour photocopies of a fairly recent Engen road atlas I was using had been excellent so far and I was reasonably confident that the turn-off would materialise sooner or later. But the challenge with these standard roadmaps when back-roading is that you need to estimate your own distances and waypoints by marking off the length of the road against the scale provided. And even using my old yachting dividers, my measurements were still prone to small inaccuracies. Often these dirt tracks also have numerous kinks in them as well and I'd sometimes been too lazy to measure each and every little twist and turn — an omission I hoped I wouldn't regret later on.

The turn-off eventually materialised at nearly treble the estimated distance, slightly more drastic than the "small inaccuracy" I'd been expecting. But, its "private farm road" appearance caused a little doubting "pop-up" to keep surfacing in the back of my mind even after I'd found it, questioning whether it really was the right road after all. And after opening and closing 15 farm gates and not seeing a soul, I still wasn't a hundred per cent sure. On any other day of the trip, time and distance wouldn't have been terribly important, yet that day, not only was petrol a concern, I'd also promised to meet Harvey in Loeriesfontein for sundowners. Yet after sitting and staring at the cracked earth of Soutpan for a while and listening to the comforting clanking of two distant windmills, I was lulled into a more peaceful and accepting mindset. Besides, what else could I do?

On a journey like this, you also learn to accept that some days are just going to be more challenging than others. After coming close to being lost and then successfully fending off the reappearance of the vultures from my nightmares the previous evening, I thought I was in the clear until I very nearly collided with a sheep just a little further on. The thing is, sheep often look like they know where they're going, but it's all just a woolly illusion. They're prone to changing tack like a politician in crisis and no amount of heckling has been known to change their behaviour. And because putting tyre tracks on someone else's sheep is generally considered bad form in the greater Karoo district, I gave the erratic ewes an extra wide berth and made myself scarce. A little further on, I cruised past a few more sheep grazing on the edge of the road outside Brandvlei. Even though I'd already gone past them, they suddenly decided to jump through the barbed-wire fence, and one of the fatter ones unfortunately got stuck. Now, an overweight sheep stuck upside down in a barbed-wire fence is not one of nature's most pleasant sights, but I still felt compelled to rush back to try and assist the poor animal. Yet, my "trying to assist" only made it struggle more. I was powerless to help. Eventually the sheep managed to break free by itself and was reasonably unscathed, its only apparent loss being the woolen jersey it left behind on the fence. It was when I thought of an itchy jackal finding this "jersey" and using it to get rid of its fleas that I knew the sheep's bizarre accident probably had some purpose.

I made for the peace and quiet of "downtown" Brandvlei, and the uncomplicated promise of a toasted egg and tomato sandwich.

⋆

"Brandvlei. Shit." So said journalist Stephen Haw in the *Sunday Times* compilation of *Rediscovering South Africa*. When I got to what looked like a decent take-away café in town and I couldn't even buy a toasted egg and tomato sandwich and a cup of tea, I felt similarly derisive about the place. But Haw and his fellow journalists had more than superficial reasons to complain about:

> We are chased back to Brandvlei by icy rain and plummeting temperatures. And then in the bar of the hotel, an incident that leaves us reeling. Simon is asked to remove his hat, while another man nearby wears his without question. I ask why but know that I already know the answer and that this is the beginning of something that ends badly.
>
> "No hats in the bar," says the bartender. Which of course means that I have to point out the man on the stool next to me. "What about him?"
>
> "*Nee. Jy verstaan nie. Ek het die reg om te diskrimineer.*" And that's it. Everything gets quiet.[50]

The man asked to remove his hat was a black photographer with the *Sunday Times* crew. While there are no doubt numerous white people in Brandvlei that respect the laws and ethos of the "New South Africa", I was still glad that I only needed petrol from the place and not a bed, or the chance of a beer served by the hand of a racist barman. I prayed that Loeriesfontein was different and got the hell out of there.

As I powered up the gentle gradient of a pass not too far out of town, a tawny eagle eyed me imperiously from its rocky perch. Normally seen in more wooded regions, I was surprised to see one in this sparsely vegetated area. With the change in altitude came a gradual transition in the surrounding flora as well, it was slowly moving from desert succulent towards the more widespread Karoo shrub and grass. The metamorphosis from Bushmanland back to the Karoo proper had begun.

The connecting road to Loeriesfontein was as bad as the petrol attendant in Brandvlei had made out. As I'd experienced between Putsonderwater and Kenhardt, these main dirt roads between two towns were often the worst. But in this case, there really was no viable alternative, especially seeing that I was still on a reasonably tight schedule. Yet, some way out of town, an enormous yellow grader signalled some respite. Working from the Loeriesfontein side, the local roads department had already got about three-quarters of the way to Brandvlei and the virgin roadway smoothed the journey forward. This was real Zen dirt — and I had it all to myself.

Rebeccasaurus was burbling along as happy as an herbivorous dinosaur in a fern forest, and I was making surprisingly good time. After my brush with getting lost among the pans, I'd made it to Brandvlei with a couple of litres still in the tank. She was not a bike that would let you down easily, and I was fast understanding why the farmers around Aberdeen were always referring to my mount as a *kanniedood* (can't die). There was just no stopping her. Yet another example of "old" technology that doesn't need improving upon: air-cooled, single cylinder, four-stroke with monoshock suspension — a winning combination.

My revised estimations were that I'd be in Loeriesfontein at around two o'clock, well ahead of my previously predicted ETA of about five in the afternoon. About half an hour away from the town, I pulled off the road and sat under an acacia tree to eat lunch and relax a while. Curious sheep from a nearby farm came to visit and bleated the silence into retreat, but I didn't mind, they were the only real company I'd had all day and they were thankfully not trying to injure themselves by jumping through fences at the sight of me. Using my rain suit as a groundsheet and my backpack as a pillow, I took in the view of a nearby koppie beyond the toe of my boot and drifted nostalgically into Herman Charles Bosman country:

> The more I screwed up my eyes and gazed at the toe of my boot, the more it looked like Abjaterskop. By and by it seemed that it actually was Abjaterskop, and I could see the stones on top of it, and the bush trying to grow up the sides, and in my ears there was a far-off humming sound, like bees in an orchard on a still day. As I have said, it was very pleasant.
>
> Then a strange thing happened. It was as though a huge cloud, shaped like an animal's head and with spots on it, had settled on top of Abjaterskop. It seemed so funny that I wanted to laugh. But I didn't. Instead, I opened my eyes a little more and felt glad to think that I was only dreaming. Because otherwise I would have to believe that the spotted cloud on Abjaterskop was actually a leopard, and that he was gazing at my boot. Again I wanted to laugh. But then, suddenly, I knew.[51]

I woke up with my body bearing the brunt of a determined assault from a colony of large black ants. Okay, so they weren't as immediately threatening as the leopard in Herman Charles Bosman's imagination, but if I'd slept a little longer, I might well have lost a couple of kilograms to their hundreds of hooked jaws. Taking a closer look at one that I'd squashed in self-defence, I noted that it was nearly two centimetres long, with a distinctive brown abdomen. After closer inspection through the magnifying glass of my Swiss army knife, I saw that it had a set of powerful mandibles, and I wondered whether it was a carnivore (army or driver ant) or if its jaws were designed for harvesting vegetal matter, or perhaps even collecting seeds to be delivered back to the nest. With their display of highly adaptive and canny behaviour, ants are regarded by a number of scientists as being near the top of the insect "intelligence" ladder. And one of the facts that make them think this is ants' remarkably human-like display of communal interaction for the common good, so that they make up a kind of "insect civilisation".

The famous Afrikaans writer Eugene Marais, who studied the behaviour of ants over a period of ten years, wrote a book, *Soul of the White Ant*, in which he formulated a theory that the sum of all the individual ants of a colony make up one organic whole. He believed that the colony is in fact a composite animal that is still evolving and that the queen was the brain and the director of all the individual parts. As for the ant's "soul", Marais philosophised over the colony's collective manifestations of sensations and "feelings" such as pain and even "love". But some are sceptical of his theories, even more so because of his reputed dependence on recreational chemicals at the time. Perhaps the jury is still out.

☙

Massed formations of pterodactyl-shaped clouds winged their way towards Loeriesfontein, while misshapen ridges led the eye to the far-distant Hantamsberge in the background. I was now definitely leaving Bushmanland and re-entering the familiar Karoo once more: grey-green bush, shale soils and shredded tyres lined the road towards Loeriesfontein. All the way from Putsonderwater I'd noticed the ominous tyre carcasses on the side of the road, but no road thus far had savaged as many tyres as I'd seen on this particular stretch of road outside Loeriesfontein. I rode very carefully, determined to protect my puncture-free record like an intact no-claims insurance bonus.

Thoughts of tyre trouble were soon eclipsed by hundreds of

lizards trying to cross the road. Dodging them was like playing a "Jurassic Park" video game; the challenge in this instance, though, being obviously to miss and not hit the mini dinosaur-like "targets". Profusions of brightly coloured daisies and *vygies* were thriving in the roadside drainage areas while more and more flat-topped mountains and koppies hove into view from the south. I was getting close to my destination after a long day in the saddle and I could almost taste that first ice-cold beer at a pub somewhere in Loeriesfontein. Although it had been a hot and tiring ride in from Kenhardt, it had not been nearly as daunting as I'd expected. Of course, it's only ever really daunting if you crash or break down and have to walk well over 100 kilometres to the nearest town. Yet on my old faithful *kanniedood* XT250, I doubted that it would ever happen. But then again, I also knew that I would have to leave the final say to powers larger than my blind faith in Johnny's mechanical ability, as well as the prowess of Japanese engineering.

As soon as I arrived in town I saw that I'd be able to kill two birds with one stone — the information office I needed to visit was joined to an inviting-looking pub. And after the manager had brought me a beer, I found she had some interesting stories to tell as well.

"You know, up until the late '50s and even the early '60s, I used to trek with my folks with the sheep up to our summer farm in Bushmanland," Elize told me.

"Oh really; did you truck the sheep up to the fresh pastures?" I enquired.

"No, man, we followed the herders in donkey *karre* with all our provisions for camping there in the veld. We had to take almost everything along with us because our land didn't have a fancy house on it or anything. In the mid-'60s my dad eventually did get himself an old *tjorrie* to drive the family across, but you know, it wasn't really the same. That time of moving along at the pace of the sheep allowed you to absorb and appreciate the change of the seasons."

I was holed up on the stoep of yet another guesthouse cum bar cum restaurant cum information office called "Boesmanland". It was very pleasant — soaking up the warm sun and the cold beer and half-listening to Elize drone on about the days of yore. She told me how she and her husband longed to get in the bakkie and just drive the back roads like I was doing. To just stop where they wanted to and sleep in the back on the side of the road when they got tired. And then also how she so wanted to swim with dolphins in Mozambique. Even though they were both tied up in jobs making ends meet for the moment, she was sure their time would come soon; they just had to plan it and be patient.

As I pulled into the Loeriesfontein Hotel's car park, I thought I heard the bike make a sort of fluty pinking noise; it was reminiscent of the noise I'd heard on my trial run when the bike's rings had gone. But after revving the bike I noticed no excessive exhaust smoke and decided to take it around the block to see if the noise disappeared. It did. I think what had happened was that in the confines of the surrounding walls of the parking lot, some perfectly normal valve noise had just been amplified out of proportion. I breathed a huge sigh of relief and made my way to my room. On a long motorbike journey like this, you become so attuned to the sound of your motor that the slightest change in pitch can set the alarm bells ringing. Then again, perhaps it was just the full moon that was making me edgy.

Being attuned to the noises of one's transport reminded me again of the ocean crossing my wife and I had made on our Miura. After a week at sea, we became aware of the significance of every single noise that emanated from a particular point of sailing. If we were on a port tack, the door to the heads would rattle, yet on the opposite tack, gravity overcame its noisiness. It was a useful system, because every noise had a known cause, like the way the dividers used to schlock in its holder above the chart table when we were wallowing around in a windless sea. Conversely, an unknown noise required investigation, yet most times, the causes were harmless enough; like the time one of my pipes made its way into the bilges. But I digress.

The Loeriesfontein Hotel was the kind of old country establishment I'd been hoping to stay at during the entire trip. Due to my own preoccupation with finding a room without first surveying the scene more thoroughly, I'd missed my chance at the Kenhardt Hotel, which had looked equally promising when I finally discovered it. I paused a while in my new surroundings and marvelled at the level of cleanliness and comfort: en suite shower and toilet, a separate hand basin in the room, TV, radio, a proper reading light above the bed (hallelujah!), dressing table, cupboard, a kettle with tea and coffee — all for about R170, including breakfast. It was excellent value and I knew Harvey would appreciate it as well.

With about three hours of daylight left, I decided to walk to the unique Windmill Museum on the other side of town. In terms of sophisticated shopping outlets, Loeriesfontein was like so many other small Karoo towns — it was not likely to earn any "Retailer of the Year" awards. Besides the petrol station — which had run out of unleaded fuel — there were a number of café cum general grocer stores, and that was about it. So when I discovered two light aircraft parked in the showroom of an old motor dealer's building, I was knocked out. After some enquiries I discovered that they belonged to Boet Loubser, who has a factory behind the showroom where he assembles Bushbaby aircraft to order. It proved to me once again never to judge a small town, or its people, before digging a little below the surface.

But with Tannie Gesina Louw, the curator at the Windmill Museum, I didn't need to do much digging to realise I'd found an absolute gem of a human being. Married to an ex-speaker of parliament during the reign of the Nats, Tannie Gesina was a down-to-earth person with a great love of Afrikaner history. I came across her sitting behind a work bench deep in concentration as she carefully painted the letters "Model B" onto the silver background of a large windmill's rudder. Absorbed and in her element restoring this antique piece of machinery back to its former pristine state, she was the quintessential Afrikaans *tannie* of yesteryear. Her silver hair was rolled into a tight bun and she even had an apron on, making her look like she could quite as easily have been baking rusks for her grandchildren.

"Good afternoon," I ventured quietly, trying not to scare the life out of her.

"Yes, hello. I did hear you come in; I just couldn't look up straight away on account of needing to get these lines absolutely straight. Would you like me to show you around?"

"That would be great," I said, steeling myself for the long "school tour" ahead.

Yet it wasn't like that at all. Even though Tannie Gesina moved incredibly slowly on account of some fairly major surgery she'd just had, it really was a most absorbing tour. Starting off with the installation of more than 20 windmills, she not only lovingly named each one and its country of origin, but she knew exactly how each one functioned and even things like whether their respective gearing systems were sump- or hand-lubricated. She reeled off names like Gearing, Springbok, Climax and — my personal favourite — the Mogul. Yet the most fascinating part of the tour was still to come. Inside a barn, which she unlocked with a large bunch of keys anchored somewhere in the depths of her skirts, a fascinating 200-year-old scene played out.

On my travels I'd given much thought to the "philosophy of travel and movement", including what makes the journey so often more exciting than the destination itself. Thus far I'd come to believe that the euphoria was partly due to the immense sense of freedom that being untethered to any particular place or life circumstance can bring. Almost as though the journey allows you to act outside who you normally are, or think you have to be, in your daily existence. Whatever the case, the barn scene revealed some of Africa's most adept and hardy travellers known as the Trekboers: itinerant farmers who were continuously on the move to greener pastures; as well as the Trek farmers: those who trekked with their families and cattle only between the seasons, often to take advantage of pastures in both summer and winter rainfall regions.

Even though these two groups of farmers worked the pasturing of their livestock differently, there were obviously great similarities between them in terms of how they lived once in the veld. The Trekboers just had no fixed home to come back to, the veld was their home and in this way they unwittingly emulated the gypsy lifestyles of the indigenous Khoikoi (Hottentots) and San (Bushmen); peoples that they, ironically, often clashed with on their travels.

Tannie Gesina walked me through the lives of these travelling farmers, from their sturdy ox wagons to the canvas bell tents they would erect at their various outspans and destinations, and then onto the bomas around their fireplaces and their ranges of wrought-iron cooking utensils. She even showed me an example of an earthen ant heap that was hollowed out and used as a makeshift oven to bake bread when in the veld. Every item of clothing, every tool, utensil, piece of furniture and luggage had been meticulously labelled by Tannie Gesina herself. "You know, when these people reached their destinations and were lying in their beds inside their tents at night, listening to their sheep grazing contentedly nearby against the sounds of the African night, they knew they were very close to heaven," she told me. After this poetic summation of Trekboer life in the veld, I had to bring her a small fold-up travelling chair so that she could sit down and get her breath back.

While she was resting, I took in the words of a plaque fixed to another smaller wagon nearby. The wagon originally belonged to two brothers, Fred and Ernest Turner, who apparently travelled all over Bushmanland in it. Originally selling bibles to out-of-the-way communities, they were often asked to bring one or another grocery or hardware item the next time they passed through. Because of this, it is said that the two brothers eventually became full-blown travelling merchants, or *smouse*, as they were known by the predominantly Afrikaans communities they served. These *smouse* were often colourful characters of Jewish or Indian extraction who, besides much needed grocery items, also brought many new-fangled city inventions to the rural folk that they didn't really need; or so we're led to believe by Oom Schalk Lourens of the Groot Marico district:

> It's funny when you come to think of it. When there is anything that we Boers don't want you can be quite sure that the Jew traders will bring it to us, and that we will buy it, too.

> I remember how I laughed when a Jew came to my house once with a hollow piece of glass that had a lot of silver stuff in it. The Jew told me that the silver in the glass moved up and down to show you if it was hot or cold. Of course, I said that was all nonsense. I know when it is cold enough for me to put on my woollen shirt and jacket, without having first to go look at that piece of glass. And I also know when it is too hot to work — which is almost all year round in this part of the Marico Bushveld. In the end I bought the thing. But it has never been the same since little Annie stirred her coffee with it.[52]

"Hey fellow traveller, how was your trip?" I said from behind him.

Harvey was checking in at reception, and when he looked up I could sense from his tired eyes and uncharacteristically grubby hands that something had gone wrong.

"Don't ask; but hey, let's go for a beer," he replied, sidestepping any discussion of some obvious frustrations on the journey from Hermanus.

Like me, Harvey always believes you can squeeze more things into the time available than you actually can. After telling him of my interesting visit to the Windmill Museum, he insisted that we pop in to have a quick look and then walk around the town to get a feel for the place. By the time we sat down for a beer at the Boesmanland pub, I was parched — we'd been walking and talking non-stop for over an hour. But it was great to have some company and I'd compressed the highlights of my trip thus far into a brisk half-hour monologue. It turned out that Harvey's Jeep had had two punctures on the way up; the first just outside Calvinia and the next just outside Loeriesfontein. The first puncture was so bad that, although they'd repaired it by putting a tube in the tyre, they'd advised him only to use it as a temporary spare. So he bought one new tyre in Calvinia, leaving him his one original good spare and an emergency one. But that was, of course, before the second puncture outside Loeriesfontein. So now he only had the emergency one left. I decided to stay well out of Harvey's path on the road in case this puncture thing was contagious.

9

More of the Unexpected

(Loeriesfontein to Calvinia: 89 kilometres)

※

By dint of going wrong all will go right.

French proverb

"Now, Nick, I don't want to hamper you or hold you up at all. You must continue with the solo journey as if I wasn't here," said Harvey in a serious tone over breakfast.

"Well, that'll only be vaguely possible if you stop getting punctures," I sparred.

He thrust out his chin and gave me his most engaging smile, but his eyes were saying something completely different.

We'd had a good evening. Despite both being weary from the day's travelling and challenges we'd faced along the way, we'd forced down a bottle or two of red wine over dinner and were feeling a little rough the next morning. But regardless of his condition and with absolutely no consideration for his advancing age, Harvey is always a tonic. His effervescence is contagious and I realised that his company was just what I needed at this advanced stage of the journey. Although I was really enjoying myself, riding a small and ageing scrambler long distance over rough terrain for eight days is physically demanding. And with a saddle aimed more at comforting the backsides of short-distance Japanese tarred-road commuters, I often found myself having to stand up for long periods to allow my blood to reacquaint itself with my nether regions.

We left the Loeriesfontein Hotel in good spirits. The new owner, an ex-policeman from Melkbosstrand who'd said he'd had enough of fighting crime with one hand tied behind his back, was making a determined effort to revive the old hotel. Both Harvey and I believed that he and his wife were doing a really good job of it, and they'd only been there a couple of months. For the two of us, it had cost under R250 per head, which included dinner, bed and breakfast plus all our drinks. No wonder we were smiling.

In springtime, the fields alongside the dirt road to Calvinia are splashed with colour from a wide variety of flowers; yet these seasonal blooms constitute only a small part of the 4,000 different plant species that are found in the wider Namaqualand and Hantam Karoo regions. But it was mid-November when we passed by, and the only remaining "spring" flowers were some resilient *vygies* that occasionally dotted the veld with reds, pinks and lilacs. Another travelling duo who must have also enjoyed the last of the *vygies* as we were doing were the early explorers Thunberg and Masson, way back in 1774.

Carl Thunberg arrived at the Cape in 1772, and its unique floral kingdom held him enthralled for three years. Wanting to collect as many diverse plant species as he could during his stay, he made three field trips into the interior. On his trip through the Bokkeveld and the Roggeveld (named after the type of wild "rye" grass that grows there) during November and December 1774, he was accompanied by the Scottish botanist Francis Masson. And because he collected over 3,000 species of flowers and plants during his stay in the country, of which well over 1,000 were previously unknown to science, Thunberg is often referred to as "the father of South African botany".

The dedication of these early botanists in venturing out into the hostile interior of a virtually unexplored land cannot be overstated. And, as Thunberg himself tells us in quaint olde English, putting together a scientific expedition of this nature not only took a fair amount of courage, it took a lot of preparation as well:

> I therefore provided myfelf with neceffary clothes, as well as with boxes and bags, for collecting roots and feeds, with boxes and pins for infects, a keg of arrack for preferving ferpents and amphibious animals, cotton and boxes for ftuffing and keeping birds in, cartridge-paper for the drying of plants, tea and bifcuits for my own ufe, and tobacco to diftribute among the Hottentots, together with fire-arms, and a large quantity of powder, ball and fhot of various kinds.[53]

I had just crossed over what I took to be the Klein-Doring

River and was taking in the view of a narrow valley between some rounded hills while I waited for Harvey. Although it seems that Thunberg and Masson may have known this as either the Klein-Toren or Naressie River, it was around here that my path actually intersected with theirs as they headed north on their journey around the back of the Hantamsberg, and then south-west through the Roggeveld. And, fortuitously, our intended route through the back roads to Sutherland indicated that this would probably not be the last time we'd intersect with the paths of these pioneering botanists.

I saw Harvey dawdling over a rise in the distance. He had the binoculars trained on something in the veld, and judging by the way the Jeep was meandering all over the road, he was steering the car with his knees. While I was waiting for him, I decided to read up a bit on some of the other early explorers who'd traversed this region so many years before.

☙

The English explorer John Barrow, who later founded the Royal Geographical Society in 1830, came within about 50 kilometres of Loeriesfontein in 1798. Secretary to Lord Macartney during the first British occupation of the Cape, Barrow's first trip into the interior required him to mediate between the eastern frontier settlers and the Xhosa chief Ngqika (Gaika). On this and subsequent expeditions, Barrow kept meticulous records, again recorded in the olde English of the day, which eventually led to the publication of his much respected work, *An Account of Travels into the Interior of Southern Africa*, in 1806. Although Barrow was also known for his somewhat disparaging views of many of the early Dutch farmers, he sometimes deigned to pass them the odd backhanded compliment as well:

> Rude and uncultivated as are their minds, there is one virtue

in which they eminently excel — hofpitality to ftrangers. A countryman, a foreigner, a relation, a friend, are all equally welcome to whatfoever the houfe will afford. A Dutch farmer never paffes a houfe on the road without alighting, except indeed his next neighbour's, with whom it is ten to one he is at variance.[54]

An explorer who displayed a less judgemental and, as we have already seen, terser style in his journal entries was Robert Jacob Gordon. During his third journey into the interior between August 1778 and January 1779, Gordon travelled through what are today the Sutherland and Calvinia districts. He followed much the same route Thunberg and Masson did in 1774, only in reverse. His two main deviations from their route were that he passed to the south of the Hantamsberg and then, unwittingly, also visited the site of modern-day Loeriesfontein.

After leaving Van Plettenberg in Somerset East and having decided to visit the colony's north-western frontier via the Roggeveld, Gordon was once again hard at work on a diplomatic mission with certain Bushman clans in the area. After a meeting with a certain Chief Doerop near modern-day Nieuwoudtville, it seems that he was encouraged to venture further north-east with him to sow more seeds of goodwill with Doerop's people and another Bushman clan under Chief Gronjam. At this "peace ceremony" on the Camdeni River, on the site of present-day Loeriesfontein, Gordon observed some Bushman rituals and made the following characteristically laconic entry in his journal:

> I was very much amused by the Bushmen who are good people. Saw an old woman performing sorcery. From her son's body she snorted forth a devil (evil spirit) which she said she could see and it was like a cobra. The snorting made her nose bleed. She walked away drunkenly with the evil spirit. One of them held her under the arms. Quickly she

was given a stick which she used to walk on her own. She also beat the ground with it. She snorted once more upon her son's nose. She rubbed his belly with buchu. At the same time some of the women sitting there were smoking buchu through the nose.[55]

ॐ

Some crows were feasting on the remains of a riverine rabbit lying on the side of the road. Although the eye had already been plucked from its socket, the unmistakable white ring around where it should have been was still noticeable. Some reddish rocks amidst the fields of wild rye caught my eye, and I wondered whether it was some sort of iron oxide on their surfaces. I was thoroughly enjoying the ride into Calvinia, the dirt road was well maintained and it had just the right amount of twists and turns, as well as rises and descents, to "focus" my attention. The previous evening's paranoia over Rebeccasaurus making a "pinking" noise appeared totally unfounded; she was cruising along as reliably as always.

Looking over my shoulder, there was no sign of Harvey, so I decided to park the bike under a pepper tree in a lay-by and wait. But after five minutes or so I became restless and got off the bike to stretch my legs. I came across a sculptural memorial bound with wire to an iron fence post; it was one part heart and another part Maltese cross. Tragedy seemed so out of place in these quiet country surroundings; but then again, death and peace often precede or follow one another — irrespective of the setting. Flotillas of high cirrus clouds were making their way north. Their passage indicated that some sort of frontal system was not far behind, so I was keen to press on without further delay; but Harvey was still nowhere to be seen. Because it was important that I experienced the actual riding alone, Harvey's plan was to try and keep out of my way and then to meet up with me once we got to the towns en route.

But although I appreciated his respect for the ethos of my trip, I was also concerned about him getting more punctures, and often waited until I could see him somewhere in the distance before I rode on.

The Michelin man arrived deflated. Again. He'd had another puncture and he now had absolutely no spares left — emergency ones or otherwise. It seemed that the fairly worn "dual-purpose" Michelins that had been great on the tar were just not made for the sharp shale of the Hantam's secondary dirt roads. The verdict at the Supa Quick in Calvinia was dire. They had no more Bridgestones similar to the one Harvey had fitted there the day before, or for that matter, any other brands that matched his wheel size. They said they could order one overnight and repair the other punctures so Harvey could still have two spares. Yet I somehow doubted that two would be enough.

After the reality of the delay had sunk in and the initial disappointment was over, we decided to ponder our next move over a cold beer at the Hantam Hotel. It was such a friendly place and, like the Loeriesfontein Hotel, so reasonably priced that we booked in immediately. While quenching my thirst I'd picked up a brochure that briefly outlined the hotel's history: it was first called the Royal, and then, suitably, in 1926, a banquet was held there to honour the visit of the Earl of Athlone and Princess Alice to the town. With a base from which to explore, we set out to see what the town had to offer. Pep Stores seemed like an unlikely place to start, but I needed to buy some airtime and Harvey needed to buy another pair of longs now that an extra day, or possibly more, had been added to his trip.

Named in memory of the champion of the Reformation movement, John Calvin, it might be expected that the town of Calvinia would be full of overly pious people. And although it does reflect a certain old-world conservatism and a great reverence for history and old buildings, the people we met seemed like the average friendly small town folk one finds all over the *platteland* (countryside); certainly far from sanctimonious anyway. Our first impressions were that it had much the same well preserved character and feel as Graaff-Reinet in the Camdeboo. For one, the town's national monuments and other historical buildings appeared to be similarly cherished and well cared for by the townsfolk.

It was on the "Historic Walk-about" with its fascinating array of interesting old buildings that we discovered an institution that was close to both of our hearts: the Karoo Boekehuis (Book House). Built in 1855, this house was restored in 1993 as a retreat for writers. It has a library stocked with inspiring books by a wide variety of Karoo authors and other "Africana" titles from all over the country. And because of this intriguing collection, Harvey and I were already setting a date to return long before we'd left the building.

Maxine Hugo at the town museum was another unlimited source of inspiring information. I had only been expecting to pick up on the Karoo fossil trail again on my planned outride to Fraserburg from Sutherland. But Maxine had other news for me. On a visit to the Calvinia region in 2000, the well-known palaeontologist Bruce Rubidge made the following interesting observations:

> From a scientific point of view our trip was also most successful. Nobody has ever discovered fossil reptiles in that part of the Karoo and we have now been able to demonstrate that there are fossils present. Most of what we discovered are Dicynodonts. This was a large and diverse family of plant-eating reptiles which lived in the Karoo between 200 and 260 million years ago. Because the specimens collected from Middelpos are still enclosed deep within the rock it is not possible to determine what species they are, and they may very well be a species which is new to science as was the case with the specimens we collected around Williston a few years ago .... What we are pleased about is that we were

able to recognise the ancient Karoo shoreline in your area and that these fossils occur immediately above the shoreline as is the situation in the rest of the Karoo basin where we have worked.[56]

The "Karoo shoreline" that Rubidge refers to is the western edge of the ancient inland sea that filled the Karoo basin. By about 250 million years ago it was mostly silted up by deposits brought in from great rivers to the north and south, and had by this time become a shallower lake. In a matter of days I planned to be standing on the south-western extremity of this same ancient lake near Fraserburg: a vast alluvial plain that in the late Permian age was home to mammal-like reptiles, as well as other more primitive reptilian species, fish, amphibians, molluscs and insects. It was a very exciting prospect.

ଔ

I couldn't help thinking just how serendipitous our being delayed in Calvinia was turning out to be; particularly when we were holed up for much of the time in the town's impressive museum. I mean, where else would I have made the acquaintance of a stuffed sheep that was lost in the mountains for a few years and when it was found, its fleece was a record 38 centimetres long? And in what other small town museum could you expect to find a four-legged ostrich? But besides these obvious circus trophies, Maxine was digging up all sorts of interesting anecdotes relevant to our route, and these included some startling revelations concerning certain events that took place during the Anglo-Boer War in the Calvinia region.

Coincidentally, the two Anglo-Boer War stories that really resonated with me related to unacceptable conduct from both sides. And the first account that follows, is loosely translated from a report in Dutch that I was given by Maxine. It's the laconically written yet engaging story of a Boer boy called Frederick Loubser:

> On the 9th of December, I, Frederick Loubser, was on a horse riding through the wheat fields of Diepdrif.
>
> We see the English at about one hundred yards. Myself and Frikkie Strauss, Gert Steenkamp, Koos Nel, Jan Steenkamp en Frans Vlok ride away fast in the direction of Zantkoppe.
>
> One Englishman catches me. I stop and jump off and put my hands up. He then comes and pulls my knife out by its cord and the two chains of my watch, and then he pushes me in the chest and shoots me. Then I fall. I wasn't armed. I lay where I fell. He reloaded but didn't shoot again.
>
> It was about ten o'clock when he shot me. I lay there until after midday the next day and then I walked away from there.
>
> On Wednesday morning I arrived at Rodevlak and found three female staff and a boy in a hut. I told them that I was an English spy. I was scared I would be caught if I said otherwise.
>
> On Thursday I arrived at De Puts. I rested there until Saturday afternoon. Then a young boy came across me at De Puts. I ask him to walk to Brandwacht and arrange a cart to come and fetch me because I am sick.
>
> I didn't tell him that I was wounded.
>
> On Saturday afternoon Mr F. van der Merwe, Magrieta van der Merwe and the same young boy I sent, came in the cart to fetch me.[57]

While the above incident reflects the hair-trigger tensions that existed between the Boer and British adversaries in the region at the time, the one that follows below indicates the British apathy for the safety of the northern border towns of the Cape Colony on the one hand, and merciless treatment by the Boers of the indigenous population on the other.

The far-flung towns of Kenhardt, Prieska, Williston and Calvinia, to name but a few, in the remote and thinly populated regions of the north-western reaches of the Cape Colony were always going to be susceptible to Boer incursions from the northern territories. An example of this is the Boer uprising, already covered in chapter 6, known as the "Prieska revolt" that took place in February 1900. Central to this problem was the fact that the British war effort, from the Orange (Gariep) River in the south, primarily concentrated on the progressive defeat of the Boers and the subsequent control of their territories in the eastern and central parts of what is today a united South Africa. As a result, British protection of the remote towns in the north-western regions was often left up to poorly armed and ill-trained town guards who had little real hope of repulsing a well-organised Boer attack. In addition to these feeble forces, there were also a few intelligence officers based in selected towns whose job it was to warn the Cape-based colonial reinforcements of ominous movements of Boer forces and other threats. Yet, even with prior knowledge of an impending attack on Calvinia, the British reacted very slowly and in the end, allowed it to take place virtually unopposed.

Abraham Esau, a prominent "coloured" blacksmith and dedicated British loyalist, had been campaigning for some time for the magistrate to supply the locals with arms to stave off the Boer attack that he knew was imminent. The magistrate was in an unenviable position. If he supplied Esau and his followers with weapons, he risked the wrath of the Boer farmers with "republican" loyalties, and if he didn't, Calvinia risked being occupied by the Boers. Many months later, again under threat of a Boer attack, he made a weak conciliatory gesture: he supplied Esau and his followers with a number of old sabres. Unhappy but undeterred, Esau and his "militia" set about organising themselves into a kind of town guard. Armed only with the sabres, pickaxe handles, stones and other assorted weaponry, they held regular drills and manned strategic points around the town, as well as setting up a system of early warning signals to alert the town in the event of a Boer attack.

The militia's enthusiasm for protecting the rule of British law was certainly not only inspired by blind allegiance to their colonial overlords; it was mainly due to the racist treatment they knew they would suffer at the hands of a new Boer government. Since May 1900 Calvinia's black population had been intimidated with reports of Boer malfeasance perpetrated against their compatriots in the surrounding countryside. Acting like tyrannical warlords, the Boers demanded food, livestock and other property belonging to black civilians as "tributes" to their cause. Those who didn't comply were terrorised into submission, and many of them were executed in front of their fellow citizens.

Esau's following, predominantly among the black population of Calvinia, grew daily. He organised a number of public meetings, and perhaps his biggest display of allegiance to the British occurred when he led a victory parade through the streets of Calvinia to celebrate the relief of Mafeking. But without proper training and weaponry, Esau knew that the town would succumb to a coordinated Boer attack. Because of this, he built up a friendship with a British intelligence officer called Preston stationed in Clanwilliam. His motivation was ultimately to have Preston use his influence in persuading the British that the "Native Levy" he had been petitioning for to protect Calvinia from the Boers, was absolutely necessary.

With an understanding between the two men that, at the very least, Preston would ensure that British troops would be ready to rush to Calvinia's aid in the event of a Boer attack, Esau established an effective spy network of some 100 comrades who reported on "rebel" or other Boer commando activities in an area that included the towns and surrounding regions of Clanwilliam, Williston, Carnarvon, Loxton and, of course, Calvinia.

It was because of these successful intelligence efforts that when the Boers, under Commandant Niewoudt of the Orange Free State force, entered Calvinia on 10 January 1901 against little effective resistance, the first man they sought was Abraham Esau. By the end of the first day of their tyrannical rule he was in jail. The normally peaceful town was in chaos. Niewoudt imposed himself on the populace as their new *landdrost* (magistrate) and enforced what was known as "Republican" native law. This was a means of suppressing the black population via a system of menacing regulations that included the establishment of a special court to punish "idle" or "disorderly" black citizens, the requirement for all unmarried black male labourers to be gathered into yearly "service", and the introduction of taxes and labour tributes from "Hottentots and Kaffers". Niewoudt even encouraged farmers to send him "insubordinate" and "troublesome" labourers, who were summarily punished, often on the strength of petty grudges between a farmer and his staff.

Against the background of this tyranny, and even in the face of being betrayed by the non-existent British support in repelling the Boer invasion, Esau stood firm. He refused to supply the Boers with the names of any of his informants or the location of an arms cache he was alleged to have stashed. He also flatly refused to publicly renounce his allegiance to the British. These acts of defiance, combined with damning evidence against Esau from farmers who claimed that he had incited their labourers to commit arson, led to Esau's first public punishment. He was beaten, covered with dung and offal, tied to a stake and then left to burn in the excruciating midday heat. The very next day he was sentenced to further "punishment". As the new *landdrost*, Niewoudt sentenced him to 25 lashes "for having spoken against the Boers and for having attempted to arm the natives." After receiving 17 lashes from Niewoudt himself, Esau fainted and when he was untied and fell to the ground, it is said he was kicked where he fell.

During the next two weeks Esau received further public floggings and on one occasion, was even stoned by some of Niewoudt's commandos. Throughout their hero's torture, Esau's followers displayed resolute and loyal support for him with little regard for the consequences. They defied curfews, sang insulting songs aimed at the Boers and helped Esau through his public torture in which ever way they could. But all their support could not save Esau from his final fate. On 5 February 1901, Abraham Esau was put into leg-irons, tied between two horses and dragged out of town just beyond the municipal boundary, where he was executed.

Although the Boers murdered Esau, it was ultimately British indifference and incompetence that sacrificed him.

☙

Later that afternoon Harvey and I were looking for black springbok in the Akkerendam nature reserve on the edge of town. We saw infinitely more walkers and joggers than animals, and the black springbok eluded us completely. Yet the inspiring view of the flat-topped Hantamsberg with its crown of dolerite "organ pipes", cloaked with the soft orange and yellow light of the setting sun, went some way in helping to exorcise the tragic discoveries we'd made at the museum earlier on.

10

Over the Hills and up to the Stars

(Calvinia to Sutherland, with an excursion to Fraserburg: 404 kilometres)

He who has a why to live can bear with almost any how.

Friedrich Nietzsche

We headed out early the next morning across the wide and dusty plain between the Hantamsberg and the Roggeveldberge to the south. I was in front of Harvey's Jeep, and his new tyres were cutting a confident trail across the parched valley. The Supa Quick team had come good with their promise to have us safely on our way by 8 a.m. and Harvey now had two new front tyres, two of the best of the remaining Michelins on the back, plus one good spare and one "emergency" spare in the boot. Hopefully this would be enough to see him through to Sutherland, about 180 kilometres away. Hopefully.

A pair of black eagles circled the heights above Keiskie se Poort. I let Harvey go ahead to position himself for some photographs and then I tried my Alfie Cox impression up the pass; yet the results were somewhat tamer than I'd hoped for. When we scrutinised the old maps along the way, it turned out that we were still following the old trails of Thunberg, Masson and Gordon pretty closely. Of course, when they were reconnoitering the area over 200 years ago, there was no town of Sutherland to visit, so no detour was necessary. We would be turning south-east at the Fish River, whereas Thunberg and Masson had carried on south to intersect with the Tankwa River. And they'd reached this point after descending from the heights of the Roggeveldberge at a place on their map called Uitkijk.

I was relieved that we'd managed to get away from Calvinia on time. I'd originally thought that the leg from Kenhardt to Loeriesfontein was going to be my longest stretch, but at over 400 kilometres, day 10's journey made it look like a stroll in the park. The ride to Sutherland was only half that distance, but once I got there and offloaded my bags at a B&B somewhere, I planned to head straight off on my Fraserburg fossil excursion and still be back before sunset. It was some ask. Because of this hectic itinerary, I kept up a pretty fast pace. At times Harvey must have thought he was back on the Roof of Africa rallies of old where he used to navigate a modified VW Beetle for Clive Smith. Apparently, they had their fair share of punctures as well.

And quite coincidentally, that first half of the journey to Sutherland, on the dirt tracks along the high plateaus of the Roggeveld Mountains was actually quite similar to some regions of Lesotho. Yet no matter what kinship it may have shared with other parts of southern Africa, the pristine and peaceful nature of this Bo-Karoo track made us feel like we were discovering it for the very first time. We didn't see a living soul until we intersected with the main gravel road from Calvinia, some two hours later.

"Wasn't that road the most rewarding find?" said Harvey after finishing a mouthful of Salticrax and olives.

"Ja, it had such an amazing variety of scenery and surfaces: those smooth plateaus, challenging passes, the old settler ruins; but best of all, we didn't have to share it with anyone," I replied dreamily.

We were languishing under a huge pepper tree at the bottom of a pass called Oupoort. Since connecting with the main gravel road from Calvinia we'd been bouncing around like a couple of rag dolls on an unsprung ox wagon; the road surface was impregnated with numerous large rocks and stones that repeatedly attacked our respective suspension systems. It was also well over 30° C, and I decided to dip my hot head and rattled brain into the cool waters of a neighbouring farmer's reservoir. It wasn't quite as invigorating as a swim, but we needed to press on and there wasn't time for a full immersion.

"Harvey, you're not going to believe this."

"What? What have you seen?" he asked from his horizontal position, his head propped up against the tree trunk with one disinterested eye peering out from beneath his wide-brimmed hat.

"It's a Jeep with another flat tyre."

Neither of us could believe it, but there was no denying that the car was listing increasingly to the one side and the rear right tyre was about to expel its very last breath.

Puncture number four in well under three days; even if we were rally drivers sliding sideways around corners on sharp fragments of volcanic rock, this surely had to be some kind of record. We decided it was open season on the French: *I mean just where did they expect you to drive with your "dual-purpose" Michelins — only on a beach or salt pan covered with baby oil, perhaps?* It's amazing how loosing off a round of vitriol can strengthen one's resolve. We replaced the wheel in record time and took off for Sutherland with renewed purpose; Harvey's "emergency" spare — the one that had an irreparable hole in the tyre itself — needed a back-up. The craggy old farmer in a floppy bush hat who'd warned Harvey at the Supa Quick in Calvinia had been right: "Man, that road to Sutherland just eats tyres; I always carry at least two spares." Perhaps the French weren't really to blame.

Since ascending the Roggeveldberge we'd seen many animals and birds: red duikers darting through the golden brown rye, graceful grey herons riding on slow wings and numerous steppe buzzards sky-perching in the fresh breeze, casting their acute eyesight into the veld for signs of breakfast on the move. There were also large herds of cattle that grazed contentedly on the wild rye behind mountain stone walls — monuments to the early settlers and their labourers who'd pioneered this sort of solid enclosure together. I pictured the hardy Boers with their indentured San (Bushmen) or Khoi (Hottentot) workers toiling side by side under a blazing 18th century sun. In places, rows of equally spaced menhir-type rocks stood behind the modern wire fences. At first I fancied that these might be the relics of some ancient sect, but soon realised that they were just ingenious fence posts of old.

The vegetation on the ascent to Sutherland is probably best described as a kind of rugged montane grassveld. As I rode through it, I noted many flat-topped rocky ridges that framed farmstead scenes and their surrounding blue gums in the distance — and the pleasing picture just kept on repeating itself. The area reminded me quite a lot of the Belfast/Dullstroom districts in Mpumalanga, and in winter, at 1,456 metres above sea level, it is often just as cold. While hard to believe, Belfast has actually recorded more extreme winter temperatures than Sutherland, but Sutherland's average minimum winter temperature of just -6.1°C is certainly cold enough; and definitely not a place to be sleeping out under the plentiful stars without thermal everything. As we rose in altitude and got closer to Sutherland, the cattle of the lower Roggeveld gave way to flocks of sheep, obviously better equipped to cope with the frosty winter chill.

I stopped at the base of a boulder-strewn ridge just outside Sutherland. The stacked assortment of lichen-encrusted rocks was fascinating; it looked as though a once frozen-solid ridge had thawed too quickly on a sunny winter day, and then simply split into thousands of odd-sized pieces. I was about to get back on the bike when I saw Harvey coming up the hill in the Jeep. Miraculously, all four tyres were still intact, but he nonetheless had an anxious look on his face: it was getting on for lunchtime on a Friday afternoon and he had a tyre to repair in a sleepy little hamlet that wasn't really given to rushing, even on Mondays. We'd arranged earlier that I'd go ahead and find a suitable B&B, let him know where it was and then catch up with him later after I'd been to Fraserburg. He'd decided not to join me and rather to have a look around Sutherland instead. I think all the punctures were starting to get to him.

The man at the information bureau showed definite signs of tourist fatigue. Yet, you could hardly blame him; he'd been answering hundreds of enquiries over the past week concerning the opening of the new Southern African Large Telescope (SALT for short — the largest telescope of its kind in the southern hemisphere) by President Thabo Mbeki, supported by a host of associated dignitaries and wannabees. But despite his somewhat flagging demeanour, he still provided me with a number of accommodation options, as well as enough tourist literature on the region to keep me busy for weeks.

After paging through the brochures, I made a shortlist and decided to call on the Sutherland Inn first. On arriving there, a lanky man with little hair and an engaging smile welcomed me to have a look around. It was a tastefully renovated old house with three en suite bedrooms and an outside cottage, a communal dining room and lounge area with well-worn armchairs, plenty of books and a telescope. It was absolutely perfect. I told Johan we'd take two rooms and immediately set about getting my luggage inside and preparing for my afternoon ride to Fraserburg. When I got to my room, though, and sat down for a few minutes, enjoying a cup of tea and a homemade rusk, I was tempted to have a long soak in the shower and just curl up for an afternoon snooze. It hadn't been that long a ride in from Calvinia, but it had been quite rough on the body and a rest was an attractive alternative to another long journey on the bike.

Yet with imprints of large mammal-like reptiles in the offing at Fraserburg's renowned Gansfontein palaeosurface, it didn't take me too long to shake off my lethargy, and I was back on the road by half past one. I had less than four hours to do the 220 kilometre round trip so that Harvey and I would still have time to visit the extinct volcano, Salpetrekop, before sunset. I was going to have to really move it.

ଔ

Vincent Opperman was a man of many talents and as many

titles: economics officer, tourism officer and Fraserburg Museum's curator. But he was also one of those rare individuals who manage to be both self-assured and self-effacing at the same time. I'd phoned ahead and asked him if he could show me around the site, so he was kindly waiting for me at the entrance to Gansfontein when I got there.

"We're so lucky to have this site near Fraserburg; it's really a great tourist attraction. And if it wasn't for the heavy rains that broke the dam wall above the site all those years ago, it probably wouldn't have been discovered in the first place," said Vincent with a reverent expression.

"Oh, so did the flood expose the surface we're going to see?" I asked.

"Ja, Mr van Gass noticed it a short while afterwards, but it was only in 1983 that a visiting geologist was taken to the site and then he reported the importance of it to the scientific community. Some years later, Sanlam donated money and the site was prepared to receive tourists, but it only officially opened in 1990."

"Doesn't all the tourist traffic damage the footprints?"

"Ja, you're right, too many people walking over the fossil imprints is going to eventually destroy them. That's why the whole area needs to be covered and walkways constructed just above the surface to preserve it properly."

"And that's going to take quite a bit of money, I suppose?"

"Yes, but there's a lot more public interest in palaeontology these days, so hopefully, between government and big business, it'll soon become a reality."

Looking over the simple barbed-wire fence surrounding the site, I was stunned at the quantity and quality of footprints I saw. It was like a unique collection of ancient languages just waiting to be translated; a kind of prehistoric hieroglyphics that had the ability to bring these extinct animals back to life. Apart from footprints of the mammal-like reptiles such as the five-toed dinocephalians and the large primitive reptile known as bradysaurus, there were also imprints of ancient water and wind-formed ripples, as well as traces and trails of fish, insects and gastropods. It was a fossil wonderland, and after taking the tour with Vincent, I sat quietly by myself and read through the comprehensive information supplied by the museum to try and let it all sink in.

With my thoughts still somewhere in the Permian age, I found it hard to concentrate on the rigours of the road on the way back to Sutherland; in my mind I was still on all fours at the Gansfontein palaeosurface with my hands in some ancient footprints doing my impression of a lumbering bradysaurus, a comical yet enlightening experience. And then I thought back to Elma le Roux and the "seven-toed footprint" in Kenhardt and wondered what she'd make of it all.

※

I got back to Sutherland at quarter to six and found Harvey sitting next to a towering pile of astronomy books in the lounge.

"You won't believe it," he said, "but as I was having the last puncture fixed, one of the other tyres went flat. But never mind that now; I'm trying to find out where we should point this telescope tonight; I mean, we're in the stargazing capital of southern Africa after all," he continued, his eyes wandering over a map of the heavens.

"Good idea, but I need to go and wash off this road dust quickly and then we need to head off to Salpetrekop first."

"Ja, sunset is in less than an hour's time, so we'd better hurry."

It was due to Lawrence Green's friend Denis Wood that Harvey and I were on our way towards an extinct volcano. I'd read about how Wood had scaled Salpetrekop sometime in the 1950s and then remarked when he'd reached the top, "Only the fitful moan of the wind disturbs the still, silent wastes."[58] And just reading those poetic words was reason enough for both of us to want to make the trip. But by the time we'd driven the 15 kilometres out of town, the sun was sitting just above the horizon. There clearly wasn't enough time or light to climb it, but we still felt we needed to get close enough to sense the mountain's fiery old aura. At around 300 metres above its surroundings, Salpetrekop is certainly not the type of mountain that instils awe by its large and looming presence. In fact, from the angle we saw it at and without record of its mercurial past, it could probably pass for just another koppie. Yet, standing at the base of the slopes leading to the rocky dome that caps this small mountain, we both sensed its appeal — an inexplicable energy. Perhaps the void created by so much outgoing tumult was still being filled. But then again, maybe it was just our own sense of reverence for such an ancient and powerful force.

It was later in the Sutherland Hotel bar that we discovered a number of experts on Salpetrekop. In fact, of the four people in the pub, one of whom was the daughter of an accomplished pool-playing mom, three were virtual fundis on Salpetrekop. And it also became evident that this extinct volcano still manages to get some people hot under the collar. For starters, the farm where it's located belongs to the local mayor, and he's apparently thinking of banning further visits due to a number of tourists taking souvenir rocks home with them. The pool-playing mom downed her neat vodka shot, turned to me, wiping her lips with the back of her hand, and said: "Ja, that little mountain has caused a fair amount of *kak* around here already."

"What sort of *kak* would that be?" I asked, smiling at her expressive choice of words.

"Well for one, De Beers was convinced they were going to find diamonds in the kimberlite rock up there, but they discovered uranium instead. And there's also old South African rock art up there, and I'm not just talking about Bushman art, I'm talking about Nguni finger paintings on the walls of certain caves that very few people have seen."

"Sorry, but you've lost me. What are Nguni finger paintings?"

"Well, just what they sound like, really: artworks or murals painted by dipping one's fingers into the oxide pastes of the time and depicting scenes and designs on the walls of caves. The secrecy surrounding these works goes back to the old Nationalist government. They didn't want to attribute these works to black Africans, because they're said to date back to a much earlier period than the Nats would have had us believe. You see, it wouldn't have sat well with their history books, which depicted the Nguni peoples as only having entered South African territories in the middle of the 17th century, and not the 4th century as is now widely accepted."

"Whew, that's quite a story. But you say there's Bushman art up there as well?"

"Oh yes, but you have to know how to find it. There are only a few of us who know the way to those caves. But there's a hell of a lot of San art around these parts, not only at Salpetrekop. The problem is, many farmers are too scared to let others know that they have rock art on their farms due to possible future land claims and other problematic heritage issues. I've heard that some have disguised the entrances to sites and even destroyed some paintings to protect their farms from these threats."

We were just about to leave for our prearranged dinner back at the Sutherland Inn when the hotel manager, Riaan, introduced himself as a guide to Salpetrekop and invited us to go up with him the next morning. But we unfortunately had to be on the road too early, so we declined; yet I knew one thing for sure: even though the volcano was extinct, its aura was still very much alive and kicking. And the locals were determinedly keeping it so.

Back at the Sutherland Inn, Johan had prepared a superb

dinner. I'd told him that I would prefer a vegetarian dish and that Harvey wasn't too fussy; the result was a cordon bleu-style stuffed butternut and assorted roasted vegetables, certainly the best meal I'd had on the trip so far. Harvey got slightly fewer vegetables and a giant Vienna schnitzel. I poured him a glass of well-shaken red wine from my indestructible plastic mineral water bottle and we toasted our good fortune at discovering so many interesting stories in the bar.

"You know, Nick, if I were still an active journalist, I wouldn't have believed my good luck at stumbling over such a well of intriguing information as you did," said Harvey, after clearing his throat with a draught of well-travelled wine.

"Ja, I know. I was sitting there thinking that if she revealed any more secrets and scandal about Salpetrekop, I was going to fall off my barstool."

"Well, while you were being regaled by the pool player, I had a rather interesting chat to the young barman. Turns out Thunberg and Masson's pioneering trail cut right through their family farm south-west of here, and my favourite explorer, Burchell, made tracks over another farm he knows not too far to the east."

ଓଃ

It was only sometime after the trip that I got to grips with Burchell's journey through the Sutherland region. He was apparently on his way north to Kuruman via Klaarwater (now Griquatown) when he passed just to the east of present-day Sutherland, and only about 20 kilometres west of modern-day Fraserburg. He was even closer to the Gansfontein site that I'd visited when I was there, and I wondered what he would have made of it all if it had already been exposed by the flood and he'd stumbled across it back then.

Because his expedition had been sanctioned by the colonial

government, Burchell carried a letter from the authorities in Cape Town requesting the various field-cornets' assistance, when and where it was required. But, even with official sanction, and despite being adequately compensated for their services in the field, Burchell found the Boers to be often less than forthcoming. Yet, Field-Cornet Gerrit Maritz, seemed an exception:

> He offered his services with great civility and readiness, and concerted the order for the *voorspans*, with Snyman, who was equally ready to fulfil his duty. I mention this with pleasure, because I experienced on other occasions, afterwards, a very different treatment; and ascertained, to my mortification, that an order from the government will not always procure for an Englishman the necessary assistance from the boors; nor, though they receive a remuneration, ensure even their civility to him, or their respect for a higher authority.[59]

But it could be construed that Maritz's helpfulness may have had something to do with a favour he was to ask of Burchell, because soon after making his acquaintance, he asked him to deliver an official letter to the missionaries at Klaarwater. It requested the missionaries there to "deliver up and send to Cape Town, certain runaway slaves and Hottentots who had taken refuge at the settlement."[60] It seems that, Maritz, like many other "employers" in the colony, thought of Klaarwater as something of a blight on the landscape as fugitives from the colonial and farm labour systems — and even common criminals, for that matter — were often able to find refuge behind the robes of the well-intentioned missionaries there.

In terms of the assistance he now required, Burchell's chief necessity was the provision of fresh teams of oxen to help him and his expedition over the steep pass leading up the Roggeveldberge. After being delayed a couple of days by cold and rainy weather,

Burchell describes part of this hazardous journey:

> August 6th. The day was occasionally showery, and extremely cold. The boors came again with their oxen, and at noon we commenced the ascent of the mountain. The road was exceedingly steep, winding in different directions to avoid the deep ravines; but was less rocky than the other kloofs of the colony which I had passed, although the rain had now rendered it slippery and dangerous.
>
> At one spot towards the top of the mountain, where the acclivity was the greatest, the oxen slid from side to side, unable to keep on their feet; and the great weight of the waggon began to drag them backwards, in spite of their utmost exertions. The two boors, who were driving, were in the greatest anxiety and alarm, not only for the fate of the waggons, but also for the safety of their own cattle. Witnessing their perilous situation from below, I scrambled hastily out of the road, to save myself among the rocks, expecting to behold everything hurried headlong down the steep, and for some moments giving up all for lost. By singular good fortune, the wheel took a direction against a large block of stone, which lay on one side of the road, and thus gave the cattle time to recover their feet, and take breath. The drivers debated whether it would be possible to reach the summit till the ground was become dryer. At length, after allowing the teams to rest a few minutes, they resolved to make the attempt, rather than having the trouble of coming again another day. Accordingly, two Hottentots followed each waggon with large stones, ready to scoat the wheels the moment they began to run backwards; and, by a smart application of the whip, and loud whooping, the oxen made an extraordinary exertion, happily surmounted this dangerous place, and safely gained the summit of the pass.[61]

☙

I was paging through the index of Conan Doyle's *The Great BoerWar* after dinner and was surprised when I happened across an entry for Sutherland. I'd not thought that any influence of the war had reached this remote and lofty region, but it seemed that I was mistaken.

By the beginning of 1901 Hertzog's eastern invading force of around 1,200 mounted men was already about 240 kilometres into the Cape Colony. It was after taking the town of Calvinia — which we know they used as their regional headquarters for a short time — that the Boers started to spread their forces wider afield. Doyle reports on the Boer movements that followed:

> From this point their roving bands made their way as far as the sea-coast in the Clanwilliam direction, for they expected at Lambert's Bay to meet with a vessel with mercenaries and guns from Europe. They pushed their outposts also as far as Sutherland and Beaufort West in the south. On January 15th strange horsemen were seen hovering about the line at Touws River, and the citizens of Cape Town learned with amazement that the war had been carried to within a hundred miles of their own doors.[62]

According to Doyle, Esau was executed by the Boers just a day before Calvinia was retaken by the British on 6 February 1901. The British forces under De Lisle had been waiting for reinforcements to arrive before they could initiate an attack on the significant Boer force stationed in the town. Bethune's column, consisting of a mixed bag of predominantly colonial forces and a few British regulars, arrived in Clanwilliam on 28 January. Had it not been for the difficult nature of the terrain that stretched over the 80 kilometres separating the enemies, it seems that Calvinia could have been liberated earlier.

One can only wonder if Esau might have been spared had the British arrived earlier or if the Boers only executed him when they knew that they would have to give way to the British forces after 5 February. Perhaps if he'd been a white British loyalist, things would have been different. I thought back to my earlier judgement of the British being responsible for sacrificing Esau, and that seemed a bit harsh in light of the new information I'd learnt, but whichever way you look at it, they still really took their time to answer his numerous calls for help. Doyle's sentiments on Esau's execution are clear: "The flogging and shooting of a coloured man named Esau forms one more incident in the dark story of the Boer and his relations to the native."[63]

Both Harvey and I were yawning our way through the covers of some dusty old books in the lounge. It had been a long and eventful day, and I was just about to nod off when Harvey jumped to his feet.

"Hey, Nick, we haven't looked through the telescope yet," he said, flailing his arms about enthusiastically. I tried to ignore him, but he just wouldn't go away.

"Ja, okay," I said, trying to feign some enthusiasm.

Harvey had the eyepiece to his eye and was twiddling knobs and wheels like a submariner practising a crash dive.

"No, man, there are no stars where they're meant to be," he said incredulously.

"Have you taken the lens cap off?" I asked helpfully. I received a withering glance and an acid smile that spoke volumes.

But stepping closer to the open window in front of the telescope, I soon had my sleepy finger on the problem; the night sky had clouded over and not a star was to be seen. Not one to have his enthusiasm dampened by mere murk and mist, Harvey suggested that we walk around the town in the hope that the sky would clear up by the time we returned.

Yet with street lights at a minimum to facilitate astronomical endeavour, Sutherland is not the easiest place to walk around after dark. After turning down a number of dead-ends, we managed to find a dirt track that headed off into the veld. As we stood there in the darkness, the church bells struck eleven and a small patch of sky opened up on cue. We looked up through our small window on the night sky and saw hundreds of tightly clustered stars there.

"If only we'd brought the telescope," Harvey lamented.

But then a shooting star trailed its way across that small gap in the clouds, and we made our way home, tired but replete.

11

Passes, Poorts and Pausing

(Sutherland to Kruisrivier: 270 kilometres)

I love the Karoo. The effect of this scenery is to make me so silent and self-contained. And it is all so bare, the rocks and bushes, each bush standing separate from the others, alone by itself.

Olive Schreiner

With Salpetrekop on my left, I waved goodbye to the town of stars and secrets. Sutherland had produced more than its fair share of intrigue, enigmatic characters and a good number of humorous moments, and remembering another one of the previous night's bar stories, my helmet was soon filled with laughter.

Apparently, a short while ago there was a bad epidemic of sheep poaching in the Sutherland district. The farming community were up in arms, as no matter what precautions they took, they couldn't seem to catch the culprit in the act. The police detective connected with the case intimated that he was also frustrated, but, nevertheless, still felt confident that a breakthrough was imminent. But more and more sheep were disappearing daily and the farmers were becoming very impatient. Then one night a group of farmers were stalking some jackal when in the distance they saw someone carrying a sheep towards a bakkie. For the farmers, this occasion was even better than shooting jackal, because jackal only follow their instincts, whereas thieves — well thieves had no excuse, they'd mused to themselves. Duck-walking on their haunches between the low-lying Karoo bush they surrounded the thief and at a given signal they all sprang up and pointed their rifles at the villain. Blinded by the powerful torch beam, the thief dropped the big ewe he was carrying and made a run for the bakkie. And then the booming voice of one of the farmers said: "You can run all you like, but we know where to find you, *detective!*"

During dessert the previous evening, Harvey had related another story with more than a touch of black humour that had also really tickled me. It concerned an account by a gung-ho foreign correspondent who'd been sent to Luanda in Angola during the 1960s. It was a time of great political upheaval in the then Portuguese colony and the correspondent, Donald Wise, decided he would have a beer and a bowl of shrimp at a local pavement café before he set off in search of the big story. He was just getting into his beer and soaking up the delightful pavement atmosphere when he heard the sounds of a struggle from the building above. As he looked up he saw the bloodied body of an African man falling towards him. Luckily, the body just missed him and landed on the sidewalk next to his table. Wise was apparently quite shocked and said that the incident "fair put me off my beer." But regardless of the fact that the falling body had upset the pavement café's convivial atmosphere, Wise was quick to appreciate the intrigue of the story that had virtually fallen into his lap. He introduced his report by saying: "The first African to be killed in Portuguese Africa nearly fell into my beer today ...."[64]

This story, and the light relief it brought at the time, had thankfully saved us both from descending into an intellectually bankrupt stupor. We'd been discussing the wonders and the magnitude of the universe and everything else in between, and despite the handicap that the inclement weather later cast on our star-gazing aspirations, Harvey and I had already discovered a common bond of startling astronomical ineptitude. No matter how hard either of us tried to remember the names and the relative positions of the major planets, stars and constellations, we just couldn't get it right. It was as though the subject were just too huge to grapple with, and once you started to get the vaguest handle on it, you wondered what the point was anyway. I mean take our solar system, for example, and our infinitesimal part in it. The sun is more than a 100 times bigger than the Earth and is roughly 150 million kilometres away. The Earth spins on its axis at an average speed of about 1,550 k.p.h. while moving around the sun at approximately 106,660 k.p.h., and then the whole solar system moves through the Milky Way galaxy at around 1,120,000 k.p.h. And when you've finally come to grips with all this mind-blowingly fast movement and incomprehensible size and distance, you ask yourself: *Okay, but where is it all going, and why? And if the whole solar system, as a* unit, had to suddenly stop moving at such a speed through the galaxy, would this deficit of motion affect our lives, and if the answer is "Yes", surely we need to know how long it can keep moving at such a speed? Then, of course, there are all those other galaxies; immeasurable, but nebulous nebulae; other universes ....

I rest my case.

ଔ

Riding out from Sutherland across the Bo-Karoo plateau to the edge of the escarpment, we noticed that the surrounding veld looked in really superb condition. Large and healthy-looking grey-green bushes were spaced almost a metre apart and, especially when viewed from afar, gave the impression of a verdant landscape — far removed from the biome's supposed semi-desert classification. Adding to the natural bounty, and our enjoyment, were a number of springbok and steenbok that accompanied us as we wound our way along the 40 kilometres of good dirt track to the shoulder of the plateau.

Yet although we'd seen what looked like good grazing in the region, the early farmers often had to move their livestock into the slightly more temperate neighbouring districts during winter just to ensure their survival. On his travels through the area in the early 1800s, Lichtenstein recorded some of the hardships these local farmers faced at the time:

> Snow falls earlier here than in the Lower Roggeveld; and as the cold and thick fogs are very injurious to cattle, the inhabitants are driven down in winter to the Karroo. In October they return home, but they are not long at rest, for in summer they are often compelled by the drought to go northwards to the banks of the Riet-river.[65]

At the top of Komsberg Pass we paused to take in the spectacular view. In the middle distance, just after the initial precipitous pass, lay a fertile valley that wound its way more gently down to the lower-lying Karoo landscape beyond it. At this point, a wide sandy plain stretched to the staggered rows of jagged black and purple mountains, the Swartberg range, on the horizon. According to Harvey's GPS in the Jeep, we were at a height of 1,722 metres above sea level. And with Laingsburg sitting at an altitude of only around 675 metres, we expected to roll downhill pretty much the whole way for the next 140 kilometres. But, as we discovered later, the sheerest drop occurred over the first few kilometres of the descent and the gradient reduced significantly when we reached the flatter Moordenaars-Karoo.

When Lichtenstein stood in the vicinity of where Harvey and I were admiring the view, he was no less taken aback by what he saw:

> The hill we were now to descend is called the Komberg; it takes this name from the valley below, which is called the Kom-valley (the Tub-valley), as being enclosed with hills, so that it has the appearance of a vast tub. It is impossible to give an idea by any description of the prospect which at this spot opened upon us. It is one of the most extensive that I saw in all my travels over Southern Africa. Never having appeared during the last fortnight to ascend very much, we were exceedingly astonished to find ourselves at such a height, to see what a depth below was the country that lay spread before us.[66]

As we descended the pass in our modern off-road machines, I spared a thought for Lichtenstein's small expedition as it edged itself down the twists and turns of this initially steep gradient. The grip of the horses' hooves and the iron-rimmed wagon wheels on the loose stones was tenuous at best:

> We began to descend, leading our horses in our hands, slipping over the loose rolling stones which crossed our

> way at every step. The first quarter of the way is steep as a staircase; all the wheels of the waggons were locked, so that they slid down over the loose slates with which the whole way was strewed. The road then begins to take a different direction, and after many turnings and windings, comes to the front of the declivity, when, looking down, a house is seen so directly below that we seem almost upon it, yet there is a full hour still to wind and turn before it can be reached. The African hills have this resemblance to Mount Sinai that they are much less difficult to ascend than to descend.[67]

It seems that Lichtenstein was quite impressed with the welcome and the hospitality he received in the "Kom-valley" at the time he passed through it. He was also astonished at the average size of the Boer families, said to exceed ten children per unit — the five families he met there had, between them, spawned no less than 62 children. In contrast to the high and arid plateau he'd just descended from, the valley's numerous springs provided water all year round, which not only allowed for good grazing for the cattle, but the cultivation of fruit, corn and wheat as well. After a good dinner of mutton soup and roasted goat, Lichtenstein must have been somewhat fortified for the sight that greeted him later that night:

> Our waggons did not arrive till late at night, and had suffered so much from the bad roads, that they came in at last with broken shafts and axle-trees, so that they were with difficulty got on at all …. The object in which their lading consisted had not suffered less: the furniture of our table was almost all broken to pieces, as were many of the bottles of wine and oil; and we considered ourselves as very fortunate that we were now approaching a more inhabited country, where we could repair our misfortunes, and make some fresh provision for our future travels.[68]

I watched a herd of grey rhebok from the shade of a giant blue gum. As they ran over the veld their short and fluffy white tails bobbed in time to their graceful strides, and then they vaulted a farm fence on their way up a hillside and were gone. I'd been waiting for Harvey for some time and was beginning to suspect that some of the Komsberg shale might have found its way through one of his not so formidable tyres. So it was with some relief that I caught sight of him ambling around a corner on the final descent into the lower-lying Moordenaars-Karoo. The Kom Valley is made up of a series of small terraced plateaus, and it's easy to see why Lichtenstein was so impressed with its relative verdure and fertility. And the handsome farmsteads and promising-looking grazing that he saw all that time ago still abound today.

The collective opinion in the Sutherland Hotel bar had been that the average ambient temperature increases by about 0.7° C for every 100 metres one loses in altitude. This made sense to us, and certainly accounted for the greater variety of crops and livestock that we noted as we descended from the cooler heights of the Bo-Karoo through the more temperate valleys on our way to the lower-lying plains in the distance.

As we headed into the Moordenaars-Karoo itself, the change in vegetation was quite dramatic: the brittle-looking and smaller Karoo bushes were spaced much further apart and sat in a composite soil of sand and shale. Yet the landscape was still undulating, with a number of small rocky ridges shepherding the road on its downward trajectory towards Laingsburg. We crossed numerous drifts and not one of them appeared to have seen water for quite some time. It was hostile country: a region that looked like it may well have once served as a place of refuge for murderers, fugitives and other desperadoes — perhaps the South African equivalent of the "Badlands of San Hernando". But, as with many intriguing names, the origin of the term Moordenaars-Karoo has reputedly more than one explanation. Yet none of the versions that were later told to me by Laingsburg tourism was entirely convincing.

In the early days of the settler farmers there was apparently a jail situated close to the Anysrivier. One of the jailers was said to be a brute of a man with a short temper. It was also claimed that when he was irritable, or simply bored, he would take it out on his prisoners by chasing them up and down a nearby mountain and firing live rounds of ammunition among them. The flaw in this story seems to be that while he might have terrorised the prisoners with these antics, it is not said whether he actually killed — or murdered — any of them.

The next explanation suggests that prisoners who managed to escape from the jail were not able to survive in the hot and hostile conditions of their surroundings, and that many of them died before they could free themselves from its murderous clutches.

The final version, and perhaps the most plausible, suggests that a band of local farmers had had enough of the marauding tactics of the Bushmen (San) and banded together in a commando, hunted every last one of them down, and killed them.

Although the problem of conciliatory agreements between Boers and Bushmen being regularly broken was purportedly a national one, if we are to believe Lichtenstein's appraisal of what he witnessed in the area, then this region seems to have suffered more than its fair share of deception at the hands of the wily Bushmen. And, as happened elsewhere, an agreement with one clan of Bushmen often didn't hold good for another clan. This seemed to happen mainly because they were a people without national rule, and because of this, one clan was largely independent of the others. From Lichtenstein's reports, it appears that many of the Boers really made an effort to be hospitable to the various clans that visited them and often provided them with gifts and large quantities of food for weeks at a time. He also stated that it was sometimes the case that the very "guests" the Boers had been entertaining would come back and rob them after they'd enjoyed generous shows of Boer hospitality. In certain instances, the Bushmen were also said to have not been satisfied with their plundering raids until all a farmer's cattle were killed or maimed, and because of this, the injured cattle would often have to be butchered by the farmers where they lay. There are, of course, always two sides to any story, but even if these accounts are somewhat exaggerated, which Lichtenstein is not known to have done, it is easy to understand how the Boers would have wanted to put an end to this sort of deception and harassment. Lichtenstein's views on punitive expeditions led by the Boers in retaliation for these ongoing attacks are clear:

> It cannot, therefore, be a matter of surprise if the antipathy of the colonists to like plunderers is carried pretty far, and that it is scarcely considered as a crime if in pursuit of these flying hordes some of them are, from time to time killed. That regular parties, however, are made by the colonists to hunt them down, as some late writers have asserted, I must say is untrue.[69]

These assertions of Lichtenstein's may also appear to put the final version of the origin of the name Moordenaars-Karoo into question. But how much Lichtenstein was privy to during the relatively short period that he stayed in this region, and how much he was perhaps shielded from the Boers' real feelings and deeds, is unknown. What we do know with certainty, however, is that the San as a group were eventually exterminated in this region, and those that could escape the borders of the colony eventually crossed the Gariep — and kept going.

CB

I'd just ridden past a lovely old farmhouse that was in the process of being restored when a thicket of reeds lining the road ahead signalled the presence of water. And according to my faithful dog-eared copies of the Engen roadmap, it was none other than the infamous Buffels River. Even though there was only a trickle of water in it, it was still a pleasant place to idle away the time as I waited for Harvey to catch up. Having Harvey come along for a short part of the trip had been a great success. He was always careful to ensure that he wasn't interfering with my "solo" journey, and I was equally insistent that I carried all my own tools and luggage as if I were still travelling completely on my own. In fact, sitting there on the side of that concrete drift on the Buffels River, I chuckled to myself at the irony: with all Harvey's punctures, I'd certainly been more of a back-up team to his "expedition" than he'd been to mine.

Even though some of the solo dynamics, such as that acute and singular awareness of my surroundings as well as the undisturbed clarity of my own thoughts, had obviously changed, the trade-off for the company of a kindred spirit was more than fair exchange. It was our last day together, and I felt sad that he would be leaving me in Kruisrivier the next morning. It was also hard to accept that my circumnavigation of the Great Karoo was coming to an end, as it was proving to be one of most educative and rewarding journeys I'd ever made.

With my upcoming crossing of Seweweekspoort and brief foray into the Little Karoo, I was about to make a small deviation from the "true" circumnavigation trail. I had chosen this route over the one to Prince Albert and then on to Aberdeen because of my desire to predominantly follow secondary dirt tracks rather than long stretches of tar. But in the end, it only meant I was following the Great Karoo's southern boundary, the great Swartberg range, just to the south of the line, rather than just to the north of it. There really wasn't much in it.

Not long after Harvey and I had turned off into the

Moordenaars-Karoo, we'd stopped for a cool drink near some old stone ruins near the side of the road. We'd trudged around them and pondered over when the various kraals and buildings had been built and theorised about why they'd been deserted. Was it a family's dreams that lay in ruins at our feet, were they perhaps driven off by drought or Bushmen, or had the size of their farm just become too small in time to support an economical quantity of livestock? In the end we couldn't make up our minds, but a Cape Town historian, Dr Cyril Hromnick, believes he has found some interesting answers to the origins and history of other stone ruins in this region, yet his discoveries relate more to ancient temples than mere farm dwellings.

The foundation for a lot of Hromnick's controversial assertions is the theory that the Khoi (previously known as Hottentots or Ottentotu) race was formed by the interbreeding of Khung women (San/Bushmen) with early Indian gold miners and their Indonesian labourers. He asserts that these miners and their labourers had initiated gold-mining operations from the Mozambique coast across Mashonaland (modern-day Zimbabwe) to present-day Angola and that these could have started as early as 600 BC. It's a theory, of course, that does not sit well with some Afrocentric views that great ancient cultures such as Mapungubwe on the South African border with Zimbabwe and Great Zimbabwe itself were purely African in origin and were not learnt cultures, or even remotely influenced by foreign civilisations such as the great ancient trading nations of the Arabs or the Indians. Much of Hromnick's back-up evidence is based on linguistic links and other purported cultural ties between certain African tribes and the Dravidian Indians from the south of the sub-continent. As physical proof of the cultural links between Indians and Quena (Hromnick's Khoikoi or Khoi, pronounced "Kena"), Hromnick cites, among others, his findings of two "cosmological temples" uncovered in Komatiland and the Moordenaars-Karoo.

On my return from my Karoo circumnavigation, I unfortunately missed a one-off lecture in Graaff-Reinet given by Hromnick entitled "Stone ruins in the Karoo", and also learnt only after the event that he was conducting visits to the "temple" site in the Moordenaars-Karoo. Yet when speaking to him after the lecture, he kindly arranged a copy of an article for me, entitled "South Africa Is Denied Its Rich Cultural History", published in the December 2005—January 2006 edition of *Village Life*. An extract from this article sheds some light on the Moordenaars-Karoo "temple" as follows:

> The temple in Komatiland may have been constructed by immigrants from India, but that is unlikely in the case of the Summer and Winter Solstice temples which Dr. Hromnick has identified in the Moordenaars-Karoo near Laingsburg and which he ascribes to the Quena. (The Karoo, one of the most quintessentially South African landscapes, also bears a Quena and Dravidian name: Karu = arid country.) The various structures comprising this temple complex were disregarded by locals as remnants of kraals or game traps. They stretch over a distance of 51 km and the largest among them consists of two parallel and 530 m long solid walls. Dr. Hromnick has shown that this temple is precisely aligned with the rise of the sun on the two Equinoxes and with the lowest orbit of the Winter Solstice, 22 December.[70]

☙

Harvey eventually came around the corner; he'd been held up trying to identify some small waders in a large muddy pool a little way upriver. As he continued to wrestle with the identity of birds as we travelled the last stretch into Laingsburg, I wondered about the significant variations between the San (Bushmen) and Khoi

(Hromnik's Quena or Ottentotu). They were different in so many ways: stature, looks, as well as certain cultural practices. But their main difference was the way they put food on the table, the San being hunter-gatherers and the Khoi pastoralists. And in many instances, their differing economies brought them into conflict with one another. Yet they did share similarities in their style of language and certain religious practices, and this has led some students to believe that the Hottentots might have been Bushmen that had simply evolved from one economy into the other.

But the exact lineage and origins of the Khoi are still somewhat mysterious. Were they an earlier Negro race from central or east Africa that were driven before the first wave of accepted Negro migrations (said to have occurred around the time of Christ), and did they perhaps take San (Bushmen) women as wives and form their own unique Negro-Bushmen race? Or were they simply an offshoot of the first recorded Negro arrivals? Did numerous San (Bushmen) woman accept marriage proposals from the ancestors of the modern-day Hereros and Ovambos in Namibia and the Tswana in Botswana, and did this mixture of genes eventually give rise to the Khoi? Or were the Khoi the eventual result of certain Bushmen clans being conquered by the more powerful Negro tribes that arrived from the north? It is also possible that certain Bushmen clans situated in present-day Namibia and Botswana learnt the Negroes' pastoral practices (perhaps by herding their sheep and cattle initially), gave up their previous leaner hunter-gatherer ways, and then migrated south to greener and less crowded pastures in what is today the Cape.

What we do know for sure is that many hundreds of years later, the Xhosa and the Khoi of the Gqunukhwebe group intermarried and that their association gave rise to a cross-pollination of cultural mores, not least of which are the many click sounds adopted by the Xhosa from the original Khoi-speak. It is then surely also not impossible that this sort of intermarriage between other black African "tribes" and different Khoi groups occurred more frequently and earlier than was previously thought.

Perhaps the Khoi's uniqueness in relation to both the black African "tribes" and the San, as often described by the first European sightings, is simply a product of assimilation of many different groups and cultures over thousands of years. But wouldn't it be fascinating to know exactly how the process first started?

⋘

No matter which direction you come from, all the roads that lead into Laingsburg slope down into the town. Even to the inexperienced eye, it seems that the position of the town — largely situated in the greater part of a drainage basin and flanked on one side by the seasonal Buffels River — was always going to make it prone to flash flooding. When Stephanus Greeff acquired the farm "Vischuil aan de Buffelsrivier" for the establishment of a village in 1879, the dangers of floods in a region that received only about 50 millimetres of rain a year were probably the last thing on his mind. But the devastating floods of 1981 were so powerful that they all but eradicated Laingsburg's well-loved Victorian architecture: only 21 houses were left standing and, more importantly, 104 people lost their lives.

Sitting at a smart forecourt restaurant in the centre of this small and orderly town, it was difficult to imagine the devastation that was wrought by the floods all those years ago. Yet when you look to the water-level marks indicated high up on some of the lamp-posts running down the main street, you understand what mayhem the raging torrent must have caused. My own experience of a flood in Napier in the Western Cape in April 2005 has left me with great sympathy for flood victims. In our case, over 400 millimetres of rain had fallen in under 24 hours and a tiny seasonal stream that ran down the one side of our property, which was normally only about two metres wide and less than half a metre deep after good winter rains, became a raging torrent of 40 metres wide and well over two metres deep. A 30-square-metre shed weighing several tons and a VW caddy bakkie were whisked away as if they were children's toys. With a metre-high wall of water rushing down the side of our house, it was a miracle that it too hadn't succumbed.

"Hey, Nick, you know of course that the Springboks are playing Wales later this afternoon," Harvey blurted out from behind his newspaper in the Whistlestop Café.

"Oh, great news, but I'm not sure whether our cottage on the farm at Kruisrivier has a TV. I'll call Mandy later and find out."

After a good greasy lunch followed by wicked chocolate brownies and coffee, we were suitably refuelled for the second half of the day's journey. It was to take us through the Rooinek, Seweweekspoort and Huisrivier Passes to Calitzdorp and then via Groenfontein to our farm retreat in Kruisrivier, a distance of around 140 kilometres or just over three and a half hours in the saddle, and this meant we needed to go a little faster if we wanted to be there in time for the rugby.

A lady from Laingsburg tourism had told me that the origin of the name Rooinek Pass had nothing to do with the Afrikaans slang term for pale Englishmen who suffered sunburn above their short collars. Apparently the name came from the red oxide content seen in the surrounding rocks when the pass — or "*nek*", as the Afrikaners termed passes — was cut through the mountains. When Harvey and I later took a wrong turn on the pass, we were put back on the right track by some helpful Afrikaans folk. The irony of two "*rooinekke*" being inexplicably lost on "Rooinek" Pass and then steered in the right direction by the old "enemy" made Harvey and I have a good chuckle. It was the type of moment that would have had Oom Schalk Lourens shaking his head and saying something like "Englishmen are queer." In fact, there was such a time during the Anglo-Boer War when Oom Schalk and his nephew, Hannes, were keeping a watch out for English troops from an elevated position on a road near Dewetsdorp, when two English horsemen came into view. After shooting one of the riders, Oom Schalk and Hannes couldn't believe how casually his compatriot retrieved the wounded man without so much as a second thought for his own safety. Yet when the uninjured Englishman gave the two concealed Boers a friendly wave, Oom Schalk thought he'd pushed his point a bit too far:

> But when he waved his hand I thrust another cartridge into the breech of my Martini and aimed. I aimed very carefully and was just on the point of pulling the trigger when Hannes put his hand on the barrel and pushed up my rifle.
>
> "Don't shoot, Oom Schalk," he said. "That's a very brave man."
>
> I looked at Hannes in surprise. His face was very white. I said nothing, and allowed my rifle to sink down on to the grass, but I couldn't understand what had come over my nephew. It seemed that not only was that Englishman queer, but that Hannes was also queer. That's all nonsense not killing a man just because he's brave. If he's a brave man and he's fighting on the wrong side, that's all the more reason to shoot him.[71]

After floundering around on the Rooinek Pass, we eventually discovered the correct dirt track and found ourselves in a valley between two parallel mountains of the Swartberg range. It felt like we were entering the mythical fortress of some ancient civilisation. Huge shards of rock were pegged in staggered formations into a series of black ridges that made up the mountain barrier on one side of the narrow valley. It was a though we were passing through an ancient battle site in a war fought between a nation of giants. The sharp pieces of rock angled into the earthen ridge were the javelins that they'd hurled at each other during a bitter fight to the death that had left few standing. But then again, perhaps I'd just read too much Greek mythology as a kid.

After the unavoidable stretch of tar through Laingsburg and the Rooinek Pass, it was really good to be back on the dirt again. Somehow the tar always spoiled the illusion that the secondary dirt tracks brought — being a modern-day explorer on a quest of discovery in your own time and space. The more remote dirt tracks carry an added thrill as well: that recurring hint of fear that you might just break down and then have to walk miles over veld and mountain to solicit the help of the hairy hermit who lives in a cave in a hidden valley. This was a tantalising thought, and the main reason I rode in good hiking boots.

Our journey through Seweweekspoort made me realise that it must surely be one of South Africa's most stimulating and scenic passes, and it's a well-maintained dirt track as well. The road was completed in 1862 by a Mr A. Smidt, the brother-in-law of the famous South African pass builder Thomas Baines. Twisting and turning through this magnificent window on ancient geological activity, you cross the Huisrivier some 23 times. And the crush of stony skyscrapers towering above make you feel like an undersized midget in a kingdom of giants. The highest of these is the Seweweekspoort Mountain at 2,326 metres above sea level, and from your ground floor vantage point you're able to witness evidence of the anguish and the drama that lies behind their ancient formation. Great layers of lichen-encrusted "Table Mountain" sandstone are folded into peaks and troughs that are reminiscent of huge curling waves in a stormy sea. Some of these layers of rock were exposed to forces so violent that they were bent over double, testimony to the prehistoric turbulence that was unleashed by the fault systems that run from just outside Port Elizabeth all the way to Tulbagh. In their excellent book, *Geological Journeys*, Nick Norman and Gavin Whitfield summarise the causes of this activity:

Both the faulting and the spectacular folding around Oudtshoorn were brought about by forces deep below the surface, causing dramatic compression of the crust, with the subterranean movement directed from the south. The horizontally deposited sediments of the Cape Supergroup and their basement became folded, pushed up along east-west elongate axes and dragged down along the adjacent belts. Folding could only accommodate the strain up to a point, then rupturing began. The whole of the southern mass became dislodged and thrust over the northern block in a series of steep faults and thrust faults, which are nearly horizontal.[72]

If it weren't for the stoically erosive activities of powerful ancient rivers flowing out of the Karoo basin over many millions of years, the geological wonderlands of, amongst others, Seweweekspoort and Meiringspoort may never have been exposed to us. Perhaps T.V. Bulpin captured the "rich warmth of colour" and overall beauty of these poorts best when he said:

> In fact, the only way to picture some of the great gorges and river passages — notably Seven Weeks Poort — is to draw a poker across the embers of a dying fire; the passage left by the poker, glowing red and orange on either side in all manner of surprising shapes and beautiful tones, would not be more colourful than Seven Weeks Poort or the precipices of Meiringspoort.[73]

Seweweekspoort has also given rise to its fair share of tales and legends, and one of these concerns a toll-house keeper's ghost. The story goes that on dark and stormy nights, the ghost of the first toll-house keeper can be seen at the poort's northern entrance. Apparently this old man with a long grey beard and a typical Boer hat, carries a hurricane lantern and stops cars as they enter the poort from that side. Once the car has stopped, the ghost is said to laugh mischievously and rush back to his hideout in the ruins of the old toll-house. But as Harvey and I entered the poort in broad daylight, it is impossible for us to vouch for the veracity of these claims.

☙

I exited the poort in a bit of a daze. Not only was the scale of the geological activity I'd witnessed almost incredible, I was also battling to comprehend the strength of the torrents that had eventually torn the heart out of the mountain and formed the poort millions of years ago. These same torrents had then deposited the resultant sediment from this and other poorts into the coastal basins that stretched all the way to the sea.

Riding through the pass, I'd been conscious of eyes watching me from the rocky ledges above. At one point I looked up and in the dark cleft of a large fractured rock, a flash of movement caught my eye. I thought I saw a hint of yellow and stared at the spot for a long while hoping that a leopard would slink out of the darkness and into the light. But the hoped-for sighting didn't happen. Yet with my eyes sensitised for the slightest movement, I'd then seen numerous other animals including: dassies (hyraxes), baboons and klipspringers. At that point, my mind had cast back through the eons and I wondered what ancient reptiles and dinosaurs may have passed this way in the early years of the poort's evolution. Nearing the end of the journey through the pass, Harvey and I decided to stop for a cool drink and a snack. We sat there appreciating the silence in the shade of an overhanging ledge, the stream bubbling along behind us and the martins providing a spectacular air show above.

After the sublime dirt riding through Seweweekspoort, the tarred Huisrivier Pass on the way to Calitzdorp was a bit of an anti-climax. But the faster riding on the tar did have one major advantage — and that was the cooling effect of the fast-flowing wind: the temperature was 35° C and climbing. Yet, in fairness, it cannot be said that the Huisrivier Pass is boring; especially on a motorbike. With the road scaling and falling through twisted mountains covered with dense green bush, I was able to fill my goggles with many striking scenes. One of the outstanding features of this pass is the regular sightings of quartz veins that run through the cuttings in the mountainside, some of them about half a metre thick.

But even though I was still thoroughly enjoying the journey, I was also really looking forward to resting up the next day. The plan was just to sit and bloom in the sunshine, sip cold beer and mumble pleasurable noises to myself all day. Harvey planned to leave early in the morning and head home to Hermanus via the scenic Rooiberg Pass on the way to the small town of Vanwyksdorp. Dependant on the prevailing weather, it's known that the road can get quite rough in places and I just hoped his tyres would hold out, because at 77 years old, changing large 4X4 tyres can certainly take it out of you. I'd read about a "luck heap" situated on the summit of the Rooiberg Pass where you can add a stone to the pile in order to ensure a safe onward journey, but the problem was that with Harvey's penchant for punctures, it would have been preferable to have one at the start of the pass.

It was also difficult for me to accept that my short odyssey was coming to an end. It had been so much more than a motorbike trip through an ancient and mysterious landscape; it had been a journey that had thus far satisfied much of my long-held desire to piece together some of the scattered mosaic of South Africa's prehistoric and more recent past; an attempt to better understand where we've come from and where we might still be going. Yet I also knew that even once the trip was over, the journey of discovery would really be just beginning. But the trip had broken the inertia — an all important first step.

The first thing we did when we got to Calitzdorp was call our host to see if we would be able to watch the rugby test there. Great relief. Mandy said that they had a TV at the farmhouse and we could watch it with them: "The more the merrier, just as long as you don't shout for Wales, hey!" So after topping up our transports with petrol, Harvey and I shopped for some provisions for the braai we'd planned for after the game and, threading our way through some promising looking port vineyards, exited the town.

Cresting a rise shortly after leaving Calitzdorp, we were met with the sparkling blue surface of a large dam in the distance. It marked the start of one of the most scenically spectacular and enjoyable back roads sections of the whole trip. The Great Swartberg range rose on our left, and the rolling green foothills that led to them were dotted with quaint farmsteads that rode comfortably on their backs. The dirt track wound through a number of narrow cuttings, from the sides of which creepers and a multitude of different aloes seemed to grow straight out of the dripping ledges of dank and dark stone.

(I discovered later that many of the old cottages that were visible from this road are currently in the hands of city dwellers, most of whom have renovated the formerly dilapidated buildings and now use them as tranquil weekend and holiday sanctuaries.)

After an hour or so of stop-start meandering along this dirt track, we found Kruisrivier Guest Farm and stopped outside our whitewashed cottage. Apparently an old stable, it has been converted into characterful self-catering accommodation with a double bed and four singles set into a row of old horse troughs; a kind of linear progression at rest. The side timbers of the wooden troughs have been polished smooth and shiny by the countless horses' necks that have rested there, contentedly eating their fill over hundreds of years. Besides the possibility of confronting the ghosts of hungry horses, I decided to donate the double bed to Harvey. After all, he had a tyre-threatening pass to conquer in the morning and I had little planned. We chuckled at the bathroom mirror which had an old toilet seat for a frame, a window on someone's quirky sense of humour. In fact, it was really only the kitchen that was not full of novel décor pieces; but despite the allure of these quaint old touches, in the stifling heat, it was the long cool stoep that received our most enthusiastic thumbs up.

Although I normally prefer to be completely out of sight of the main house — just in case I have the urgent and inexplicable desire to bay at the moon in the nude, or something similar — our cottage faced away from the nearby farmstead and looked out onto a large pond set in a lush green garden. A fast-flowing water furrow, which I later learnt was part of a small river system, cascaded into the pond and convinced us that it was time for a swim. The swirling orange-brown waters were a great tonic for our weary and well-travelled bodies, and, feeling greatly refreshed, we sat down on the stoep and nodded off.

But it takes more than mere tiredness to keep a loyal Springbok fan away from his rugby. At one stage both Harvey and I had battled to separate ourselves from our chairs on the stoep, yet in the end, the promise of cold beer and surging Springboks, or so we hoped, won through. The Strydoms gave us the best seats in the house, and we watched the Springboks triumph in a match that see-sawed back and forth far more than the 32-16 score line would have suggested.

Yet, I found the family dynamics almost as interesting as the rugby game. The three well-groomed children were on their best behaviour, dad (Basie) was still in the fields planting *mielies* (maize) after the recent good rains, Ouma Hessie was having a brandy and water on the couch and was full of chirps about the voluptuous anthem singer's revealing tight T-shirt as well as the good-looking rugby players, and mom (Mandy) managed the children, as well as the needs of the whole gathering, with a deft hand. Just before half-time, a local school principal wandered in with his son, they were Ben and Klein-Ben. Ben was a Castle man and keen to share his allegiances with any would-be converts in the room. Knowing that it was getting late and that we still wanted to braai, Mandy had thoughtfully asked the kids to start our braai fire during half-time. It was a godsend, because when we got back to our cottage, tired and hungry from the long day in the saddle, the coals were just right and we were able to cook right away.

Neither of us spoke much through dinner; we managed a collection of satisfied sighs through mouthfuls of boerewors and red wine and were content to let the eloquent silences have their say in between.

12

Taking the Long Road Home

(Rest day in Kruisrivier then the return trip home via Willowmore: 369 kilometres)

The most powerful thing you can do (and it is very powerful) to change the world, is to change your beliefs about the nature of life, people, reality, to something more positive ... and begin to act accordingly.

Shakti Gawain

I felt as apprehensive of Harvey's leaving as I had prior to his arrival three days before. He'd enhanced my journey with his enthusiasm for everything that went on around us and he'd also managed to let me be alone to do those bits of absorbing that are important to do on your own. As I waved him goodbye, I realised again that there is no substitute for quality time spent with those you love. I said a silent prayer for his safe passage, which mainly entailed a plea for the longevity of his tyres, and then he was gone.

Though sad to see him go, I was also looking forward to some time to reflect on the journey and to try and piece together the huge amount of varied stimuli I'd processed — as well as the piles of information I'd gathered — along the way. I was sitting there lost in these reflections when I felt a wet tongue licking my calf. It belonged to Mandy's beautiful golden labrador, and she herself followed close behind.

"So did you guys sleep well?" Mandy said, beaming at me with her farm-fresh glow.

"Ja, like the dead, thanks. In fact, how we managed to still braai after we left you is a bit of a mystery."

"And what have you got planned today? — because there's a lot to see around here."

"Well, I was planning just to take it easy and read up on the area from all the brochures and magazine cuttings you gave me last night. And then maybe take a stroll later."

"Okay, but do you know that the red stone hills in our region are one of only three such formations found in the world? I think the other two are in Arizona and the Canary Islands, if I'm not mistaken."

"Yes, I was just reading an article on them. Apparently they resulted from a mixture of compressed sediment and varying sized boulders and cobbles that were formed during the break-up of Gondwanaland."

"Ja, that's what they say, and I suppose you know that their distinctive red colour is caused by traces of iron oxide in that sediment."

"I was just getting to that part. I'll probably make a turn past Redstone Hills farm before I leave tomorrow. I'd like to see some of the unique formations that they're speaking of in this article."

"It'll be well worth it. But if you've got a minute now, I'd like to show you around some of the other old buildings on the farm."

Mandy first took me to the adjoining cottage next door, known as "Die Waenhuis". As she opened the door, the appropriateness of the name was obvious — standing in one corner was the family's old "communion" wagon. Apart from its named function, this wagon was also used to fetch family members from the nearest railway station in Leeu-Gamka, which entailed a long and perilous trip over the Swartberg Pass. We then walked to the old mill house, which has also been converted into self-catering accommodation. It was plain to see, everything Mandy and Basie (real name, Johannes) had put their hands to had been done with the greatest respect for balance between the original architecture and modern comfort. But what struck me most about this unit was its unique veranda. It was built virtually on top of the fast-flowing water furrow; the same strong water source that apparently used to turn "one of the quickest mills in the area", and which also ran past the cottage I was staying in.

On our way back to the farmhouse, Mandy walked me past the well-equipped and neatly kept campsite. Like many modern-day farmers, the Strydoms have had to look to ways of supplementing their traditional land-based income from cattle, maize and tobacco. And paying guests are a way of doing this that the Strydoms seem to really enjoy. I followed Mandy into one of the front rooms of her farmhouse and was confronted with all sorts of tourist memorabilia, home-made products and a wealth of literature on things to do in the area. She offered me a cup of coffee and we sat down to chat some more.

"So how long has the farm been in your family?," I asked, dipping my home-made *boerebeskuit* (rusk) into my coffee.

"One of Basie's forefathers of seven generations ago, also Johannes Strydom, was the very first registered owner of this land way back in 1759."

"That's a long tradition of farming. Do you think any of your sons will carry it on?"

"Well, we rather want them to study for other careers first and then if one of them still wants to farm after that, that's fine."

"Are you a bit worried about the future sustainability of your farm as an economic unit, or is it more a concern for the lot of white farmers in general under an ANC government?"

"You know, these days you need to really mix up the type of farming you do in this area to get some sort of decent return, and especially with the minimum wages the new government wants us to pay now. You know, Nick, we wouldn't mind so much if there was a minimum output we could expect in return, but there's no such thing."

"Did you grow up on a farm around here?"

"No, I'm actually from the Boland and after school I studied to be a teacher. But after travelling around Europe in an old Kombi camper, I really wanted to get into tourism, as a tour guide or something like that. Yet when I got back, there didn't seem to be any vacancies open in that line, so I carried on teaching in the Cape."

"But how did you land up married to a farmer in Kruisrivier?"

"I was offered a teaching post at the Calitzdorp school, and I took it because I needed a change. And then one day when I was helping the matrics organise a charity ball, I joked with them that they should find me a blind date so that I could go to the dance. Well, they put forward a number of candidates: the first had bandy legs, the next guy had one funny eye and the third was going bald. In the end I decided I would take a chance with the baldy, and Basie and I fell in love!"

"That's a romantic story. And it looks like you two have a good life here."

"Nick, God has been good to us, but then I suppose we try to play our part too."

I strolled back to my cottage thinking of the Strydoms. They appeared to be a hard-working Christian family who were determined to adapt to the new economic realities of farming, and this seemed to mean increased diversification. But I couldn't help thinking that I might have met the last generation of farming Strydoms, and after nearly 250 years of wringing an existence from the soil, that was quite a sad and sobering thought.

∞

My plan just to bloom in the sun was in tatters. After my tour with Mandy I got to grips with giving Rebeccasaurus the once over: poking and prodding her innards and attachments for signs of anything that might have shaken loose, lubricating parts that didn't really need it and of course my favourite tinkering activity, tightening screws and nuts that were perfectly happy just the way they were. Luckily, I didn't "over fix" anything this time, and after giving her a bit of a clean-up, I felt quite pleased with myself.

But my inexplicable restlessness didn't stop there. I proceeded to mumble all sorts of inanities and the odd profundity into my dictaphone. It was as though I'd been bottling up all these thoughts and records of the trip, and since there was now no Harvey to share them with, I put them down on tape instead. It was sometimes disquieting to realise just how companionable my dictaphone had become. It gave me a reason to express myself, note my feelings on a range of issues and, of course, record interesting things that I'd seen. In some ways it played the part of a mechanical therapist, allowing me a window on my innermost thoughts, and I didn't have to lie down on a couch and pay a lot of money for the privilege either. Although, of course, if any therapist ever analysed the content of these tapes in any sort of depth, they would probably recommend that I lie down for a very long time.

One of the more cogent thoughts I had during this rambling monologue was just how different modern "canned" exploration was to that of the Bushmen or even Trekboer times. I had been able to explore the back of beyond, as we think of it today, on existing roads and tracks. And no matter how rough their surfaces were, they still led you pretty much from point to point. The Bushmen and the Trekboers, on the other hand, not only blazed their own trails through the virgin veld, they often had little idea of where they were going to land up. Both of these traveller types would only stop when the surroundings suited their needs, the Bushmen to stalk the prey they'd seen or to harvest plants, roots and bulbs that presented themselves, and the Trekboers only when a suitable and unoccupied pasture was found. Perhaps the only way to emulate this sort of freedom today is to have absolutely nothing planned and to stop only where you find something really interesting, and, of course, to rest. I promised myself that this would be the way I'd do it next time. I realised I was going to have to make a lot of money in between.

Every now and then my casually wondering mind was directed back to the moment by one of the numerous birds that caught my eye. Without stirring from my slumped position in the chair on the stoep and even trying to look for them, I notched up well over 20 birds in the course of a couple of hours. Among the most memorable was a steppe buzzard that perched in the crook of a tree overhanging the pond; it was so close that I could see the red lining inside its beak without binoculars. And then there was the dazzling European bee-eater and the paradise flycatcher that both flitted about snatching small buzzing insects from the air above the gurgling stream. It was an idyllic afternoon.

When we'd chatted earlier, Mandy had pointed out an article in a local magazine called *Landscapes* that she thought I might be interested in. It concerned some unusual rock art discovered at Eseljachtpoort near Oudtshoorn that had some interesting mythological explanations. And although the figures in the painting did look decidedly like mermaids, they may, of course, simply have been the depictions of trance visions seen by the Bushman shamans, and could therefore also be related to the "swallow-tail" images found at other sites in South Africa. But it is also possible that they actually did represent the mythological creatures that were said to live beneath the waters of the very poort the painting was discovered in. Stories about scary water creatures among the Khoi and San peoples were common and varying accounts stretched from the Gariep (Orange) River to the Cape. In William Dicey's book, *Borderline*, he recounts one of the popular myths of the Gariep River's Richtersveld region:

> The Grootslang appears to be the only surviving legend of the Orange. Sober accounts tell of a great snake called Kiman, cruising the remote canyons between Augrabies and the Richtersveld, preying on stock. The colourful ones claim the snake has a diamond embedded in its forehead; that it entices young girls into the water and knocks men down with its breath. "Kiman", a shepherd near Kum Kum warned us, *"moenie hom vaskyk nie, hy's aantreklik."* All drownings on the Orange are the snake's work.[74]

It has been said that these myths were used by the Khoi and San elders to foster the clan's respect for rivers and make them aware of the danger of drowning, particularly among children. So perhaps it is not surprising that the Eseljachtpoort's legend originally told by an old Bushman called Afrikaander concerns a young girl who was lured into the water by one of these mythological creatures:

> She stopped at the hole to look at some flowers, which were very attractive and drifting near her, till one came so near that she stopped over the water to pluck it, but she had hardly touched the flower when she was caught by a hand and dragged into the water.
>
> As the girl did not come home, her mother went to look for her and traced her tracks to the hole. When she saw that the tracks did not go further, she knew that the Water Woman had caught her child, for she was a clever woman.
>
> She ran into the veldt and gathered some shrubs, she ran home, dried them by the fire and ground them into a fine powder. Then she ran back to the hole and threw the dust over the water. She went and stood a little way off and waited.
>
> She saw her child coming out of the water and walking towards her. She was unhurt, but the Water Woman had loved her so much that she had licked her cheeks white and this remained so afterwards. She told her mother that the people who live under the water had fine houses and live in great abundance.
>
> The girl's mother had instructed her child from her youth how she should behave and what to eat if she should fall into the hands of the Water Woman. "If they ask you: 'What will you eat, fish or meat?' you must say, 'I eat neither, give me

bread to eat.' If you ask for fish or meat, it will mean certain death to you, as the Water Women are half fish, half flesh, they would think that you would want to eat them."[75]

Even though it was well located near the stream, the Kruisrivier Guest Farm was set in a bit of a dip, so it was only during my walk that I was able to get a broader picture of the surrounding landscape. I strolled up a short incline in the road and when I rounded the first corner, the long lush valley opened up and led my eye along the dark slopes of the Swartberg in the direction of Oudtshoorn.

I stopped above a rock pool in the river and thought about the mermaids that may be lurking there. It was an enchanting thought, especially as this distant rock pool was set among lush fantasy foliage: various aloes, mosses, lichen-covered rocks, with long succulent grasses growing in between. And the picture was framed by two drooping Karee trees on opposite banks, their crowns pushed together as if contemplating what other bounty they should allow to sprout beneath their boughs. It was the perfect setting for mythological water creatures of some kind. Yet the compressed fantasy world I saw through the binoculars gave up a creature of another kind: it was a large rock monitor and it had just snatched up a sizeable dragonfly. Perhaps the Khoi and San tales were passed on to warn children of these and other more dangerous animals, such as crocodiles, lions and leopards, that may have lurked near pools like these in days gone by. But probably the most dangerous thing was the water itself, an element that would swallow and kill a young child who couldn't swim just as easily as if it had been crushed by a leopard's jaws.

My walk took me along the meandering dirt track that wound through rolling green hills and ran parallel to the towering Swartberg Mountains. Whitewashed farm labourers' cottages leaked tendrils of wood smoke from their chimneys, while smiling children in tatty clothes pushed toy cars made of fence wire around dusty yards; they looked determined to use up the very last rays of sunlight before being called for dinner.

I'd had a wonderfully relaxing day and the sunset stroll had been the perfect way to end it. But the walk had also exposed part of the interesting-looking new road I was to travel the next day and I was soon itching to get back on the bike again.

ॐ

I set off for Redstone Hills farm at around half past six in the morning. I decided I would leave my luggage in the cottage and collect it on my return, as I needed to come back past Kruisrivier anyway. When I got to the farm turn-off, the orange sun was still low in the sky and its soft glow highlighted the red cliffs that rose high in the distance. Their strangely eroded shapes formed a fairy-tale backdrop to one of the farm's self-catering cottages nestling in the fields beneath it. I felt it was too early to disturb the farm's owners and visit some of the other spectacular formations I'd read about, but I was content to study those I could see from the road through binoculars. I was particularly interested in these enon conglomerate deposits, as they were part of a greater trail of quickly eroded and deposited material that extended all the way to the coast, and even offshore. And in some of these related coastal deposits, the rare fossils of some of South Africa's first dinosaurs were found — finds that I was hoping to learn more about later.

It was my second-last day on the road and I was still thoroughly enjoying myself. The dirt track I'd seen disappearing into the distance yesterday turned out to be a gentle roller-coaster ride through undulating oceans of variegated green. The farmlands had shifted inland from the road and I was riding through such a quiet corridor of indigenous spiky vegetation that it felt like my very own private nature reserve. The stark contrast between this verdant section of the Little Karoo and the far more arid reaches of the Great Karoo, reminded me that I would be entering the latter's hot climes later on in the day.

But seeing this unspoilt stretch of the Little Karoo for the first time also made me think of one of the Cape's very first European explorers: Ensign Izaak Schryver, an official in the service of the Dutch East India Company. Although there were doubtless other wandering *vryburgers* ("free" farmers/citizens) who may have happened across certain areas of the Little Karoo that Schryver is credited with discovering, as well as the Khoi and San, who had already been there for thousands of years, his was the first recorded "Company" expedition into these parts. In 1689 Simon van der Stel sent Schryver and an armed contingent off to answer an invitation from a reputedly powerful and cattle-rich chief of the Inqua Hottentots who was based near modern-day Aberdeen. It appeared that Hykon was keen to trade some of his cattle for European goods and other newfangled curiosities. To get there, Schryver had to cross a number of mountain ranges, among which was the formidable Outeniqua barrier. Approaching from the southern side, Schryver and his party had eventually found their way into the Oudtshoorn basin by way of the Attaqua's kloof, named for the Khoi tribe that had once lived there. The path he followed was tramped through the undergrowth by hundreds of migrating elephants over thousands of years.

It took Ensign Schryver's expedition a total of 39 days from leaving the Cape to locating the Inquas on the plains of Camdeboo. From Theal's description and Gordon's early maps, it would appear that Hykon's settlement could have been located on the banks of the Camdeboo River in the shadow of that western part of the Camdeboo Mountain range that ends in the formation known as the "Sleeping Giant", about 25 to 30 kilometres north-north-east of present-day Aberdeen. According to Theal, the trading expedition was a huge success, and Schryver returned home with "over a thousand head of horned cattle". There was only one recorded occasion during all their dealings when there "was a slight misunderstanding between the two parties". Theal explains:

> It was a law of Hykon's tribe that anyone killing game was not to eat of it until a present had been made to the chief. In ignorance of this custom, one of Ensign Schryver's party shot a bird and cooked it, upon which Hykon expressed his displeasure. As soon, however, as the ensign was made aware of the circumstance and of the law of the tribe, he sent the chief a present of beads, which was received as ample atonement for the mistake.[76]

(Note: The Attaqua's kloof trail is said to lie only about five kilometres west of the Robinson Pass, the magnificent pass that links Mossel Bay to Oudtshoorn. Bulpin tells us that although "it has now reverted to an overgrown and forgotten track," it can be found in the vicinity of the Ruiterbos Forestry Station.[77])

ଔ

After a blissful half an hour of having the nature-bound dirt track from Kruisrivier all to myself, I arrived at a busy T-Junction with a tar road. To my left lay the famous Swartberg Pass, a pass that Lawrence Green described as only being rivalled by "the fifteen thousand foot Darjeeling that leads into Tibet." At the very least, most would agree that it is one of Africa's most spectacular passes.

Though the call to ride the Swartberg Pass was strong, I needed to turn right to continue running parallel to the southern side of the Swartberg range via the back roads to De Rust, and then re-enter the Great Karoo at a later stage through the tarred, but equally spectacular, Meiringspoort.

Quite how I got lost looking for my back roads turn-off to De Rust in Schoemanspoort is still a mystery to me. It had looked dead simple on the map, but in the space of less than five kilometres I'd already turned into a number of dead-end farm roads. I passed the same municipal road gang about five times and eventually saw the foreman shaking his head and muttering to himself, words that surely had to do with the sanity of tourists on old motorbikes who couldn't find there way through an open barn door if their lives depended on it. I was beginning to feel the same.

Then, miraculously, a previously "hidden" turn-off suddenly revealed itself to the left. It had been cannily camouflaged between two rocky spires and had eventually decided to stop being childish and come out and show itself. I felt relieved, because I knew that my confused meanderings had been starting to upset a lot of farm animals, not to mention road gangs and their incredulous foremen.

But the back road to De Rust was well worth the initial confusion it caused me. I'd only been riding it for about five minutes when a well-treed and well-watered camping resort came up on the left. Now I'm not a big fan of camping at resorts, or camping anywhere for that matter; in fact, I firmly believe that camping is a thing you only do in a remote place of wild beauty where it is absolutely impossible to build comfortable chalets. But this resort looked like it would certainly appeal to those that had grown up on a diet of scout jamborees and were partial to the communal camping thing, shared ablutions and all.

And just a little further up the road I discovered the reason for the resort's verdant disposition. The Koos Raubenheimer Dam presented a picture of deep blue molten glass that secreted its way into the trunks and folds of the valley that wound into the distance. I was standing at the view site, munching on some trail-mix and mouthing off to my dictaphone, when a couple from Gauteng arrived. Most people from Gauteng are so used to being hectored and bullied by gangsters and other rabble that they'll speak to just about anybody not hefting an AK47, even a bleary-eyed biker talking to himself early in the morning. As it turned out, they were actually not from Gauteng at all: it was their son's car, and they were just the friendly Wheelers from Glentana near Mossel Bay. It was Mrs Wheeler's birthday, and, after wishing her well for the year ahead, I went in search of some more enon conglomerate that they'd told me was lurking behind some distant hills, not too far from De Rust.

The hills and mountains around Oudtshoorn through which I was passing had played host to a number of small and highly mobile Boer commandos, offshoots of the main invading forces of Kritzinger and Hertzog, under local leaders such as Scheepers. Although the uprising of the Cape Afrikaners that was feared by the British, and especially Milner, never gained the momentum anticipated, these invading bands continued to harry the British within their own colonial territory. And it was almost impossible for the British to prise the Boers out of their mountain fastnesses; these sorts of exercises required a disproportionately high number of troops, and because the Boers were invariably strategically placed to pick off the approaching British, the latter's casualties were often unacceptably high.

But the British had their own bulldogs in the field who could be relied upon to take on these sort of challenges, men who commanded small detachments, such as "Gorringe, Crabbe, Henniker, Scobell, Doran, Kavanagh, Alexander, and others." A number of these regional detachments succeeded in at least keeping the Boers on the move and preventing them from doing more infrastructural damage to the colony than they did. Yet, while neither side seemed to gain much from these games of fast and loose in the mountains, the mobility of the Boers and the logistical support they received from their Cape cousins, certainly gave them the edge in this sort of warfare. Their main achievement appears to have been that they sucked up British resources, resources that Kitchener certainly could have used in his determined efforts to bring the war to an early close in the main arena of conflict to the north of the Orange River. And if the British had been able to capture some of the other generals that were invading the Cape, such as De Wet, Smuts or Steyn, it would have freed up even more of these resources, and might well have added impetus to Kitchener's efforts to persuade the Boers to accept the Middelburg peace terms that he'd been discussing with Botha.[78]

Kitchener's frustration with the Boers' increasing reluctance to fight a conventional pitched battle and their growing preference for guerrilla warfare was escalating daily. As Pakenham explains further:

> It was the guerrilla's refusal to play the game and fight like men that appalled Kitchener, not his doubts (though doubts he certainly had) about his own troop's ability to fight. Hence the policy that he now proposed to London: a policy for progressively adopting more drastic methods of forcing the enemy either to give battle or throw in the sponge.[79]

It was this type of frustration that led Kitchener to eventually adopt his "scorched earth" policy, or as Milner called it, "the policy of punishment". The flushing out of Boer guerrillas by Kitchener's sweeping operations was, as has already been discussed earlier, not the military success it should have been with the huge resources allocated to it. What he definitely did succeed in doing was to displace tens of thousands of Boer women and children. They were accommodated in hastily organised and poorly staffed camps at 24 different locations strategically placed near railway lines. From Pakenham we learn that Kitchener saw the need for this action as two-fold:

> To prevent the guerrillas being helped by civilians was his first priority. He had also to protect the families of the Boers

who were at risk because their men folk had surrendered: Botha, Smuts, and De La Rey had made it official policy to drive these unfortunates from their homes.[80]

Kitchener's blinkered focus to get the war over and do whatever he believed necessary to achieve these aims sidetracked his attention from the monster concentration camps he was creating. Yet, contrary to what some Afrikaners may believe, this was not a planned and deliberate genocide, but the result of Kitchener's seemingly cavalier handling of the whole affair, as well as the apparent gross ineptitude of the officials charged with the implementation and administration of the individual camps themselves. The totally unacceptable conditions and loss of lives that resulted, especially of woman and children as well as their black labourers, was a tragedy for both the Afrikaner and black African nations. It was also a disgrace for the British authorities and their appointed lackeys. In explaining Kitchener's apparent indifference to the situation, Pakenham recorded:

> He was simply not interested. What possessed him was a passion to win the war quickly, and to that he was prepared to sacrifice most things, and most people, other than his own small "band of boys", to whom he was invariably loyal, whatever their blunders.[81]

୧୨

The smell of garlic wafted through my helmet; yet there seemed to be nothing growing in the adjacent fields which explained the source of this pungent aroma. But with my legendary lack of vegetable growing skills, I wasn't surprised that I might have missed the crops which sprout this strongly scented vegetable. It was only when I stopped to ask a farmer what the rounded pin-cushion flowering plants in his fields were, that he finally solved the conundrum for me. I was surrounded by acres and acres of onion-seed plants.

The ride from the Raubenheimer Dam towards De Rust had been really enjoyable so far. It had many of the qualities that one looks for on a back road journey such as mine: short and narrow poorts and cuttings, lush farms growing maize and lucerne, beef and dairy cattle, great mountain ranges rising high in the distance and, of course, the peace which results from virtual solitude. Many of the homely farmsteads were surrounded by well-tended, lush gardens, and the presence of numerous weeping willows scattered about the valley indicated that the area was certainly not short of water either. It had so much scenic variety it was the type of dirt track that would probably even hold a teenager's attention, or at least steal it away from the iPod or portable DVD for long enough to give him or her a healthy dose of natural greens. And, of course, on a motorbike, the many ascents and descents, as well as the unknown twists and turns coupled with the challenging gravel surface, were enough to focus even the most adept rider's attention. Zen dirt was the only appropriate descriptor — and I didn't want it to end.

About five kilometres out of De Rust it was time to focus on some attractions of another kind. Across a patchwork of fields on the far side of the valley rose a beautiful example of an enon conglomerate mountain. I looked at it for a while and was amazed at how much the one section resembled Salpetrekop, back in Sutherland. But this red-coloured formation was far from a volcanic mountain. Its relatively soft sedimentary rock surface was gouged and severely pockmarked, demonstrating that it is more easily eroded by weather in a shorter space of time than most other mountain surfaces. I resolved to read up more on these and the other similar formations that stretched down to the southern coast, especially those between Plettenberg Bay and Port Elizabeth; but my curiosity would have to wait until I'd had some brunch in De Rust.

After my meal, I felt I had a fresh understanding of why many cooks refer to eggs as "comfort food". And this is especially fitting, in my view, when they're accompanied by a piece of medium-rare ostrich fillet, fried mushrooms with fresh coriander and a handful of potato wedges. I was ensconced on the veranda of a small new eatery in De Rust, and my riding kit, research notes and other equipment engulfed an entire table for four. With a large plunger of filter coffee as companion, I settled in for a leisurely read in the sunshine.

I learnt that certain rocks found on the narrow coastal plain of the south-eastern Cape often indicated that fast-flowing rivers had been involved in the deposition process. And this was the same process that deposited the sand, gravel and cobble formations of many different-looking types of enon conglomerate that stretched from here to the coast. I also learnt that the fast deposition process is not conducive to the formation of fossils. The fine sand, or silt, contained by these fast-flowing currents is suspended in solution and is not able to settle around an animal carcass in the speedy manner required. In contrast, the slow-moving and silt-laden rivers of the Karoo floodplains produced almost ideal conditions for the formation of fossils. Once an animal had died either in or around these rivers and floodplains, conditions often existed where their bodies would be buried quickly, thus preserving their shell or skeleton shapes for later discovery in the hardened mudstone or shale. That's why fossil finds on the coastal plains are rare and, where they are found, the remains are often fragmentary. But conditions for fossil formation seemed to improve somewhat once these fast-flowing rivers entered the more calming influences of the sea shallows. And although South Africa's first dinosaur fossil was apparently uncovered along the Bushman's River, it is in some of these so-called "near-shore" deposits that a number of other impressive dinosaur fossils were also discovered.

My photocopied notes went on to speak of some of the specimens uncovered:

> Other dinosaur remains from this period in South Africa are the vertebrae of a large sauropod dinosaur called Algoasaurus (similar to but smaller than its North American cousin, Apatosaurus), which were discovered in near-shore marine deposits of the Algoa Basin. A life-sized reconstruction is on display at Bay World, Port Elizabeth. This plant-eating sauropod probably browsed on the leaves and cones of the tall pine-like trees growing on the coastal floodplains of the Algoa basin.[82]

I was over the moon. My personal fossil trail, one of the chief side-interests of my trip, had fortuitously led me to uncover a link to some true dinosaurs in the south. Rebeccasaurus had at last come home. And if I hadn't drifted into the Little Karoo for a while and been curious to discover more about the formation of the magical red enon conglomerate that abounds here, I probably would never have found it.

వ

As I crossed "Ghost Drift" I saw a giant kingfisher and took this as a good omen. It was at this drift, the first of 25 (Bulpin says 26) that you cross in Meiringspoort that one of the early pioneers reputedly witnessed "a supernatural light, in the form of a ball of fire..." Although Meiringspoort showcased much the same thrusting and dramatic folding activity in the strata of its sandstone cliff faces, it was somehow not quite as spectacular and awe-inspiring for me as the Seweweekspoort. Besides the Swartberg range not being quite as high here, it probably also had something to do with the fact that the smooth tar road and plentiful tourist lay-bys had unwittingly stripped it of some of its natural drama. Yet, by the number of cars and tourist busses I witnessed, it was clear that these features were highly popular with many mainstream travellers.

It was at one of these lay-bys that I noticed a sign directing tourists to a waterfall. Helpful staff at the information kiosk persuaded me that the short walk up the mountain would be well worth the effort. I met a young American couple from Minnesota who'd just had a swim in the deep pool below the slender waterfall and they were brimming with good cheer. It was their first time in "Airfreekah" and they were amazed at just how "civilised" it all was, almost a little disappointed, I sensed, that the continent wasn't one big and dangerous expanse where wild animals roamed freely. They were on their way to the Addo National Park and were being shepherded by an attractive woman from Cape Town. She told me that next year, she and one of the American couple's moms were going to ride Harley Davidsons from Miami to Chicago. She was my kinda gal.

Besides knowing by now that one never regrets a swim, I decided not to strip off all my biking gear and risk becoming a tourist sideshow in my briefs, and settled on just dunking my head instead. Cooled from the top down, I crossed the remaining eight drifts and exited the poort, heading towards the tiny hamlet of Klaarstoom. I was still smiling at the ghoulish and grammatically challenging description supplied by the tourism people for the 21st drift that I'd just passed over:

> 21. PEERBOOMDRIF (PEAR TREE DRIFT): An enormous saffron pear tree grew nearby making this a popular gathering place and outspan. Along the road was a house where two spinsters lived in, with the dead of one of them the other buried her in the dining room. The survivor disappear without anybody seeing her.[83]

I stopped at the dirt track turn-off to Willowmore, just beyond Klaarstroom. The trip through the Little Karoo over the last few days had been a most interesting and revealing diversion, but standing next to the bike, I realised that all I could hear was the ticking of the hot exhaust as it cooled down. The singing silence, the brown stubble covered ridges and the crisp blue light welcomed me back to the edge of the liberating vastness — it was good to be back in the Great Karoo again.

Before Harvey had left me in Kruisrivier, he'd given me a copy of one of his earlier books, *Have Wings Will Fly*. It is a book that showcases, among other things, a great variety of people's interactions with birds in many different environments. Sitting there in the hot silence on the side of the road, I found some of his musings about the Karoo landscape:

> The Karoo has stood motionless for millennia .... Yet, within that vast stillness you become aware, of the smaller paradoxes it offers you, and of their constant movement. The Karoo changes from the shimmering summer heat under a solitary, shady peppercorn tree; to the steaming cold rising from a horse's back on a winter's morning. The Karoo reflects the shifting patterns of the Autumn clouds. In bright Spring sunshine, it turns like clockwork to the movement of mountain shadows. Every hour, the Karoo changes colour; from the red of dawn, to a grey-green-yellow botanical carpet in the slanting sun; to the white heat of noon, to the blue pencil-lines of hills in front of a developing sunset. All this against a background of black stones, and toasted brown earth, curling at the edges. It is a harsh, dry world, but with room for the imagination to soar upwards to the eagles and to swoop freely with the falcons.[84]

It was after reading this that I decided on something I'd been mulling over all day: I was going to compress my two-day journey into one and try and reach Aberdeen that night.

☙

Once I'd made the decision to make for home, I focused on the dirt track as though I were trying to win a desert enduro. Since leaving Klaarstroom, the dry Karoo ridges on the left and the Swartberg Mountains on the right had closed in on the road, making me feel like I was running a narrow gauntlet of dry sand and stone. About half-way to Willowmore the valley opened up again, and soon afterwards something shining in the veld caught my eye. It was the hubcap from an old Chevrolet, and I wondered who the people were that had lost it and where they were going at the time. As I stood there examining the shiny relic, being blasted by waves of dry heat, I thought I picked up a flicker of movement on the stony ridge to my right. The whole trip I'd wanted to see a caracal so badly and then suddenly there it was — just a fleeting glance of the black tufts of hair on the tops of its erect ears and the quick movement of muscle beneath its tan-coloured pelt as it sprang effortlessly over some large rocks, and then it was gone. With my head still in the clouds after this serendipitous sighting, a number of badly eroded drifts saw me bottoming out my suspension a few times, but I made it through to Willowmore intact and filled the bike up with petrol for the final 140 kilometre push home.

I threaded my way through the crusty sugar-lump hills that partnered the Grootrivier towards Fullarton. I was preoccupied with thoughts of being reunited with my small Karoo family a day earlier than I'd planned and I was struggling to focus on the challenging riding at hand. It wasn't easy. I had only been away for two weeks, but with the great distance I'd covered and the incredible amount I'd experienced and learnt along the way, it seemed a whole lot longer.

At the top of Swanepoel's poort, I had a very close call with a natural biking hazard. A large hadeda ibis wasn't looking where it was flying and we very nearly collided in a mess of dust, feathers and foul language; but, judging by its hysterical lamenting, I'm not sure who got more of a fright, the bird or me. Yet, after a calm caravan of leopard tortoises shepherded me through the poort's final cutting, and I saw the vast plains of Camdeboo shimmering in the distance, I knew it wouldn't be too long before I'd be relaxing at home with my Karoo clan. From the tiny ghost town of Miller, the plains stretched uninterrupted to the hazy-purple forms of the Camdeboo Mountains, some 90 kilometres distant. Recent thunderstorms had savaged the dirt track's surface, and I bumped and rocked all the way to the T-junction with the tar road, just 24 kilometres out of Aberdeen.

As I came abreast of the "Sleeping Giant" reclining peacefully in the twilight, I thought of Ensign Schryver on his way to see the Inqua chief Hykon nearly 320 years ago. And then I thought of those travellers in the future that may pass this way in 300 years time and wondered how they would cover the distance, and what they would see. But whatever their mode of transport, I felt sure about one thing: the Great Karoo will continue to provide its boundless and mentally invigorating space to all those who cherish and respect its ancient beauty.

APPENDIX - 1

BACKGROUND TO THE KAROO'S 80-MILLION-YEAR-OLD UNBROKEN FOSSIL RECORD

In order to achieve an understanding of the flora and fauna of the "Karoo period" that occurred between 260 and 180 million years ago, it is first necessary to understand a little of the global environment in which the early Karoo found itself, as well as to discuss some of the major events that were instrumental in its formation.

Around 300 million years ago, when Africa was still part of the super continent, Gondwanaland, the part we now know as southern Africa was positioned over the South Pole and was covered in thick sheets of ice. McCarthy and Rubidge elaborate:

> Extensive glaciation occurred. As Gondwana moved northwards from beneath the icecap, the ice melted and retreated. Thick accumulations of glacially derived sediment were deposited (Dwyka Group). As the ice disappeared, large rivers were formed and discharged sediment into the Karoo Sea from the Cape Mountains in the south and the Cargonian Highlands in the north, depositing the Ecca Group of rocks. Extensive swamps developed on the deltas at river-mouths in the north, giving rise to South Africa's coal deposits. The Karoo Sea gradually filled with sediment, derived mainly from the Cape Mountains in the south, and the deltas gave way to extensive flood plains bordering meandering rivers. These deposits form the Beaufort Group.[85]

But what formed the Karoo Sea "basin", which was able to collect the water from all the melting ice sheets, as Gondwana moved towards the warmer northern climes? Before answering this question, it is necessary to know something of plate tectonics. Very briefly, there are zones (known as "trenches") on the Earth's outer crust that pull sections of the crust deeper into the Earth's many layers, and other zones that spew out "new" crust at fractures (called ridges) in the form of rising "lava", known as magma. Scientists first discovered this phenomenon when they noticed that the sea floor was spreading and therefore enlarging over time. They realised too, though, that because the Earth's total surface area was known to be pretty constant, if the sea floor were spreading, somehow and somewhere it must be being absorbed as well. The area where one tectonic plate is caused to slide under another is called a subduction zone. McCarthy and Rubidge contextualise this explanation by saying:

> About 330 million years ago, a subduction zone developed along the southern margin of Gondwana, causing compression in the interior. Sedimentary rocks of the Cape Supergroup began to fold, forming a mountain range. Rhyolite magma rising from the subduction zone produced volcanic activity. The weight of this growing range caused the lithosphere to sag and a depression formed along its northern side, in which an inland sea formed — the Karoo Sea.[86]

Although described as an inland sea, the Karoo Sea was, however, still connected by channels to the surrounding oceans for a very long time. Yet due to the generally small tidal ranges that have been uncovered by palaeontologists, these connecting channels were thought to have been relatively narrow. As the sediment brought in by the rivers from the north and south grew in volume, so the Karoo Sea became more and more silted up, until eventually the once huge inland sea was reduced to a large, yet shallow, inland lake.

Around the end of the Permian period (approximately 250 million years ago) the lake became filled with sediment deposits and eventually dried up completely. It is from the ten million years or so before this, though, during the continued depositing of the Beaufort Subgroup of rocks (see detail Chapter 2), that fossils of the earliest terrestrial reptiles of the Karoo period are found. The habitat that these animals lived in ranged from huge floodplains to marshy river deltas and riverbanks covered in a variety of edible vegetation. This vegetation consisted mainly of club mosses, true mosses, liverworts, horsetails (which were similar to bamboo) and a great variety of ferns. Also present were the numerous species of wide-ranging Glossopteris trees with their characteristic tongue-shaped leaves. During periods of heavy rainfall, the floodplains would be awash with thick mud comprising many layers of fine alluvial silt. As can be imagined, these were extremely fertile breeding grounds for the types of vegetation already mentioned; and herds of herbivores, as well as the numerous circling carnivores, thrived in this nutrient-rich environment.

The swamps, marshes and pans of the Karoo period were ideal fossil-creating biomes, as many animals that died there were quickly buried in shape-preserving mud; and it was doubly beneficial to fossil formation as it was also deficient in "corrosive" oxygen. Although the Karoo became less muddy and increasingly arid towards the Triassic period, conditions were still able to support the creation of fossils, albeit to a somewhat lesser extent.

In terms of the fauna that inhabited Gondwana during the Karoo period, it is useful to divide the presence of various animal populations into three main sub periods, i.e. Middle to Upper Permian (270 to 248 million years ago), Triassic (248 to 206 million years ago) and Lower Jurassic (206 to 180 million years ago). In terms of the limited scope of this overview, it is also important to note that while there were a multitude of other types of fauna such as insects, amphibians and fish, this brief exposé of the Karoo period deals predominantly with the reptiles, mammal-like reptiles, early dinosaurs and first pure mammals.

THE MIDDLE TO UPPER PERMIAN PERIOD

Two main groups of large terrestrial animals roamed the Karoo of this period. They were the remainder of the more primitive pareiasaurs (reptiles originally from cotylosaurian roots) and the more advanced therapsida (mammal-like reptiles), which eventually developed into mammals. The pareiasaurs were represented by bulky reptiles such as bradysaurus (an anapsid — see explanation under: "The Classification of Reptiles through the Ages", detailed below) — a 2.5-metre-long plant-eater protected by a thick armour of bony scales. In reconstructions from fossil skeletons, these fearsome-looking creatures resemble crocodile-sized leguaans (rock monitors), but have thicker armour. Certain schools of thought believe that their tough outer scales were the evolutionary beginnings of the "modern" tortoise shell.

Therapsids, on the other hand, were divided into a number of different subgroups. These, and examples of some of the animals found within them are listed below.

Dinocephelians ("terrible head"): These animals were so named because their heads were made up of very dense, fused-bone skulls. It is thought that their thick heads were used for head-butting either in defending their territory or as part of some sort of courtship ritual. Their teeth comprised incisors, as well as canines and post-canines, which are said to be the forerunners of the more sophisticated pre-molars and molar dentition of the mammals that were still to evolve. An herbivorous example of this group would be moschops, a 2.5-metre-long animal with specially adapted, interlocking incisors for the grinding of tough plants like horsetails. A carnivorous dinocephelian, the three-metre-long anteosaurus, probably would have preyed on a variety of the plant-eating dicynodonts, another group under the broad therapsid umbrella. Although the reasons are still unknown, dinocephelians became extinct before the end of Upper Permian times.

Gorgonopsia ("terrible eye"): The gorgonopsians were the main carnivores of the period and were equipped with large deadly canine teeth for cutting through and ripping off their prey's flesh in great chunks. Only having incisors and canines and no post-canines meant that these animals were forced to swallow the whole chunks of meat they bit off, similar to today's crocodiles. A well-known example of this group is the lion-sized rubidgea, a reconstruction of which can be seen at the Kitching Fossil Exploration Centre in Nieu-Bethesda. The gorgonopsians were unfortunately wiped out by the end Permian mass extinction event of 251.4 million years ago.

Therocephalia ("beast head"): This group represented the line of mammal-like reptiles that were eventually to evolve into pure mammals. Even though it is only speculation, it is possible that these reptiles developed progressively more mammalian traits in order for their bodily output, and general behaviour, to be less controlled by temperature in an increasingly harsh and arid environment. Considering this, perhaps it is expedient to first look at the main distinguishing differences, and their outcomes, between reptiles and mammals.

Reptiles are known as "cold-blooded" creatures because their more primitive bodily systems are unable to maintain a constant body temperature. Their energy levels are thus governed by the temperature of the environment in which they find themselves, meaning that they will be more inactive in a cold environment than a warm one. Mammals on the other hand, are able to either generate heat or dissipate it through various adaptive bodily functions. Their brains are also generally larger, better enclosed and more sophisticated than their reptilian counterparts. But all this sophistication comes at a price. The mammal's higher metabolic rate, generally greater mobility and more active brain requires a higher level of nutrition on a more consistent basis. The mammal's food intake also has to be chewed more thoroughly than a reptile's, and, because of this, their dentition and jaw structures vary considerably. The main difference is the presence of pre-molars and molars in mammals for the crushing and fine grinding of foods before swallowing. As the therocephalia evolved into more mammal-like animals, so did their teeth. An earlier example of a carnivorous therocephalian, such as the 2.5-metre-long scymnosaurus, thus differed greatly from the later and much smaller insectivorous form, scalaposaurus, which was said to have tiny cusps on its post-canine teeth. This represented a move towards the more complex and purer mammalian dental patterns.

The last of the therapsid groups is the successful dicynodontia. They were generally well-adapted herbivores that ranged in size from the initially very small examples of around 20 centimetres long, such as emydops, to those over two metres in length, which included the large daptocephalus. Most dicynodonts' teeth were replaced over time with a horny beak-like structure — much like that of a modern-day tortoise — that was well suited to shredding plant material. They also had two medium-sized tusks that protruded downwards from their upper jaws and were said to be used in defence against predators. They apparently moved in large herds close to the river banks and, while abundant during this period, the group only survived the end Permian mass extinction by virtue of one species: lystrosaurus.

Before crossing over to the Triassic period, it is perhaps pertinent to briefly mention one other group of small reptiles present in Upper Permian times, the ancestral group of "modern-day" lizards and snakes: youngina. Youngina also eventually gave rise to another very significant group, known as archosaurs ("ruling reptiles"), which appeared around Upper Triassic times and whose line eventually leads to the first dinosaurs. They are also said to be linked to the ancestors of crocodiles and birds.

It was originally thought that the Karoo's early terrestrial fauna migrated to the Karoo basin from the northern hemisphere. These "immigrants" were believed to have originated from the early reptile group, the pelycosauria. Yet recent findings of the therapsids — patranomodon and anomocephalus in the southern Cape rocks of early Gondwana — have put the earlier theory in question.

THE TRIASSIC PERIOD

After the "mother of all mass extinction events", which took place 251.4 million years ago (see detailed explanation Chapter 2), most therapsids took on increasingly more mammal-like features. Again, it is not known exactly why this happened, but it could well be that the environments had become too extreme for cold-blooded animals to thrive in. As detailed in the previous period, the main terrestrial animal groupings and examples of each are listed below.

Of the therapsid groups of the late Permian period, only a few therocephalian species and one dicynodont seemed to have made it through to Triassic times:

Dicynodontia: As mentioned earlier, lystrosaurus was the only dicynodont species to survive into the Triassic period. This herbivore was between one and two metres in length and stood about one metre high. Being semi-aquatic, it is thought to have spent much time in the plentiful pools of its lower Triassic environment. Lystrosaurus seemed to thrive in its Triassic surroundings and is said to have successfully radiated into a number of other species as well. One such species was the large flesh-eating dicynodont, kannemeyeria, a two-metre-long resident of the Middle Triassic period.

Therocephalia: This successful Permian group of mammal-like reptiles and their distant relatives, the first mammals, were more and more dominated firstly by the early archosaurs and later by their descendants, the dinosaurs, as the Triassic period progressed. Of examples of this group that made it into the Triassic period from the advanced therocephalians, such as scaloposaurids, Cluver tells us:

> Descendants of Cistecephalus Zone scaloposaurids persisted into early Triassic times and a related form, Bauria, was a specialised herbivore with flat-crowned crushing teeth. Once considered to be close to mammal ancestry, Bauria is, in fact, an advanced member of therocephalian stock.[87]

Cynodontia ("dog tooth"): It has been suggested that the cynodontia group evolved from late Permian therocephalia. This group had evolved significantly closer towards the true mammals of the early Jurassic period through advances such as those found in thrinaxodon. This small flesh-eating cynodont (about 50 centimetres long) had post-canine teeth with definite cusps, thought to be the forerunners of the more advanced, faceted and occluding dentition of later true mammals. The presence of a bony secondary palate meant that this animal was able to chew food in the front of its mouth while still keeping the airway at the back of the mouth open and thus breathe at the same time. These and other mammal-like improvements, such as a more completely enclosed brain, show why thrinaxodon, and some of its later Middle to Upper Triassic period descendants, is considered to be one of the closest ancestors to the first pure mammals of the early Jurassic period, such as megazostrodon. Thrinaxodon, which in reconstructive drawings looks like a cross between a mammal-like reptile and a small dog, is also a good example of how therocephalians and cynodonts successfully reduced in size over time, which was necessary to avoid detection and predation by the dominant archosaurs and dinosaurs of the period.

Early Archosaurs ("ruling reptiles"): This reptile group was of a new type, and while it was a member of the diapsid group, it actually had a third opening on the side of its face between the eye and the nose, the function of which is still unclear. It is thought that archosaurs originated outside of southern Africa and migrated to this part of Gondwana in the early part of the Triassic period. It seems that after the end Permian extinction event they became the most fearsome predators, while their flesh-eating competitors, certain lines of the therapsids, generally became smaller and more reclusive. From the fossils of these early archosaurs, palaeontologists have noted another of their distinguishing characteristics: their back legs were well developed and longer than their forelegs, allowing them to lift the front part of their bodies when they ran, thus greatly increasing their speed and agility. One of the early forms of archosaur was proterosuchus, a crocodile-like predator of around two metres in length with a uniquely mobile snout. Then, in the Middle Triassic period, some new forms took over at the top of the food chain; one of these was the fearsome predator erythrosuchus, a four-to-five-metre crocodile-like monster with large jaws and rows of serrated teeth that waited in ambush for its prey. Another important, but much smaller, archosaur arrived on the scene soon afterwards. Its name was euparkeria and it was only around 65 centimetres long. Yet to see a reconstruction of this reptile standing on strong hind legs with short powerful arms outstretched and dextrous-looking hands seemingly waiting to grab hold of its prey, and then presumably to slash it to pieces with its sharp rows of teeth, is to witness a very fearsome predator indeed. And with fossil records having indicated that its eyesight was very well developed as well, much like those of some "modern" birds and crocodiles, its hunting prowess seems to have been assured. Due to its early bi-pedal running style and other physical behavioural traits, euparkeria is seen as a significant link in the chain between early archosaurs and true dinosaurs. It is also thought to be distantly related to the ancestors of all of today's birds and crocodiles.

THE EMERGENCE OF DINOSAURS

The first true dinosaurs in southern Africa are reputed to have left footprints in the Molteno formation (the first layer of the Stormberg Subgroup of rocks) in the upper part of the Triassic period, around 210 million years ago. While little fossil evidence is available on these animals, their footprints seem to clearly indicate that the individuals in the groups ranged from small to medium-sized two-legged (bi-pedal) creatures. Michael Cluver of the South African Museum tells us more:

> Dinosaurs are divided into two large groups, which are probably only distantly related to one another. One group, the Saurischia, included flesh-eating and plant-eating animals, whereas the other branch, the Ornithischia, were exclusively plant-eaters. Red Bed dinosaurs such as Massopondylus and Melanorosaurus were primitive Saurischia, and are grouped in the infraorder Prosaurapoda. The Karoo dinosaurs did not achieve the immense proportions or bizarre appearances of the later dinosaur groups, but the herbivorous Melanorosaurus, which reached a length of up to 12 metres, must have been an impressive animal. Massopondylus, which seldom exceeded a more modest 6 metres, was a partly bi-pedal plant-eater and is known from several complete skeletons.
>
> Of great importance among the Red Bed dinosaurs are fabrosaurus and heterodontosaurus, among the earliest

Ornithischia known. In these plant-eating animals the teeth in the rear of the upper and lower jaws lay in closely packed rows, and vegetation was broken up in the mouth by crushing and slicing movements between upper and lower tooth rows. In some Ornithischians the front teeth were replaced by a horny beak, reminiscent of that found in dicynodont mammal-like reptiles.

Although dinosaurs are classified under the class Reptilia, they differed in several important respects from living reptiles such as lizards and crocodiles. Recent research has reinforced earlier suggestions that the dinosaurs were not "cold-blooded" and could, in fact, maintain a reasonably constant body temperature and a high metabolic rate. Dinosaurs achieved this in a manner altogether different from that of mammals and it is clear that the dinosaur's metabolic mechanism, for which large body size was a requirement, was much better suited for Mesozoic conditions than was that of the early mammals. Older concepts of dinosaurs as slow-moving and sluggish creatures have today been replaced by proposals that these huge monsters were, in fact, active and mobile, and in some cases very fleet of foot[88]

The early prosaurapoda dinosaurs found in the Red Beds of the lower Elliot formations around the Maluti and Drakensberg Mountains are said to have still walked on all fours. Like the traditional picture most of us have of these weighty lumbering giants, most of their body length was made up of the neck and tail regions, while their small heads looked greatly out of proportion to their large barrel-shaped bodies. As the Triassic period drew to a close, harsher climatic conditions had a dramatic impact on some of the early dinosaur species. McCarthy and Rubidge elaborate:

> Towards the end of the Triassic Period (about 210 million years ago) the climate in southern Africa became more arid.

Tannie Gesina Louw hard at work restoring the rudder of yet another windmill – Loeriesfontein.

Examples of a Trekboer wagon, tent and other memorabilia – Windmill Museum, Loeriesfontein.

Climbing up Keiskie se Poort across the plain from Calvinia.

The Hantamberg as seen from the Akkerendam Nature Reserve on the outskirts of Calvinia.

Surrendering to the fiery old spirits of Salpetrekop just outside Sutherland.

On the trail of the "Moordenaars Karoo" heading toward Laingsburg.

Harvey and myself deeply perplexed after contemplating the mysteries of the universe in Sutherland.

Exiting the pristine and magnificent Seweweekspoort on the way to Calitzdorp.

Ferns survived, but the seed ferns did not. Not much fossil plant evidence is present for the succeeding Jurassic period in South Africa, other than a few cycad fronds. In other parts of the world cycads, cycadeoids and conifers flourished at this time. And as the Triassic gave way to the Jurassic, the large early prosauropod dinosaurs were replaced by smaller relatives typified by the medium-sized plant-eater Massopondylus and its relatives.

Also sharing the Upper Elliot floodplains were flocks of small, bi-pedal, group-hunting, meat-eaters formerly known as Syntarsus, but now considered to be a local species of the American genus Coelophysis. These small dinosaurs, about the size and weight of a modern secretary bird, are thought by some to have been covered in primitive feathers mainly to protect them from the rapid, severe fluctuations in temperature in the harsh desert-like conditions of the late Elliot and especially the Clarens Formation. They are early members of the group of dinosaurs known as the Theropoda, which were to rise to great prominence in later times. It is to this group that the world's largest ever land-dwelling meat-eaters, such as Carcharodontosaurus, Spinosaurus and Tyrannosaurus belong.

One reason why the theropod dinosaurs are considered important today is because it is from this group that most scientists now believe modern birds descended.[89]

THE LOWER JURASSIC PERIOD

Probably the most important evolutionary event of this period was the appearance of the world's first mammals. In an increasingly arid environment, these tiny animals, such as the shrew-sized megazostrodon and erythrotherium, lived with their few surviving therapsid forefathers as well as the early dinosaurs and archosaurs, consisting of a number of crocodile-like predators — and, of course, a range of amphibians, fishes and insects.

THE FIRST MAMMALS

After the end Permian mass extinction event, the remaining lines of therapids began to evolve more mammalian traits, and at an accelerated pace. One such therapsid, a cynodont the size of a suricate (meerkat) named trirachodon, seems to have survived the end Permian event by living in burrows. And judging by fossil finds of the Lower Triassic period, its numerous and reasonably well-advanced mammalian features appear to have already started evolving in Permian times.
With archosaurs and dinosaurs set to take over from the carnivorous therapsid predators, from the Triassic to the end of the Cretaceous period (a period of around 150 million years), the evolving mammals had no choice but to become smaller, smarter and more unobtrusive.
One such result of this evolution was the shrew-sized megazostrodon, the first ever pure mammal discovered in South Africa. It is amazing to think that it is to this species, and other tiny mammals like it, that the entire spectrum of modern mammals, including man, owes its existence.

THE END OF THE KAROO PERIOD

Around 190 million years ago the climate of the Karoo became progressively drier and more arid. And it is reasonable to assume that because of this and other influencing factors, many of the resident animal species would have begun to leave for "greener pastures" in the north. Assuming this was the case, it was certainly just as well, because 182 million years ago, the already cracked

"Karoo" earth split open further and violent eruptions of lava poured over the area in an almost consistent stream that lasted two million years. In certain places it reached great heights, and huge basaltic mountain ranges such as the Malutis and the Drakensberg were formed.

It is not clear whether the earlier dinosaurs or their larger successors ever repopulated the Karoo region after these eruptions. What is clear, though, is that the successors of these early dinosaurs went on to dominate habitats all over the rest of the world, as Cluver elaborates:

> In the Jurassic and the Cretaceous periods, together representing a time span of nearly 130 million years, a dinosaur radiation resulted in overwhelming numbers of medium-sized to very large forms. Some, such as the 9-metre-long Tyrannosaurus were among the most formidable predators known, while the plant-eating Diplodocus reached a length of 27 metres. Diplodocus belonged to a group known as Sauropoda, and these animals included the largest four-legged animals known: Brachiosaurus, for instance, reached a body length of 24 metres and a body mass approaching 50 tonnes.
>
> Dinosaurs, the undisputed rulers of the earth, filled almost every available habitat, and mammals probably survived this long period of subordination only by virtue of their small size, which allowed them to exploit habitats inaccessible to the almost universally large-sized dinosaurs."[90]

The dinosaur trail in South Africa only seems to pick up again along the eastern and western coastal plains of the Mid-Cretaceous age (about 100 million years ago). Discoveries of dinosaurs such as paranthodon africanus and algoasaurus found near Port Elizabeth show that descendants of the early Karoo dinosaurs eventually returned to the same latitudes as their Karoo ancestors.

As is now well known, the dinosaurs were wiped out after another "mass extinction" event that took place 65 million years ago. Although some believe that it has not been conclusively proven, there seems to be mounting evidence pointing to a large meteorite strike that caused dramatic and fatal changes to the global ecosystem. It has been claimed that this extinction event killed about 75 per cent of all species living at the time.

The Classification of Reptiles Through the Ages

In order to follow the evolutionary chain from the first reptiles through to mammal-like reptiles and their modern-day descendants, it is first necessary to list and classify the three main reptile groupings. These classifications are largely based on the existence or not of a temporal opening (hole) in the skull behind the eyes, which allowed for the attachment of more powerful and sophisticated jaw muscles. Courtesy of the Kitching Fossil Exploration Centre in Nieu-Bethesda, these three groups can be simply summarised as follows:

Anapsids — Reptiles with no holes in the skull behind the eye (e.g. the tortoises and turtles of today).

Synapsids — Animals with one hole behind the eye. Animals in this group include the sail-backed pelycosaurs and the Therapsids (mammal-like reptiles). There are not many fossils of pelycosaurs in South Africa, but there are many Therapsids.

Therapsids are divided into six different groups: Dinocephalians, dicynodonts, therocephelians, biarmosuchians, gorgonopsians (and) cynodonts. (The ancestors of all modern day mammals.)

Diapdsids — Reptiles which have two holes behind their eyes and constitute the Archosaur Group, which includes crocodiles, snakes, lizards, pterosaurs (flying reptiles), dinosaurs and birds.

Author's Note: Although every attempt has been made to ensure the accuracy of this overview, the author accepts no responsibility for any errors that may occur due to his misinterpreting the material researched. As stated in the main "Author's Note" in the front of this book, the author does not claim to be a palaeontologist, and has attempted to convey a complicated subject in an easily accessible manner. It is therefore recommended that the reader consult the bibliography provided below to check the veracity of the information contained in this overview, should any doubts exist.

APPENDIX - 2

OTHER KAROO ADVENTURE-BIKING ARTICLES BY THE AUTHOR.

This appendix contains three articles detailing additional dirt track journeys through the Karoo. They first appeared in BIKE SA during 2007.

☙

David and Goliath
A dirt-track journey from Aberdeen through the Karoo to 'Die Hel' (Gamkaskloof)

The big machine came to a practiced emergency stop a few inches from my left toe. I didn't flinch. Bravado is a prerequisite greeting between old biking buddies; especially when his bike is almost five times more powerful than yours.

After months of persuasion, my old S.A.C.S school mate, Ian Huddlestone — a.k.a the "Stone"— had eventually arrived in my dusty Karoo hometown of Aberdeen. Pretty much a novice on dirt, I'd promised him one hell of a test-ride for his new dual-purpose BMW GS1200. Since moving here about 18 months ago, I've clocked up close to 5,000 kilometres on my faithful old XT250, covering dirt tracks all over the surrounding Karoo landscape and far beyond. For me it's seldom about blazing through the bush, often I trundle along as though I'm looking for parking; only then do you notice the otherwise small and well-hidden treasures of the Karoo. Mostly travelling deserted secondary dirt-roads only used by the occasional farmer, I've plugged into routes which offer a kind of adventure-biker's Nirvana. I call it 'Zen-dirt' and I planned to give the "Stone" a very good taste of what I was on about.

Day 1: *Aberdeen via Bultfontein to Klipplaat, then to Fullarton via Grootrivierhoogte and finally on to our overnight farm stop: "Stoepies" via Swanepoelspoort and Miller — approximately 230 kilometres, all on dirt tracks.*

Our pre-departure photograph displayed a paradox of imagery: the "Stone" kitted out in his immaculate two-tone BMW Motorrad outfit alongside his gleaming beast of a bike, and me in my homemade protective jeans and faded old top standing in front of the plucky little Yamaha XT250. I'd set an almost circular course for the day, destined to take us through a mixture of vlaktes, poorts, mountain passes, some smooth gravel and a series of rough farm tracks.

Once on the dirt, the "Stone" stood up and surveyed the surrounds like a Germanic Lord of the Manor. The road stretched lazily ahead to the small hills in the distance. They looked like the backs and buttocks of sculptured maidens with incongruous tufts of grey-green hair dotted sparingly around the contours of their bodies. Karoo dirt tracks can be remarkably deceptive; once you're out of the compacted narrow tyre tracks and strike the almost imperceptible 'middel-mannetjie', the front tyre often wants to wash away. We stopped to look at a large herd of springbok and the "Stone" decided to deflate his so-called 'dual-purpose' radials for better traction. A curious bat-eared fox looked on from a distance.

Having limbered up, we expressed new confidence and took to ramping some of the rainwater humps in the road. It was one of these humps, though, that nearly had us doing cartwheels through the veld as, just at the point of no return, I noticed a three-metre wide and one-metre deep chasm yawn open beneath me. I opened up and leant forward, willing the bike over the trap, but I'd not hit the ramp at a high enough speed. The front wheel hit the edge of the donga, yet, miraculously, the momentum carried the bike over. Well almost. It was the complete compression of the back shock that had me dodging and weaving over the road like a small drunken dinosaur. Luckily the "Stone" had seen my goofy antics and gave the big GS a bit of extra pepper and landed with a smile on the other side. He was having a ball.

With the old railway junction town of Klipplaat behind us we rode towards the gnarled heart of the day's journey: an ancient poort through the Grootrivierhoogte. Great mountains reaching hundreds of metres into the air provided a backdrop to a wide sandy river course, hinting at the poort to come. And then the mountains began to rise up all around us. They were the type which exposed their inner make-up to you, showing that they had once been liquid magma halted in its tracks when the cooling process had begun. Their exposed igneous layers were curled over in whorls, some of the higher peaks looked like huge rocky waves threatening to break across our path.

A magnificent female kudu broke cover and dashed across the road. Riding on, we were increasingly stunned by the rugged beauty and timeless aura of the place. A giant rock monitor lizard the size of a small crocodile scurried into the bush in front of us. Exiting the poort, we stopped to compare notes on the beautiful and challenging terrain. The "Stone" was gob-smacked and kept shaking his head and muttering: "F***ing awesome mate, f***ing awesome." After this eloquent outburst, we breezed down a smooth gravel road and entered another series of poorts, eventually arriving at the rail-side hamlet of Fullarton. I was glad that I'd prearranged a jerry can of fuel at our overnight stop as there appeared to be little chance of filling up en route.

I'd been through Swanepoelspoort a number of times before, and although it exposes some interesting rock formations, the ride was so much tamer than the one we'd experienced earlier through its less-travelled neighbour. The poort soon emptied us back onto the vast plains of the Great Karoo. Another old railway town, Miller, welcomed us with views of its dilapidated Victorian buildings and deserted streets. We watched as rampant tumbleweeds rolled about as if they owned the place and felt like we were slap-bang in the middle of a Wild-West film set, only our mounts were made of iron, not horseflesh.

The slopes of the Skoorsteenberg offered panoramic views of the Camdeboo Mountains: hazy-violet heights framed the vast plains of Karoo scrub that stretched out languidly to the north in front of us. And then, in the late afternoon sun, our overnight stop, "Stoepies", welcomed us with its rolling green lawns and cool blue swimming pool. As I lay on my back in the water, watching the impossibly beautiful sunset of iridescent pinks and oranges unfold, I marked a moment where everything was sublime. And that was before an ice-cold Heineken and a braai: "F***ing awesome mate, f***ing awesome," gurgled the "Stone" once more.

Day 2: *"Stoepies" via Beervlei Dam and Rietbron to Prince Albert, Swartberg Pass to Gamkaskloof (Die Hel) — approximately 285 kilometres, 80% on dirt tracks.*

It was my turn to be Goliath. The big Beemer burbled throatily as I twisted the throttle. We'd decided that I should try it out on the tar first, and when I got on it, it felt like a Cadillac compared to the bony little XT. For the first 10 kilometres I got to grips with the feel of the silky torque and tested its awesome brakes. And then I opened it up. At just over 200 kilometres per hour I tapped off the power and coasted to a stop with a coat hanger grin. It was surreal: the smooth power delivery, the excellent balance and the sheer solidity of the machine made me feel almost detached from the road. Almost invincible too.

We stopped in at my cousin Richard's house in Rietbron. And although he wasn't there, an enormous Coke bottle standing in the outside loo gave us cause to smile at his quirky sense of humour. Storm clouds were gathering on the horizon. We paused for some tuna and Salticrax, and also to decide whether we needed to get our rain suits on. Even though the storm was moving slowly away from us, it was trailing an ominous tornado-like finger, so the rain suits were donned just in case.

With 55 kilometres to go to Prince Albert, the terrain threw down a slick challenge. After a downpour, the talcum powder-like dust on most Karoo dirt tracks turns to slippery brown ice. And it was while negotiating one of these patches that the "Stone" took a tumble. Or, should I say, a long slow slide. His beautiful BMW Motorrad rain suit was dripping in chocolate-coloured mud, an image which only heightened my desire to burst out laughing. Now, it's an odd quirk I have, I know, but dirt-bike prangs of this nature have always seemed to tickle my penchant for slapstick comedy. The more the "Stone" said: "Scheez broe, there was just nothing I could do!" the harder I had to pinch myself to stop laughing uncontrollably. With the track this slippery, it took us nearly two hours to cover the remaining distance. The moral of the story: fit proper dual-purpose tyres (not hybrid road radials), or preferably knobblies, before tackling serious off-road conditions.

We topped up our tanks and our supply of red wine in chichi Prince Albert and headed for the hills; it was past four o'clock and we still had at least two hours of gruelling riding to 'Die Hel' (Gamkaskloof). Entering the Swartberg Pass from the Prince Albert side is a spectacular experience. Sheer cliffs form the sides of a multi-coloured canyon, the tortured rock faces reflecting their ancient and tumultuous past. Near the top of the roller coaster ride, we began our descent into 'Die Hel'. We raced against the flagging light and the threatening cloud that continually dogged our progress. Between the parallel ranges of the lofty Swartberg mountains, the hairpin bends, switchbacks, streams, loose sand and flight-enticing humps all conspired to spark the remaining reserves of adrenalin through our exhausted bodies. After an exhilarating age, we stopped above the final descent. Gamkaskloof stretched out before us, a narrow finger of green seen through the smoky glare of the setting sun. Never has a view been so far from hell.

The "Stone" went on a wood mission for the fire. Sucking on a cold Windhoek, I became immobile in a plastic chair outside our hired caravan. It was my turn to just sit there and shake my head saying: "F***ing awesome mate, f***ing awesome."

This article first appeared in the February 2007 edition of BIKE SA.

Cruising the Camdeboo

When Eve Palmer wrote her classic: "The Plains of Camdeboo" in the mid 1960s she said: "It is a country flooded by sun; lonely, sparse, wind-swept, treeless on the flats for many miles." And thankfully this countryside remains virtually unspoilt to this day, its stark beauty a timeless reminder of an extremely well-preserved ancient landscape. With a network of dirt-tracks just waiting to be explored by those who appreciate the liberating appeal of 'deep space', Nicholas Yell asks: "So what are you waiting for?"

On the day the *manne* from the *dorp* invited me to go riding with them, I was expecting a couple of country boys on 'farm scramblers'. So when a collection of pedigreed dual-purpose bikes thundered to a stop outside my front door, I was somewhat surprised. Derick, the town's truck, car, bike and windmill mechanic led the pack on a brand new BMW1200 Adventure. Behind him was John, a local farmer, on a KTM990 Adventure and his brother Koos on a BMW1200 GS. Bringing up the rear was Ignes, Aberdeen's long-haul transport man on a BMW GS650. So in the end it was actually only me on my trusty Yamaha XT250, that had arrived on a 'farm scrambler'. Not only were these local *kêrels* and their ladies on smart bikes, but they all looked to be dressed in the right gear as well. Or so I thought, but then that was before the accident.

Even though I've not lived in Aberdeen that long, with my numerous motorbiking forays into the veld on my own, I have built up a good knowledge of the dirt-tracks leading in and out of the town and consequently, was asked to show these locals the way. Perhaps the *manne* were just trying to save me some embarrassment by not blasting off into the distance on their big, meaty machines. Yet, to my mind, the purpose of dirt-track cruising is to immerse yourself in the veld around you, so speed is certainly not one of my main goals — even if I had a faster bike. I'd far rather stand up on the pegs and watch the springbok herds gambol off into the middle-distance, the kori bustards lumber into reluctant flight and most importantly, for any negative thoughts to unravel in the meditative peace of slow dirt-track travel. That is the catharsis of Zen-dirt.

Just as I was enjoying my dusty séance with nature, a family of guinea-fowl filled my goggles. How the mother and her two large chicks missed me I'll never know, but I somehow managed to cleave the smallest of gaps between them. Ignes came alongside me and shook his head in disbelief. I was watching a pair of blue cranes bowing and burbling during their courtship ritual when the next obstacle zigzagged across my path: a steenbok desperately trying to escape the perceived threat of the gang of metal monsters bearing down upon it. The problem with these bambi-like creatures, is that even if you stop and wait for them to find that elusive hole in the fence, they are so panicked that it still takes them the same amount of time to escape, so you may as well continue riding slowly by.

My route was to take us on the Bultfontein farm road to Oatlands and then a little way back to Aberdeen Road — the old station that once served Aberdeen, Murraysberg and Beaufort West — then onto Marais siding and our turnaround point of Jansenville, a round-trip of about 250 kilometres. As I looked towards the north I knew I should have brought my new rain suit with me. Unexpected thunderclouds were rising up above the Camdeboo Mountains, the result of the 38°C heat sucking the moisture out of the desert soils which were still sodden from the recent rains.

The stretch of road just before Oatlands provided some absorbing challenges. Tight twists and turns, scary patches of loose sand and a series of water run-off humps that had us all airborne and whooping with delight. But there was a greater challenge a little way ahead. A chocolate brown puddle the size of a car and of indeterminate depth, blocked the road. I took a route just to the left of middle and sailed through. Ignes was not so lucky. At the last minute, he decided to go the middle route where he estimated the water to be shallowest. He must have hit it at a slight angle and I saw the crash video play out in my rear-view mirror. In what seemed to be a slow-motion action replay, I saw him go right, then he corrected left, but his angle of lean was just too great, and with one desperate heave to the right the bike ploughed into the stony soil beyond the puddle. It slid away from him and his passenger and their hands were left groping the air in its wake. When I got to Ignes he was writhing in agony on the ground. I was sure he'd broken something. His girlfriend, Talana, was sitting in the road a short distance away. She looked like she was in shock as she stared ahead vacantly and clutched her bleeding foot. After plying both of them with painkillers and Coca-Cola, we ascertained that they were fortunately not too badly hurt. And had they both been wearing all the right gear, they probably wouldn't have hurt themselves at all. The GS 650 had also fared pretty well — only a broken mirror and indicator light plus a few small scratches. The verdict: if you're going dirt-riding fit proper dual-purpose knobblies, and dress for the crash, not the weather.

※

When we'd picked up a few Cokes at the Aberdeen 'Padstal' earlier in the day, we'd met a Harley rider from Mossel Bay. Chatting to him about our intended route, he shook his head and said: "Give me smooth tar any day, brothers," to which Ignes retorted: "We're still too young to ride on tar, boet." The comment obviously found its mark, as even though the Harley rider wore a wry smile at the time, he made graphic references as to what Ignes should go and do to himself.

I wondered just how 'young' Ignes was feeling as he hobbled to his mount after the accident. Yet he seemed determined not to let the unfortunate event put a dampener on his day, he was first off after the accident and left us standing at the crash-site in a cloud of dust and testosterone. Young *and* tough it seemed.

The closer you get to Jansenville the pricklier the surrounding flora becomes. With so much spiny 'soetnoors' (euphorbia coerulescens) about, we knew we'd left the plains of Camdeboo to the north and had crossed into a region known locally as the Noorsveld. It was in a cutting through a small range of mountains, about 40 kilometres out of Jansenville, that we came across Ignes and Talana again.

They were in good spirits and had obviously shaken off their earlier trauma:

"You land in one of these things and you know all about it," Ignes said, pointing warily at a Noors bush behind him.

"Didn't the San use the sap as poison for their arrow tips?" I asked.

"Not from these, the plant's flesh was sometimes used by the old farmers as fodder. I think the poisonous one is the Virosa variety. But these spiny little thorns will certainly cause a welt under the skin. Ask me, I've had plenty of experience with them trying to catch warthogs on a farm near Grahamstown."

"Why were you trying to catch them?"

"Well, when a farmer brought 17 of them to his game farm in the area, they multiplied like rabbits and they either had to be culled or relocated. And those things can be quite dangerous when cornered. See this scar on my arm, from an old yellow tooth."

Our first view of hell – Gamkaskloof.

The 'Stone' negotiates the tricky track through the Grootrivierhoogte.

The impossibly beautiful sunset at 'Stoepies'.

Another pit stop, another picture; from left to right: Ignes, Henrietta, Nick (writer), John and Koos.

Derick blazing a trail through the Noorsveld near Jansenville.

Sureta: the charming bride-to-be in Jansenville.

The second awesome pass after Studtis; magnificent ride, magnificent scenery.

Leaving the Nuwekloofpas after our third journey through it.

"But surely the farmer who brought them in should be responsible for the culling?"

"I met the Oom in the bar one day," replied Ignes with a wry smile, "he said he only brought in 17 and therefore he was only responsible for 17!"

We came into Jansenville over the tarred Soutpansnek Pass. I'd taken a wrong turn a while back that brought us to a T-junction with the tar about 15 kilometres from the town. The bigger bikes left me in a wake of engine noise and exhaust fumes as I maxed out at 117 km/h on the smaller Yamaha. I caught up with them a little later at the Noorsveld Padstal; they were already into their second Coke and were all munching great lengths of kudu *droëwors*, magic stuff.

On the way to the petrol station before heading back out of town, Koos led us to a biker friend's house. And as we got there, a beautiful bridal party spilled out the front door. Relatives of Koos's friend were getting married and the bride and bridesmaids had used their house to get ready before the ceremony. After chatting to us about our route plan, Koos's mate was torn between attending the wedding and joining us on the return journey to Aberdeen on his Varadero. It was touch and go, but in the end, the promise of a big party that had been long in the making, won the day and he stayed behind.

On the road to Klipplaat I thought about Sureta. Most brides look lovely on their wedding day, but she was somehow extra special, taking time to smile and pose for us in front of the bikes while having last minute touch-ups done to her make-up on the Jansenville pavement. She was going to make her groom one very happy man.

The clouds that had been gathering around Aberdeen earlier began to loose their loads. Without a proper rain suit, and a headlight that had gone on the fritz, I was keen to make tracks.

Problem was that a few of our clan had discovered the Sharks vs Cheetahs game in the Klipplaat pub. It was seven all when Derick and I decided to set out on the 70 kilometres of dirt back to Aberdeen. The rain was starting to really come down and with a strong headwind, I wished I had a bit more horsepower. But it was when I came around a corner at a modest 80 km/h that I was momentarily thankful for my lack of speed. The last of three kudu cows had just crossed the road in front of me, and if I'd been there seconds earlier there could have been some ugly biltong lying in the dirt.

A little further on I stopped to take in the drama of the storm playing out behind me. Great forks of lightning assaulted the cracked earth while enormous sheets of water silvered the sky. Brief bursts of luminous mauves, oranges and pinks coloured the horizon as the sun dipped and the dry earth released its musty-floral smell, unique to African soil when it sings in the rain.

I saw Derick and Umelda up ahead with worried looks creasing their brows.

"We thought you'd come off, I was just about to come back and look for you," said Derick with concern.

"No I'm fine thanks; just got waylaid by the mind-blowing scenery, that's all."

This article first appeared in the May 2007 edition of BIKE SA.

To the Valley of Baboons.
A long awaited and adventure-packed tour to the Baviaanskloof

The "Stone" (a.k.a. Ian Huddlestone) had been in a bit of a state when he called me last Monday. My old mate from the Cape had been dodging bullets on the domestic and business front for too long and was seeking some well deserved rest and relaxation. He wasn't particularly fussed where we went on the bikes as long as we got out into the sticks: "preferably this coming weekend," he'd said, the city strife giving his voice a jangled edge that had knifed through the airwaves.

I'd long awaited an opportunity to brave the Baviaanskloof, and in the quiet lull after the Easter weekend and the school holidays, I felt we had a good chance of getting accommodation for the two nights we required. By Wednesday morning the arrangements were sorted. My plan for Day 1 was to leave Aberdeen early Saturday morning and take the dirt track via Miller and Swanepoelspoort to Willowmore, have breakfast there, and then head through the kloof to our first overnight stop at Kudu Kaya near Cambria. On Day 2 the itinerary would see us filling up with petrol in Patensie and then heading back through the kloof and staying the second night at a cottage near Studtis. But, even the best plans are bound to come unstuck somewhere. And when this happens, it leads you on a merry dance of discovery that no amount of planning could achieve. Our journey was to be no different.

The "Stone" arrived with his riding buddy, David, late on Friday afternoon. They were trailing a golden-orange Karoo sunset and it set the gleaming paintwork of their BMW1200 GSs aflame as they burbled down my driveway. David was an old soccer-playing rival the "Stone" had befriended in the pub after a game some years back. After a few beers, they'd forgotten that they'd being trying to tackle the life out of one another a short while ago and had discovered a mutual interest in motorbiking. Much later in the evening, they'd even dreamed about buying two GSs and doing an African safari together. The GSs have now become a reality, but the African safari still needs much planning. In fact, this trip to the Baviaans was David's first outing in the rough stuff and I was pleased to see that both he and the "Stone" had changed their tyres to real 'dual-purpose' rubber. With numerous river crossings ahead of us, the last thing they needed on the big Beemers was to be handicapped by inadequate grip.

The Sleeping Giant Mountain still looked fast asleep in the cool light of a frosty Karoo dawn. We'd had to get up before the sparrows had even stirred and were making our way past this legendary mountain backdrop just as the first tentative rays of sunshine crept out from under the horizon. Chasing our long shadows into the brightening Karoo veld, we soon crested a rise and looked down upon some distant hills floating in a sea of swirling mist. To the right of the track we saw a herd of about 500 springbok bunched closely together. It looked as if they were trying to preserve their precious body heat by standing absolutely still, even ignoring any danger we might have posed to achieve this.

"Scheez Nick, what an awesome sight," said the "Stone" in his characteristic monotone.

"Ja, and it's amazing to think that herds hundreds of times bigger than this were a common sight less than a 150 years ago," I said dreamily.

"Our 'civilised' ancestors really knew how to balls things up for us, though, didn't they. I mean how did they expect the herds to last when their hunting parties used to massacre thousands at a time?" added David with contempt.

Then we were in the mist. The atmospheric blanket that had bathed the hills in ethereal charm now smothered us with its cold and clinging moisture. My goggles were totally covered in droplets of water and I wished I had Elton John's trick sunglasses of the 70s — remember, those ones that had windscreen wipers on them? There was nothing else we could do but go very slowly and keep wiping them clear every couple of minutes. After a while I decided that there was only one thing that would give us the warmth we needed — a shot of OBs. And, amazingly, soon after that the mist cleared and the tumble-down ghost town of Miller appeared out of the gloom, a golden apparition basking languidly in the sunlight.

Swanepoelspoort is a beginner's version of the far more awe-inspiring Meiringspoort and Seweweekspoort to the west. But, like its bigger brothers, there are sections of this poort that show beautiful layers of tilted golden sandstone, evidence of the tortuous subterranean activity that caused folding and faulting hundreds of millions of years ago. The dirt track through the poort was wide and smooth, allowing us to get some speed up and cast veils of fine dust over this unspoilt ancient landscape. Instead of turning right and following the Groot Rivier to Willowmore, I decided on a time-saving route that would intersect with the single-strip concrete road between Steytlerville and Willowmore.

"Three farmhouse breakfasts with lots of coffee," said the "Stone" to the waitress at Sophie's Choice. Like all of us, he was smiling from ear to ear at the thought of the warm food after the long cold ride from Aberdeen. I'd learnt from an early age that the "Stone's" large frame required substantial succour to keep it firing on all cylinders. At boarding school he used to lead regular raids on the kitchen after hours, first prize being leftover roast potatoes on those rare occasions when we'd had 'roasts' for dinners.

After a scrumptious breakfast and interesting chat with our

friendly host, Sophia, we were back on the road by about 10:30 a.m. By my reckoning, it was going to take us about seven hours from Willowmore through the kloof to Cambria. It was only about 145 kilometres, but I'd been warned that the rougher wilderness section from Sandvlakte — dependant on the amount of water in the rivers — could take more than three hours to cover only 55 kilometres.

The western portal to the Baviaanskloof is the Nuwekloofpas. Both the "Stone" and David had heard that the loose rock and gravel surface through this pass could easily unseat the unwary, so when we sailed through this pretty average dirt track we were all a little disappointed at how tame it was. But the challenges were to come later, and the better than expected road conditions in no way detracted from the sheer cliffs of enon conglomerate that rose on either side of us. A number of these fragile formations had been eroded into fairy tale-like turrets and spires, giving the pass a distinct other-worldly feel.

And then the narrow pass spat us out into the wider, more arable section of the kloof which stretches from the Nuwekloofpas to Sandvlakte. As you enter the tucked away wonderland of the Baviaanskloof, you notice that it is not dissimilar to 'Die Hel'. But probably the thing that the two kloofs have most in common is their wonderful sense of isolation, a fact that kept both these mountain-bound communities pretty much frozen in time for centuries.

The dirt road to Studtis was in good shape and led us through a narrow fertile valley which was home to many types of mixed farming. Combinations of sheep, lucerne, ostriches and other mixed crops, seemed to most popular. The farms were set against the jagged backdrop of the Baviaanskloofberge to the north and the Kougaberge to the south. There are also numerous tight and overgrown gorges that run up these fold mountains at right angles to the track. Many of these give rise to small streams which become swollen in the winter rainy season, sometimes causing problems for adventure-bikers, but which allow the farmers to smile most of the year round. Because of its location and topography, the Baviaanskloof — or Valley of Baboons as we came to call it — is a veritable treasure chest of unique fauna and flora, one of only 25 places in the world listed as a 'bio-diversity hot-spot.' There are reported to be over 1,400 plant types, more than 300 bird species, nearly 60 types of reptiles and about 50 kinds of mammals. And that's not even counting the diverse types of insects and fish that abound here. In the many caves found in this kloof, there are also numerous examples of rock-art, proving that the San (Bushmen) once called this area home. But, as in so many other areas of South Africa, the stronger Bantu tribes, as well as the ubiquitous and land-hungry European colonists, soon had the San on the run.

We were contemplating these facts, munching trail-mix and *droëwors* on the side of the road, when the "Stone" chipped in with some political commentary.

"But Nick, how different is what the ANC government is doing today to white people, to what both the Bantu and our forefathers did to the Bushmen? We are now marginalised by damning legislation which is just as deadly as being hunted out to virtual extinction."

"Well, the Bushmen certainly hadn't oppressed the Bantu people or our forefathers as the white man unfortunately did for hundreds of years, but ja, that doesn't mean we should be paying for the sins of our fathers forever," I replied, not really wanting to get into a long political discussion.

"There should also be a time-limit on both Affirmative Action and the current terms and conditions of Black Economic Empowerment," added David.

Luckily it was a long debate and we were short on time, so we agreed to bite our tongues until later and rather focus on riding the challenging road ahead.

The first of the three passes between ourselves and Cambria was a tight and twisting descent through lichen covered cuttings, ending in a small verdant valley below. The boys on the big Beemers behind me stood heavily on their brakes as the road nosedived towards the valley floor. David was concentrating furiously as he put his newly learnt 'stand-up' technique into practice. We came up behind a Land Rover Discovery (it was to dog our progress the whole day) and only after a very long and irritating while did the driver begrudgingly let us past.

Following the long and hot descent, we decided to take a swim. We were horsing about in the water and mooning for David's camera when the Discovery ambled over the bridge — perfect timing I thought. As my stepbrother always says: "You'll never regret a swim", and it was probably never truer than on that day, paddling on our backs through tea-coloured water with small fish nibbling our toes; sublime.

The swim also focused our minds on the challenges that lay ahead. And there were plenty of them: numerous water crossings — some were 30-metres wide and half a metre deep — tight and narrow mountain passes, and all the time riding through a gauntlet of sheer green mountains on either side of the track. As I was about to enter one of the water crossings, I noticed a large baboon sitting in the cleft of a small tree right next to the road. He appeared to be counting cars and I got so sidetracked watching him that I nearly lost it in the stream. When I eventually got through the river and looked back to see how my buddies were fairing, I could have sworn that I saw the baboon laughing and slapping his sides in mirth. It obviously wasn't the car counting that gave him his kicks, it was more the agonized expressions of the people passing through the river obstacle, and the potential for funny accidents, that seemed to appeal to the ape's slapstick sense of humour.

And then something not so funny happened at the next water-hazard. David, who'd been doing so well until this point, stalled mid-stream. After a few tries the engine took and he thundered through towards the opposite bank. His face was just breaking into a triumphant smile when he hit a small disguised rock as he cleared the water. He hit it dead centre, and in an effort to go over it, he twisted the throttle a little too vigorously resulting in the bike leaning over past the point of no return.

It was one of those annoying events that often colour our lives with frustration. The bike had landed hard on its left-hand side, smacking the front crash bar into the protruding tappet cover, which in the end, damaged one of the parts it was supposedly designed to protect. Yet, it had also probably saved the full weight of the bike from landing on David's leg and, as a result, he only had a slightly sore elbow and a bruised ego. At least there were no baboons laughing at him.

But the damage to the bike was more serious than we'd originally thought. On closer inspection we saw it was not only leaking oil, the scummy white colour sitting behind the oil window revealed it had also got some water into the crankcase. Our first thoughts of towing David out were cancelled after my 'recce' of the conditions ahead. We were at the base of the most precipitous pass we were to encounter the whole day. Not only was it steep, but very uneven and rocky as well — not ideal towing conditions. The light was also beginning to fail and there was no real alternative but to coax the bike gently over the pass under its own power, all the while watching the temperature gauge for any signs of overheating.

A photo-opportunity presented itself and I decided to catch the start of a magnificent sunset and let the big Beemers bumble on ahead without me. It had been a long day and as I stared in the direction of the setting sun a pair of black eagles circled a peak in the distance. My trusty XT250 loved the rough track, and after giving the Beemers a head start of about half an hour, I wound my faithful companion up and attacked the ascent like an enduro racer. Okay, so I'm not Alfie Cox, but in my mind I was flying like the wind, albeit in a blustery hurricane kind of way. My sojourn with fantasy nearly came to an untimely end when I came over a rise and confronted a small herd of hartebeest in the middle of the road. The brakes on the old XT are not the best and if it weren't for some thick soil on the roadside, I might well have been wearing some horns through my chest.

    I caught up with the boys on the Beemers after finally overtaking our old nemesis, the painfully slow Land Rover Discovery, just outside Cambria. David's bike seemed to be doing fine so we carried on slowly towards Kudu Kaya. It was dark when we finally met up with our hosts, Johan and Petrus van der Watt, on their nearby citrus farm. They kindly agreed to take a look at David's bike with a view to effecting a temporary repair, and Johan, a keen enduro rider himself, had the crack in the tappet cover 'Pratleyed' up in no time. By 8 p.m. we were at last sipping cold Heinekens in our cosy wooden bungalow down the road. The "Stone" took charge of braaing our game boerewors and gemsbok fillet, and as a reward for his culinary prowess, decided to fill his hollow legs with nearly three litres of wine. Okay, so David and I helped him a bit, but there was no stronger proof that the "Stone" had had more than his fair share than when I saw him wandering up a dirt track by himself much later that night. He was muttering and chuckling to himself one minute, and then gesticulating wildly at the stars the next. I decided to retire lest there were still any humour-driven baboons about that might be tempted to laugh at us again, especially seeing we were in a cottage called Bobbejaan.

    It wasn't easy to wake the "Stone" the next morning. We'd decided the night before not to brave the kloof again as we'd originally planned. Instead we opted to skirt around the other side of the Baviaanskloofberge via a 4X4 track on the Elandsrivier road and then re-enter the kloof from the tamer Willowmore end. From there, we could make our way on the good gravel road to our overnight cottage at Beacosnek near Studtis in time for sundowners. Or so we thought.

After dithering about with the bikes and persuading the "Stone" that he'd had enough recovery time, we set off for Patensie to fill up with petrol before heading out on the trail to Elandsrivier. A little way into the dirt track we arrived at a high point that saw us looking all the way to St. Francis Bay and beyond; it was a beautiful clear day and the green farmlands of the Gamtoos Valley on the way to Patensie had already treated us to the lushest landscapes we'd seen for a long time. With the series of high peaks that make up the Cockscomb Mountain ahead of us, and a lonely jeep track beneath us, things were just getting better all the time.

Even though his bike was now only dribbling very small amounts of oil, David didn't want to put undue pressure on the injured GS and was still taking it slowly. I took the opportunity to dash ahead, racing along the spine of the hills that were to lead us to our crossing of the Groot Rivier in about 20 kilometres time. Besides the adrenalin rush, it also gave me the opportunity to wait at strategic vantage points and take some photos. When we finally wound our way down to the Groot Rivier (we never did discover where the 'Elandsrivier' was) we knew for certain that this track was the bonus discovery of the trip. It had everything: an absorbing jeep track, technical sections, passes, varied and challenging road surfaces, steep ascents and descents — and all the while surrounded by natural spiky vegetation with the majestic Cockscomb Mountain in the background.

I needed petrol and the nearest town was Steytlerville, about 20 kilometres off our route. We also needed to eat something, and after persuading the owner of a B&B that we were starving, she made us the most delectable toasted sandwiches and tea — and then brought on the 'melktert' for dessert. She was a true angel of mercy. The problem was that her hospitality, combined with our tardiness in getting away in the morning, was making us hopelessly late. The sun was starting to dip rapidly and we still had 170 kilometres to go on an unknown dirt track.

The minute we turned west we knew we had problems. Not only was the sun crashing towards the horizon, it was blinding us as well. Adding to our challenges were all sorts of near misses with those many types of over exuberant fauna that come to life as the sun goes down. And avoiding fleet-footed antelope with one hand shielding the sun from your eyes and only one hand on the handlebars, was far trickier than we'd thought. By the time we got to the T-junction with the Willowmore/Baviaanskloof road, our nerves were pretty shattered, and if it weren't for a shot of OBs, I'm not quite sure what we would have done.

"Scheez David, did you see me dancing about as I klapped that deep pothole," said the "Stone" after a swig of OBs.

"You looked like you were riding one of those mechanical rodeo bulls after a bottle of tequila boet," replied David with a wry grin, "but don't worry, I nearly came unstuck myself, a pair of kudu cows decided to cross the road right in front of me."

Riding at night in these parts was not the smartest thing we'd done all weekend, but it was unavoidable; we'd totally underestimated the time required.

Riding through the Nuwekloofpas at night was like entering the dark alleyways of a walled medieval city. Strange shapes flickered into view from the casts of our headlamps; innocuous rock formations became winged monsters of elongated stone which grew and then shrank back into the shadows as we passed by. I was hoping that we might see an elusive leopard on a night-time prowl, but I had to make do with the illusory figments of my imagination instead.

By the time we got to our rented cottage, we were seriously weary. And to complicate matters further we found that the staff member who was supposed to be waiting for us had gone AWOL. We had tried to phone ahead but not managed to get hold of anyone, and being after nine at night, our go-between had decided we weren't coming. She was apparently last seen heading for the hills to a local gathering in the bush; just what we needed to hear after a long day in the saddle.

But these things have a way of working themselves out. We turned around and decided to see if we could find anybody who knew how we could get hold of a key for our cosy looking cottage. For the second time in one day we were treated by an angel of mercy. Anina Bezuidenhout of Bo-Kloof B&B and Camping came to our rescue. Somehow she'd looked beyond our dusty and dishevelled appearances and welcomed us into her kitchen. While she scurried around making plans to retrieve our errant keys, we decided it was time for a beer. David and Anina left in a bakkie to fetch the keys from the bush party while the "Stone" and I relived the day's absorbing riding in the warmth of our host's kitchen.

When we eventually opened our cottage at about 10 p.m. we were pleased that we'd not looked for alternative accommodation. It was cosy, comfortable and had everything we needed. After each having a hot, high-pressure shower, we assembled an instant breyani and in a matter of minutes were tucking in to a gourmet off-the-shelf meal. The "Stone" had stocked up on a few litres of red wine and we toasted the adventures and good fortunes that had accompanied us that day. David's ailing GS had held up well, and even though it was still slowly losing oil, it had only needed to be topped up once. Not bad seeing we'd covered over 320 kilometres. — more than half of which was on pretty challenging jeep-tracks.

The next day I awoke to the barking of baboons. Stumbling out onto the small stoep, I saw a semi-clad male figure cutting graceful swathes through the early morning light. David was practising Tai Chi — one of the physical manifestations of Taoism where the goal appears to be to strike an effortless, but effective, harmony with the powers of the universe. Whatever it was doing for him, he looked at great peace, and at one with our natural surroundings.

A short while later the "Stone" appeared rubbing his red eyes in the doorway.

"If I tried that I'd probably have to visit the chiropractor afterwards," he said with his matter-of-fact charm.

"You should try it," said David, "besides its meditative qualities, it also loosens up any aching muscles and stiff joints."

"Look, if I'm that stiff I'd rather have a vigorous body rub from a good-looking woman than get myself all contorted like that," replied the "Stone" with conviction.

I had to admit, he did have a point.

Heading west out the kloof, I realised that by the time we'd made it through Nuwekloofpas — for the third time — we would have well and truly experienced this Valley of Baboons. We'd covered over 500 kilometres in and around the kloof over some tortuous, yet exquisite, terrain; certainly, nobody could accuse us of just rushing through it. When it was time to say goodbye to David and the "Stone" at their turn-off to Uniondale, I realised why the famous travel writer, T.V. Bulpin, had labelled this valley of shadows as "an ideal place for ghosts" and why he could "understand their reluctance to leave it."

Turning back to look at the kloof, I felt a similar reluctance to leave. And then a baboon bark sounded from high-up on a nearby crag and I set off knowing that it would be left in good hands.

This article first appeared in the July 2007 edition of BIKE SA.

Bibliography

Anderson, Andrew A., *Twenty-Five Years in a Waggon*, London: Chapman & Hall, 1867.

Automobile Association, *New Southern African Book of the Road*, Cape Town: The Motorist Publications, 1995.

Ballard, Sebastian, *South African Handbook*, Bath: Footprint Handbooks, 1998.

Barnard, Anne, *The Cape Journals of Lady Anne Barnard 1797–1798*, Cape Town: Van Riebeeck Society, 1994.

Barrow, John, *An Account of Travels into the Interior of Southern Africa in the Years 1797 and 1798*, London: Cadell & Davies, 1804.

Basson, Marikie, "Mystical Mermaids of the Mountains", *Landscapes*, Oudtshoorn: Schalk and Liesel le Roux, May 2005.

Bosman, Herman Charles, *Mafeking Road*, Cape Town: Human & Rousseau, 1969.

Botha, Graham C., *Place Names in the Cape Province*, Cape Town: Juta, 1926.

Branch, Bill, *Southern African Snakes and Other Reptiles*, Cape Town: Struik, 1996.

Bryson, Bill, *A Walk in the Woods*, Black Swan, 1998.

Bulpin, T.V., *Discovering Southern Africa*, 4th ed., Muizenburg: Treasury of Travel, 1986.

Burchell, W.J., *Travels in the Interior of Southern Africa*, London: Batchworth Press, reprt. 1953 (original edition: 1822).

Burger, W.A., *Kenhardt: Uit Ons Geskiedenis*, self-published, n.d.

Butler, Guy, *Karoo Morning*, Cape Town, David Philip, 1977.

Cluver, M.A., *Fossil Reptiles of the South African Karoo*, Cape

Town: South African Museum, 1991.

Conan Doyle, Arthur, *The Great Boer War,* Alberton: Galago Publishing, 1999.

Conradie, Franz, *Stargazing for the Novice,* Thabazimbi: Kransberg Kommunikasies, 1996.

Creswicke, Louis, *The Transvaal War,* Edinburgh: T.C. & E.C. Jack, 1900.

Cullinan, Patrick, *Robert Jacob Gordon: The Man and His Travels at the Cape,* Cape Town: Struik Winchester, 1992.

Dicey, William, *Borderline,* Cape Town: Kwela Books, 2004.

Dictionary of Philosophy, Aylesbury: Pan, 1979.

Du Preez, Max, *Of Warriors, Lovers and Prophets,* Cape Town: Zebra Press, 2004.

E. Boonzaier, C. Malherbe, P. Berens and A. Smith, *The Cape Herders,* Cape Town: David Philip, 2000.

Farini, G.A., *Through the Kalahari Desert,* Cape Town: Struik, 1973.

Fisher, John, *The Afrikaners,* London: Cassel, 1969.

Forbes, Vernon S., *Pioneer Travellers in South Africa,* Cape Town and Amsterdam: Balkema, 1965.

Fraserburg Museum, "Surface Markings, Reptilian Footprints and Trace Fossils on a Palaeosurface in the Beaufort Group near Fraserburg, C.P.", Handout, 1986.

Green, Lawrence G., *To the River's End,* Cape Town: Howard Timmins, 1948.

——, *The Best of Lawrence Green,* ed. Scott Haigh, Cape Town: Howard Timmins, 1973.

——, *Karoo,* Cape Town: Howard Timmins, 1982.

Johnson, R.W., *South Africa: The First Man, The Last Nation,* Johannesburg and Cape Town: Jonathan Ball, 2005.

Joyce, Peter, *The South African Family Encyclopaedia*, Cape Town: Struik, 1989.

Juta's New Springbok Large Print Atlas, Kenwyn: Juta, 1994.

Lewis-Williams, J.D., *Discovering Southern African Rock Art*, Cape Town and Johannesburg: David Philip, 1990.

Lichtenstein, Karl, *Travels in Southern Africa*, Cape Town: Nasionale Pers, 1928.

Lockhart, J.G. and C.M. Woodhouse, *Rhodes*, London: Hodder & Stoughton, 1963.

Loubser, Frederick, "Brandwacht 16-12-1901", Calvinia Museum, 1901.

Macmillan Encyclopaedia, Aylesbury: Market House Books, 1991.

Main, Michael, *Kalahari, Life's Variety in Dune and Delta*, Halfway House: Southern Book Publishers, 1987.

Manning, John, *First Field Guide to Succulents of Southern Africa*, Cape Town: Struik, 2001.

McCarthy, Terence and Bruce Rubidge, *The Story of Earth and Life*, Cape Town: Struik, 2005.

McCrea, Pinchuck and Greg Mthembu-Salter, *South Africa: The Rough Guide*, London: Rayn Guides, 1997.

Michaels, Anne, *Fugitive Pieces*, London: Bloomsbury, 1998.

Miller, Andie, "Interview with Adam Levin", *Mail & Guardian*, 23 June 2006.

Morton, H.V., *In Search of South Africa*, London: Methuen, 1948.

Mouton, Maré, "South Africa Is Denied Its Rich Cultural History", *Village Life Magazine*, Stanford, December 2005–January 2006.

Munnion, Chris, *Banana Sunday*, Rivonia: William Waterman, 1993.

Newman, Kenneth, *Newman's Birds of Southern Africa*, Halfway

House: Southern Book Publishers, 1997.

Norman, Nick and Gavin Whitfield, *Geological Journeys,* Cape Town: Struik, 2006.

Pakenham, Thomas, *The Boer War,* New York: Random House, 1979.

Palmer, Eve, *The Plains of Camdeboo,* rev. ed., Johannesburg: Jonathan Ball, 1993.

Reader's Digest, *The Great South African Outdoors*, Cape Town: Reader's Digest, 1992.

Reitz, Denys, *Commando,* London: Faber & Faber, 1929.

Rosenthal, Eric, *Encyclopaedia of Southern Africa*, Cape Town: Juta, 1978.

Rubidge, Bruce, "Letter Written to Mr 'Oom' Wessel Brynard on 24 March 2000", Calvinia Museum, 2000.

Selby, John, *The Boer War,* London: Arthur Barker, 1969.

Stuart, Chris and Tilde Stuart, *Field Guide to the Mammals of Southern Africa,* Cape Town: Struik, 1988.

Sunday Times, Rediscovering South Africa: A Wayward Guide, Cape Town: Spearhead – New Africa Books, 2001.

Theal, George McCall, *History of South Africa,* London: Swan Sonnenschein, 1893.

——, *History of South Africa before 1795,* Cape Town: Struik, 1964a.

——, *History of South Africa since 1795,* Cape Town: Struik, 1964b.

——, *History of the Boers in South Africa,* Cape Town: Struik, 1973.

Thunberg, Carl, *Travels in Europe, Africa and Asia,* London: Richardson, Cornhill & J. Egerton, 1785.

Tyson, Harvey, *A Walk on the Wild Side,* Sandton: Zebra Publishers, 1995.

——, *Have Wings Will Fly,* Craighall: Editors Inc, 1998.

Van Jaarsveld, A.Z.A., *Die Prieska Kroniek,* N.G. Sendelingspers, c. 1965.

Van Waart, Sue, *The Hell: Valley of Lions,* Pretoria: Lapa, 2000.

Venter, Fanie and Julye-Ann Venter, *Making the Most of Indigenous Trees,* Pretoria: Briza, 1996.

Welsh, Frank, *A History of South Africa,* London: Harper Collins, 2000.

Whitehouse, Patrick, *Steam Railways of the World,* London: Chancellor Press, 1992.

Young, Mandy, "Come and Visit the Ungulungu Family", *Landscapes,* Oudtshoorn: Schalk and Liesel le Roux, May 2005.

Endnotes

1: No Turning Back
1 Anderson, p. 4.
2 Green, 1982, p. 17.
3 Joyce, p. 155.
4 Theal, 1964b, Vol. 5, pp. 121–22.
5 Ibid., p. 236.

2: From Schreiner's Tomb to a Mineral Bath Spa
6 Lockhart and Woodhouse, pp. 20 & 212.
7 McCarthy and Rubidge, pp. 203 & 206.
8 Welsh, p. 81.
9 Palmer, pp. 207–8.
10 Pakenham, p. 569.

3: Across the Gariep into the Highveld Karoo
11 Du Preez, pp. 53–54.
12 Ibid., p. 62.
13 Ibid., pp. 59–60.
14 Cullinan, p. 21.
15 Ibid. p. 44.
16 Ibid., pp. 44–45.
17 McCarthy and Rubidge, pp. 239 & 277.
18 Ibid., p. 229.
19 Green, 1973, p. 23.
20 Theal, 1964b, p. 232.

4: Battlefields and Diamonds

21 Fisher, pp. 197–98.

22 Theal, 1973, pp. 218–19.

23 Ibid., p. 245.

24 Reitz, p. 193.

25 Theal, 1893, pp. 439–40.

26 Reitz, pp. 194–95.

5: Railways, River Ways and a Well Full of Laxatives

27 Farini, pp. 5–6.

28 Whitehouse, p. 85.

29 Pakenham, p. 182.

30 Selby, p. 86.

31 Creswicke and Jack, p. 64.

32 Bulpin, pp. 205–6.

33 Ibid., p. 208.

34 Morton, pp. 262–63.

6: From the Place of the Lost Goat to a Dam of Peace

35 Pakenham, pp. 249 & 254.

36 As translated and summarised from an extract from Van Jaarsveld, p. 150.

37 Burchell, Vol. 1, pp. 221 & 225.

38 Green, 1982.

39 Cullinan, p. 117.

40 Dicey, p. 77.

7: From Cool and Rested to Hot and Bothered

41 Green, 1948, p. 90.

42 Main, p. 52.
43 Burger, p. 2, citing Lichtenstein.
44 Theal, 1964b, Vol. 11, pp. 31–32.
45 Green, 1955, p. 208.
46 Burger, p. 12.
47 Green, 1955, p. 209

8: Across the Land of Begin Again
48 Both quotes from Green, 1955, p. 203.
49 Tyson, 1995, pp. 120–21.
50 *Sunday Times*, p. 129.
51 Bosman, p. 22.
52 Ibid., p. 99.

9: More of the Unexpected
53 Thunberg, pp. 140–41.
54 Barrow, pp. 76 & 83.
55 Cullinan, p. 69.
56 Rubidge, 2000.
57 Loubser, 1901.

10: Over the Hills and up to the Stars
58 Green, 1975, p. 218.
59 Burchell, Vol. 1, p. 172.
60 Ibid., pp. 176–77.
61 Ibid., p. 180.
62 Conan Doyle, p. 574.
63 Ibid., p. 575.

11: Passes, Poorts and Pausing
64 Munnion, p. 117.
65 Lichtenstein, p. 130.

66 Ibid., p. 138.
67 Ibid., pp. 138–39.
68 Ibid., p. 141.
69 Ibid., p. 143.
70 Mouton, pp. 21–22.
71 Bosman, pp. 38–39.
72 Norman and Whitfield, p. 300.
73 Bulpin, p. 262.

12: Taking the Long Road Home

74 Dicey, p. 258.
75 Basson, p. 7.
76 Theal, 1964a, Vol. 3., p. 307.
77 Bulpin, p. 321.
78 Conan Doyle, p. 643.
79 Pakenham, p. 522.
80 Ibid., p. 523.
81 Ibid., p. 524.
82 McCarthy and Rubidge, p. 253.
83 Photo-copied document entitled: "Names Given to Drifts of Meiringspoort" as supplied by Tourism Centre at Waterfall Drift, Meiringspoort.
84 Tyson, 1998, p. 41.

Appendix-1

85 McCarthy and Rubidge, p. 186.
86 Ibid., p. 193.
87 Cluver, p. 26.
88 Ibid., pp. 37–38.
89 Rubidge and McCarthy, pp. 235–37.
90 Cluver, pp. 45–46.

INDEX

A

Aberdeen, 1, 5, 20, 70, 174, 223, 247, 257 –259, 277, 283 –285, 287 –291
Aberdeen Road, 284
Abjaterskop, 175
Afrikaners, 21, 53, 72-74, 83, 127 -128, 132, 228, 250, 252, 302
Akkerendam Nature Reserve, 197
algoasaurus, 255, 273
Aliwal North, 19, 33, 38, 45, 49 -52, 56
ANC, 240, 293
Anderson, Andrew, 4, 129, 163, 306
Anglo-Boer, War, 21, 29, 38 -39, 42, 47, 52, 72, 85, 95, 108, 192, 229
ants, 16, 176
apartheid, 13, 15, 22, 29, 51, 83, 167
Archaeopteryx, 85
Asbestosis, 137
Attaqua's kloof, 247-248
Australian, 42, 113

B

baboons, 139, 232, 289, 293, 296, 299, 300
Baines, Thomas, 230
Baker, Herbert Sir, 90
Bantu, 293
"Bantustans", 13
Barnato, Barney, 117 –118
Basotho, 52-56
bat-eared fox, 278
Baviaanskloof, 289, 292 –293
Baviaanskloofberge, 292, 297
Beaufort Group, 27, 260, 302
Beaufort West, 211, 284
Beervlei (dam), 280
Belfast, 202
Belmont, 69, 99, 105, 108 -113
Black, Week, 41, 126

blockhouse, 42-43, 72
Bloemfontein, 52, 127 -128
blue cranes, 284
Boegoeberg Dam, 121, 129, 139, 143, 154
Bo-Karoo, 200, 217, 220
Boomplaats (battle of), 80, 85 -86, 88
Bosman, Herman Charles, 37, 72, 175, 301, 308 -309
Botha, Louis General, 251-252
Botswana, 108, 145, 147, 153, 167, 226
bradysaurus, 205, 263
Broederbond, 73
Buffels River, 223, 227
Buller, General, 40, 47-48, 109, 126- 127
Bulpin, T.V., 49, 114, 117, 123, 138, 231, 248, 255, 300 -301, 307, 309
Bultfontein, 277, 284
Burchell, William, 3, 129 -131, 208-209, 301, 307-308
Burgersdorp, 33, 38, 41
Bushman, 23 -25, 31, 147, 153-155, 158-162, 188, 206 -207, 243 -244
Bushmanland, 146 -147, 149, 158 -159, 164 -165, 174, 176-177, 182
Burshman's River, 254
Bushmen, 4, 25, 52, 61, 76, 147, 150, 153 -155, 158, 161, 165, 181, 188, 201, 221 -225, 242, 293
Butler, Guy, 30, 36, 301

C

cacti, 6
Caledon River, 67
Calitzdorp, 228, 232, 234, 241
Calvinia, 146, 165, 183 –185, 188 –195, 198 -201, 203, 211, 303 -304
Cambria, 289, 292, 294, 296
Camdeboo, 24, 34, 191, 247, 259, 283, 286, 304

INDEX

Camdeboo Mountains, 280, 284
Camdeni River, 188
Campbell, Malcolm, 165, 170
Canadian, 113
Cape cobra, 34
caracal, 258
Chinese, 4, 51, 97, 154 -155
Cockscomb Mountain, 297
Coldstream Guards, 110-111
Colenso, 41, 126
Colvile, Major-General, 111
concentration camps, 30, 74, 252
Cox, Alfie, 199, 296
Cradock, 1, 16-18, 19, 20-25, 29 -32, 61
Cradock Four, 22
Cullinan, Patrick, 60, 62, 302, 306 -308

D

dassie (hyrax), 139, 165, 232
de Buys, Coenraad, 32
De Rust, 248 -249, 253 -254
de Wet, Christiaan General, 43, 65, 127, 251
diamonds, 69, 89, 102, 117, 206
Dicey, William, 135 -136, 143, 243, 302, 307, 309
dicynodonts, 191, 264 -265, 274
Die Bos, 123 -124
Die Hel, 277, 280 -281, 292
dinocephalians, 205, 274
dinosaurs, 27, 64, 85, 161, 232, 246, 255, 263, 266 -272
Doerop, Chief, 188
Doyle, Conan, 211 -212, 302, 308
Dravidian Indians, 224
du Preez, Max, 53-54, 302, 306

E

eland, 24, 132
Elandsrivier (road), 297 -298
enon conglomerate (deposits), 246, 250, 253 -255, 292
entoptic phenomena, 25, 161
Esau, Abraham, 194-197, 211 -212

Eseljachtpoort, 243 -244
euphorbia, 6, 8-10, 286
European bee-eater, 243

F

Farini, G.A., 102, 302, 307
Fauresmith, 85, 92 -94, 119
Fish River, 14, 30-33, 36, 61, 199
fossils, 2, 28, 64, 85, 162, 191 -192, 246, 254, 262, 268, 274, 302
Fraserburg, 191 -192, 198 -199, 202 -204, 208, 302
Fullarton, 258, 277, 279

G

Gamkaskloof, 277, 280 -281
Gamtoos Valley, 297
Gansfontein palaeosurface, 203, 205
Gatacre, General, 40, 126
Gauteng, 249 -250
gemsbok, 65, 145, 296
Ghost Drift, 255
Gordon, Robert Jacob Colonel, 3, 59- 62, 67, 128, 134-135, 199, 247, 302
Gqunukhwebe, 226
Great Karoo, 3 -4, 8 -11, 21, 84, 106, 141, 164, 223 -224, 247 -248, 257, 259, 279
Great River, 59, 61
Greeff, Stephanus, 227
Green, Lawrence, 8, 133, 144, 156, 159, 164, 205, 248, 302, 306 -308
grey rhebok, 220
Griquas, 76 -79, 87, 134
Griquatown, 208
Gronjam, Chief, 188
Groot Rivier, 291, 297
Grootrivierhoogte, 277, 279
ground squirrels, 145
guinea-fowl, 284

H

Hantam Karoo, 186
Hantamsberg, 176, 187 -188, 197, 199

311

Haw, Stephen,   173
Hereros,   226
Hermanus yacht club,   169
heron(s),   17, 140, 158, 201
Hertzog, James General,   72 -73, 83, 93, 211, 250
Hitchcock, Alfred,   148
Hofmeyr, J.H.,   42
Hopetown,   69, 85, 96 –97, 102 –104, 114 –116, 119
Hottentots (Khoi),   13-15, 52, 131, 152, 186, 181, 196, 209 –210, 224, 226

I

Inqua (Hottentots),   247
inselbergs,   149
Isla Grand,   146

J

jackals,   133
Jackson, Maximillian,   151 –152
Jansens, Jan Willem Gen,   12-15
Jansenville,   8, 12, 15, 284, 286 –287
Jurassic (Lower),   63, 262, 267, 271, 273

K

Kalahari,   16, 24, 57, 65, 144 –147, 157, 302 -303
Karoo basin,   8, 29, 192, 231, 266
Karoo Boekehuis (book house),   191
Karoo korhaan,   5
Karoo Supergroup,   27, 29, 44, 64
Keiskie se Poort,   199
Kenhardt,   128-129, 136, 142, 149 -151, 153, 155 -160, 163, 167, 174, 177, 179, 194, 199, 205, 301
Khoi (Hottentot),   13, 31-33, 123, 129, 135 -136, 181, 201, 224 –227, 243 –247
Kitchener, Lord,   30, 43 -44, 72, 128, 251-252
Klaarwater,   208 –209
Klipplaat,   277, 279, 287 –288

Kok, Adam,   76 -80, 87
Komsberg Pass,   217
Koos Raubenheimer Dam,   249
kori bustard,   3, 5, 284
Kougaberge,   292
Kritzinger, Pieter Hendrik Gen,   29, 250
Kruger, Paul President,   21, 38-40,
Kruisrivier,   214, 223, 228, 237, 240, 245 -248, 257
Kruisrivier Guest Farm,   234, 245
kudu,   279, 287 –289, 298
Kuruman,   208

L

Ladysmith,   126
Laingsburg,   218, 220, 225 –228, 230
Leeu-Gamka,   239
leopard,   132, 175, 245, 298
le Roux, Elma,   153, 160, 205
Lesotho,   33, 50, 59, 64, 67, 200
Lichtenstein,   3, 147, 217 -222, 303, 308 -309
Liebenberg, General,   127 -128
Little Karoo,   99, 223, 247, 255
Loeriesfontein,   156, 163, 165, 172 -179, 183, 184 -185, 187-188, 190, 199
Loubser, Boet,   179
Luanda,   215
Luckhoff,   87, 94-96
lynx (rooikat),   132
lystrosaurus,   26, 28, 265 –266

M

Main, Michael,   145, 303
Maitland, Peregrine Sir,   43, 77
mammal,   26 –29, 63 -65, 132, 192, 203, 205, 263 –267, 270 –274, 293, 304
Mapungubwe,   224
Marais, Eugene,   176
Marais (siding),   284
Maritz, Gerrit Field-Cornet,   209
martial eagle,   16
Marydale,   129, 131, 137-138

INDEX

Masson, Francis, 186-188, 199, 208
Mauser, 65, 109, 112
Mbeki, Thabo President, 203
McCarthy, Terence, 27, 64, 260 -261, 270, 303, 306, 309 -310
megazostrodon, 63, 267, 271 -272
Meiringspoort, 231 –232, 255, 291, 309
Merriman, John X., 118
Methuen, Lord, 41, 108 -111, 126, 303
Milky Way, 216
Miller, 259, 277, 279, 289, 291
mineral spa, 48
Miura, 94, 178
mixed grassveld, 84
Moordenaars-Karoo, 218, 220 -225
Moshoeshoe, 52 –56
Murraysberg, 284

N

Namaqualand, 9, 146, 186
Napier, George Sir, 76 –77
Nationalists, 72 -73, 83
Nguni, 207
Nieuwoudtville, 188
Niewoudt, Commandant, 196 –197
Noorsveld, 286
Nuwekloofpas, 292, 298, 300

O

Oatlands, 284
Oppenheimer, Ernest, 118
Opperman, Vincent, 203
osprey, 33
Oudtshoorn, 231, 243, 245 -250, 301, 305
Oupoort (pass), 200
Outeniqua, 247
Ovambos, 226

P

Pakenham, Thomas, 43, 109, 251 –252, 304, 306 –307 , 309
palaeontology, 204
Palmer, Eve, 34, 283, 304, 306

pans, 66, 123, 146, 170, 262
paradise flycatcher, 243
Patensie, 289, 297
PEAR TREE DRIFT, 256
Permian (Upper), 26, 118, 192, 205, 262 -268, 272
Philippolis, 76, 78 -79, 87, 92
Phillip, John Dr, 76
Pilcher, Colonel, 113
Plettenberg Bay, 253
Pofadder, Klaas, 144, 152
Port Elizabeth, 22, 25, 76, 230, 253, 255, 273
Pretorius, General, 86 -88
Prieska, 66, 99, 108, 114, 118, 121, 123 -125, 127 -134, 137, 143, 158, 194, 305
Prieska revolt, 129, 194
Prince Albert, 223, 281
Prince of Orange, 60
Prinsloo, Jacobus, 110
Putsonderwater, 143, 148 -151, 174, 176

R

racist, 12, 135, 173, 195
railways, 71 -72, 74, 99, 101, 103, 111, 305
rebels, 30, 86, 144
Red Star Line, 102
Reitz, Denys, 86, 93, 304, 307
reptiles, 27 –28, 34, 64, 118, 132, 191-192, 203, 205, 232, 262 -268, 270, 274, 293, 301-302
Rhodes, Cecil John, 21 -22, 117 –118, 303
Rietbron, 280
Rimington's Tigers, 109
Rio (de Janeiro), 168 -169
Roberts, Lord, 126 –128
Rock Art, 25, 160, 206, 243, 303
rock monitor, 118, 140, 245, 263, 279
Roggeveld, 10, 61, 186 -188, 199 -202 217 -218

Roggeveldberge, 119, 201, 209
Rooiberg Dam, 157-158
Rooinek Pass, 228, 230
Rubidge, Bruce, 27, 64, 191 -192, 260-261, 270, 303 -304, 306, 308 -310

S

SALT (Southern African Large Telescope), 203
San (Bushmen), 24, 123, 129, 135, 146, 161, 181, 201, 207, 220, 222, 225, 243 –245, 286, 293
Sandvlakte, 292
Schreiner, Olive, 19, 21-22, 214
secretary birds, 85
Seweweekspoort, 223, 228, 230 -232, 255, 291
shamans, 25, 161, 243
Skoorsteenberg, 280
Sleeping Giant (Mountain), 247, 259, 290
Smithfield, 59, 65 -67, 70, 75, 84, 151, 159
Smith, Harry Sir, 49, 80, 86 -87
Smuts, Jan General, 127, 251-252
soetnoors, 286
South African Railways (SAR), 111
Soutpansnek Pass, 15
springbok, 95, 132, 197, 217, 278, 284, 290
steenbok, 2 -3, 217, 284
Steenkamp (Cape "boer" rebel), 127
steppe buzzards, 201
Steynsburg, 33, 35, 37 -38, 41, 44, 61
Steytlerville, 291, 297
Stormberg, 269 –270
Stormberg (battle), 40
Studtis, 289, 292, 297
succulents, 7 -9, 303
Sundays River, 5
suricates, 5, 63, 272
Sutherland, 188, 191, 198 -203, 205 -208, 211, 214 -215, 217, 220

Sutherland Inn, 203, 207
Swanepoels Poort, 277, 279
Swartberg Pass, 239, 248, 280
Swartkoppies, 76, 79 -80

T

Taalmonument, 42
Tankwa River, 199
tawny eagle, 173
Theal, Geroge McCall, 13, 67, 79, 88, 152, 247 –248, 306 –309
therapsids, 28, 64, 263, 266, 268, 274
Thompson, George, 158
Thunberg, Carl, 3, 186 –188, 199, 208, 304, 308
trains, 71, 100, 111
trance dance, 25
Trekboers, 52, 181, 242
Triassic, 28, 63, 262, 265 –272
trirachodon, 64, 272
Trompsburg, 46, 59, 66, 69 –71, 75 –76, 80, 84
Tsama melons, 144
Tswana, 226
Tyson, Harvey, 304, 308 –309

U

Upington, 76, 128, 143 –144

V

van Gass, Mr, 204
van Niekerk, Michiel, 115
Van Plettenberg, Governor, 31, 188
Velletjies, Klaas, 159
Verneuk Pan, 165, 170
Victoria Manor Hotel, 20, 24
Victorian, 20 –21, 50 –51, 68, 75, 90, 93, 123, 227, 279

W

Wanda, 96 –97
water monitor, 140
weather-helm, 97
Williston, 165, 191, 194, 196
Willowmore, 41, 237, 256, 258, 289,

291-292, 297-298
Windmill Museum, 179, 183
Witput, 99, 101, 103-104, 108
Witsand, 145
Wolseley, Garnet Sir, 109
Wood, Denis, 205
Wyndham, John, 148

X

Xhosa(s), 13-14, 31-32, 36-37, 152, 187, 226

Y

youngina group, 118

Z

Zimbabwe, 157, 224
zuurveldt, 31

About the Author

Nicholas Yell is a 48-year-old ex-adman from Jo'burg. In 2001, he left the big smoke for the verdant hills of the Overberg where he and his wife, Lerié, dabbled in wines, art and décor in the picturesque village of Napier. They discovered that, although the roles of country shopkeepers kept them in food and wine, their hearts were set on fruits of another kind: Nick wanted to pursue his photographic, copywriting and other writing interests full time, and Lerié her passion for art. They moved to the small Karoo town of Aberdeen, on the plains of the Camdeboo, in September 2005. They lived in a lovingly restored 'Karoo-huis' on a large plot of land they shared with fruit trees, vegetables and two fat cats.

Nick also writes travel articles for a number of newspapers and magazines and has just published his new book of short stories: Karoo Tales and Images. In-between writing assignments, he is also studying to become a Life Coach.

When Nick's not working or spending time at home, he'll be riding his off-road motorbike, walking through the fynbos, listening to music or, of course, reading a good book.

Nick and Lerié now live in Botriver in the Western Cape.